Asia's Struggle for Full Humanity

To My Mother

Asia's Struggle for Full Humanity: Towards a Relevant Theology

Papers from the Asian Theological Conference,
January 7–20, 1979, Wennappuwa, Sri Lanka

Edited by
Virginia Fabella

ORBIS BOOKS

Maryknoll, New York 10545

Abbreviations

ATC	Asian Theological Conference
CBA	Chinese-Buddhist Association
CCA	Christian Conference of Asia
CSR	Centre for Society and Religion (Sri Lanka)
EACC	East Asian Christian Conference
EATWOT	Ecumenical Association of Third World Theologians
FABC	Federation of Asian Bishops' Conferences
FAO	Food and Agriculture Organization (U.N.)
GPI	Federation of the Protestant Churches of Indonesia
LWF	Lutheran World Federation
NASSA	National Secretariat of Social Action, Justice and Peace of the Catholic Bishops Conference of the Philippines
OHD	Office of Human Development of Federation of Asian Bishops' Conference
WBSC	World Buddhist Sangha Council
WBSS	World Buddhist Social Service
WCC	World Council of Churches
WFB	World Fellowship of Buddhists

The Catholic Foreign Mission Society of America (Maryknoll) recruits and trains people for overseas missionary service. Through Orbis Books Maryknoll aims to foster the international dialogue that is essential to mission. The books published, however, reflect the opinions of their authors and are not meant to represent the official position of the society.

Library of Congress Cataloging in Publication Data

Main entry under title:

Asia's struggle for full humanity.

Summary of the preparation for the Asian Theological Conference held in Wennappuwa, Sri Lanka, Jan. 7-20, 1979, and its results.
1. Theology, Doctrinal—Asia—History—Congresses.
I. Fabella, Virginia. II. Asian Theological Conference, Wennappuwa, Sri Lanka, 1979.
BT30.A8A8   230'.095   80-14923
ISBN 0-88344-015-6 (pbk.)

Contents

List of Abbreviations   iv

PART ONE
PREPARING THE CONFERENCE

1. An Introduction   3
   Virginia Fabella (Philippines)
2. Towards the Liberation of Theology in Asia   16
   Tissa Balasuriya (Sri Lanka)
3. Christianity in the Context of Other Faiths   28
   Bishop Lakshman Wickremesinghe (Sri Lanka)

PART TWO
THE LIVE-IN EXPERIENCE

4. The Live-In Plan   39
   Virginia Fabella (Philippines) and Sergio Torres (Chile)
5. The Coconut Plantation Live-In Report   42
   Cynnyc Cheng (Hong Kong) and Eunice Santana de Velez (Puerto Rico)
6. Reflections on a Live-In Experience: Slumdwellers   50
   Samuel Rayan (India)

PART THREE
THE CONSULTATION

7. Socio-Economic and Political Reality in Asia   59
   K. Matthew Kurian (India)
8. Towards an Asian Theology of Liberation: Some Religio-Cultural Guidelines   75
   Aloysius Pieris (Sri Lanka)
9. Christian Reflection in a Buddhist Context   96
   Lynn de Silva (Sri Lanka)

10. Orientations for an Asian Theology   108
     Sebastian Kappen (India)

11. Faith and Life Reflections from the Grassroots in the
         Philippines   123
     Carlos H. Abesamis (Philippines)

12. Asian Theology: An Asian Woman's Perspective   140
     Henriette Katoppo (Indonesia)

13. The Final Statement   152

                        PART FOUR
                        ASSESSMENTS

14. Notes on the Asian Theological Conference   163
     Dalston Forbes (Sri Lanka)

15. Reflections by Korean Theologians on the Final Statement
         of the Asian Theological Conference   167

16. From Accra to Wennappuwa: What Is New? What More?   171
     Rose Zoé-Obianga (Cameroun)

17. A Black American Perspective on the Asian Search for a
         Full Humanity   177
     James H. Cone (U.S.A.)

18. A Latin American View of the Asian Theological
         Conference   191
     Sergio Torres (Chile)

19. Hope for the Future   198
     Justinus Cardinal Darmojuwono (Indonesia)

List of Participants   199

Part One

Preparing the Conference

1

An Introduction

Virginia Fabella (Philippines)

"Asia's Struggle for Full Humanity: Towards a Relevant Theology" encapsules both the theme and the task of the eighty participants who gathered for the Asian Theological Conference in Wennappuwa, Sri Lanka, January 7–20, 1979. This book is about this Conference: how it was planned, what it hoped to accomplish, its key experiences, deliberations, and documents.

Though planned and coordinated by an all-Asian Organizing Committee,[1] the Asian Theological Conference (ATC) was sponsored by the Ecumenical Association of Third World Theologians (EATWOT) as part of its five-year program of intercontinental conferences promoting Third World theologies as well as dialogue among Third World Christians.[2] But as an Asian theological event, the ATC received the support of the Commission on Theological Concerns of the Christian Conference of Asia (Singapore) and the Office of Human Development (Manila) of the Federation of Asian Bishops' Conferences.

The participants came from ten Asian countries as well as from Africa, Latin America, the Pacific Islands, the Caribbean, and the U.S. (represented by a Black and a Native American theologian). There were 62 men and 18 women, mostly Catholics and Protestants. They were bishops, ministers, and

Virginia Fabella, M.M., is the program coordinator of the Ecumenical Association of Third World Theologians.

3

priests; they were religious sisters and lay people; they were professional theologians, educators, church administrators, students, and social activists. Among them were one Roman Catholic cardinal, one Orthodox bishop, one Muslim professor, and two factory workers from Hong Kong.

The Conference title selected by the Organizing Committee indicated two premises: (1) that the current Western-based and Western-oriented theology is no longer meaningful to many Asian Christians, and (2) that to be significant to the contemporary Asian, theology must be based on the concrete experience of the people and the concrete realities of their continent. The articulation of the faith response must spring from the people's lives and struggles, their joys, pains, hopes, and frustrations within their given context.

Some Antecedents

This move away from Western theology and towards one that speaks to Asians is not new. Theological adaptation, accommodation, inculturation, indigenization, and contextualization have all been used by Asian theologians towards this end. Though theologians continue to employ adaptation (which seeks to reinterpret Western thought from an Asian perspective), or indigenization (which takes the native culture and religion as its basis), there is the newer thrust to "contextualize" theology. This approach conveys all that is implied in indigenization but goes beyond it in a dynamic way. "Contextualizing theology," while not ignoring traditional culture, "takes into account the process of secularity, technology, and the struggles of human justice" which characterize not only modern Asia but other countries of the Third World as well.[3] As a dynamic process, it combines words and action, is open to change, and looks to the future. Furthermore, "authentic contextualization is always prophetic, arising always out of a genuine encounter between God's Word and his world, and moves towards the purpose of challenging and changing the situation through rootedness in and commitment to a given historical moment."[4]

The Organizing Committee recognized that there are many approaches to a relevant theology for Asia, but to be a living theology, it must take the Asian experience and context seriously. Some groundwork had been done and other efforts towards this had been made by groups and individuals in Asia. The Committee wanted to build on rather than either repeat or disregard these past achievements. It is useful to recall some of these to situate the ATC.

As far back as 1949, representatives of Protestant Asian churches convened in Bangkok, to discuss the reality of the Asian social revolution.[5] In their statement, "The Asian Church in the Political and Social Life," they defined the nature of the Asian struggle as they saw it and the nature of the Christian action demanded of the church in it.[6]

Prior to their meeting in Prapat in 1957, the church representatives gathered for a conference on "The Social Goals of New Asia," where it was recognized that the Asian revolution was a total one, affecting not only politics and economics but involving the reformation of culture and religion as well.

At the inaugural Assembly of the East Asian Christian Conference (EACC) in 1958, the delegates heard Dr. Masao Takenaka of Japan speak of five major revolutions in the West[7] simultaneously taking place within a short period in Asia, and the necessity of Christian action which aimed at changing the social and economic situation instead of merely aiding the victims of the oppressive structures.

There were other attempts of the EACC to understand and respond to the Asian struggle.[8] But despite this groundwork, it was acknowledged at a consultation sponsored by the EACC in 1965 that the churches had "not taken their theological task seriously enough," having been content to accept "the ready-made answers of Western theology." The statement continued with a hopeful note: "Today we can look for the development of authentic living theology in Asia."[9]

At that time, Protestant theologians themselves still leaned heavily on European theology. A decade later, in 1976, two anthologies of their writings were published which showed the stirrings of an Asian consciousness in their theological effort.[10] Elwood's collection includes Emerito Nacpil's "The Critical Asian Principle," outlining a method of doing theological contextualization which he had first proposed in 1972.[11] But this Asian principle did not solve the question of "authenticity" or "relevancy." In his Introduction to *Asian Voices in Christian Theology*, the other anthology, Anderson admits that the Asian theologians were not clear about the "critical Asian principle."

Assessing the state of theology in 1977 prior to its Sixth Assembly, the CCA issued a statement that theology in Asia was "still largely influenced by the theological currents of the United States and Europe," and that there was "little authentic Asian Christian theology." The statement affirmed the need for a living theology that considered the multiplicity of Asian situations, taking into account the different historical and religious traditions as well as the conditions of suffering and hope within the people's struggle.[12]

While the task for theology in Asia was becoming clearer,[13] it was not becoming any easier. The All-Asia Theological Consultation held in Manila in 1977 was to identify and understand Asian realities, and perceive in these realities, issues of faith, life, and human destiny which are the basic ingredients of theological issues. However, the Consultation failed to work on Asian realities, and in general the main lectures remained abstract and academic and dependent on Western sources.[14]

The Catholic Church has a different history in Asia. Before Vatican Council II in 1962 it was difficult for the church in Asia to think of itself in Asian terms. The concept of universal church with its Roman foundations continued to predominate even after the Council. During the decade following the Council, most of the theological input of church leaders and academic theologians kept close to the Council documents but gave an Eastern interpretation to the documents' Western orientation.

The task of indigenization encouraged by the Council was largely confined to liturgy, music, architecture, pastoral organization, etc. Dialogue with other faiths, also promoted by the Council, remained the work of individuals and research centers in countries where Christians were a minuscule minority amid an overwhelming Hindu, Buddhist, or Islamic population.

A few of the local churches in Asia experienced theological awakening in the decade of the '70s. In India, for example, the occasion was the Nagpur International Theological Conference in 1971. Some Indian theologians and theological centers responded to the Nagpur challenge in terms of their Hindu context.[15] An assessment of theological reflection in India from 1972 to 1977 showed a shift from "adaptation" to "inculturation" and from a church-centered to a Christocentric approach. There was also a move towards combining interfaith dialogue with developmental work.[16]

On the whole, authentic contextualization has not aroused the interest of professional theologians in the Catholic theological institutions and seminaries in Asia. Rather, it has been isolated theologians and other Christians engaged in research and encounter centers and/or involved in social action or liberation struggles who have done some spadework and are actively contributing to the development of a relevant theology in Asia.[17] A few examples are some of the groups that participated in the ATC: the Centre for Society and Religion (CSR) in Colombo and the Research and Encounter Centre in Kalaniya, both in Sri Lanka, and the National Secretariat for Social Action, Justice and Peace (NASSA) in Manila.

The Conference Objective and Plan

The ATC was an attempt to continue this search for a relevant theology in Asia. This time, this theological task became a joint venture of Catholics and Protestants building upon what each group had done under its own aegis. "In ecumenical fellowship" their task was "to determine theological responses that would address themselves and be addressed by the concrete struggles of the Asian peoples for emancipation from oppression and for the realization of just and human societies."[18]

In light of its theme and aim, an inductive case study approach was chosen by the Organizing Committee for the Conference. Sri Lanka, as the site of the Conference, was designated as the principal case. The Sri Lankan reality, including both the cultural-religious and the political-economic aspects, was to be analyzed and reflected upon by the Sri Lankans. This was to be examined critically and used as a basis of comparison by the other Asian Christians similarly engaged in their own countries. The Committee hoped that through this convergent process, the issues for theology would emerge from actual concrete situations and not from general understandings of, and statements about, the Asian reality of suffering and hope.

The major groups struggling for full humanity in Sri Lanka, and generally in Asia, were identified as: (1) urban and industrial workers; (2) peasants and rural workers; (3) the marginalized in the cities; (4) ethnic and other minorities; (5) women; and (6) youth and students. The case studies dealt with the issues implicit in the struggles of these groups within the context of their own countries.

To implement the aim and remain faithful to the inductive approach, the Committee organizers designated three stages for the ATC, though not all were fully carried out.

First, the identification of task groups (March–December, 1978): A local committee was to be set up in each country to seek out different action-reflection groups already involved with any one of the marginalized sectors. These groups would be asked to analyze their particular struggle, do a critical analysis of the experience of their reality, and reflect on these in the light of their Christian faith and the Scriptures. Participants for the ATC were to be nominated from these task groups by the local committee. The final selection would be the Organizing Committee's responsibility so as to ascertain a balanced distribution among the sexes, denominations, and age groups. All the participants were to be ready with a full report of their analysis and theological reflection prior to the meeting in Sri Lanka.

Second, the exposure of the participants to Sri Lanka situations (January 8–11, 1979): Participants from the other Asian countries would live in the six field situations of their Sri Lankan counterparts. Together with them, they were to articulate the perceived theological issues. At the conclusion of the live-in period, reports from each of the six situations were to be prepared and presented at the consultation. The Sri Lankans would speak from their own experience while the non-Sri Lankans would reflect on their observation from their own vantage points.

Third, the consultation itself (January 12–20, 1979): The reports were to be shared with the conference participants and the findings would then be critiqued and complemented by an Asian resource group composed of social scientists of differing ideologies, representatives of other world religions, and professional theologians, both Catholic and Protestant. The task of the resource persons would be to help sharpen the issues and put them within the total Asian as well as global contexts.

The Three Stages of the ATC

The first stage involved the preparation of the participants. The diversity of their understanding of "involvement in the struggle," the timidity of non-professional theologians to "do theology," and the difficulty of coming together for collective work and reflection, all made for the uneven preparation of the participants. However, the preparatory work of three national groups deserves mention.

As the host country, Sri Lanka's preparation, done mainly through the Centre for Society and Religion in Colombo, was admirable in its comprehensiveness. The Centre already had existing contacts with action-oriented groups and professional theologians. This facilitated not only the selection of task group coordinators but also the subcommittees responsible for the work that necessarily went with hosting an international conference.

Their preparation for the Conference included three general sessions with task group representatives, as well as separate consultations on each of the six sectors designated for both in-depth study and the live-in experience of the ATC participants. The sessions dealt with the social causes of oppression in Sri Lanka and pooled ideas for new alternative approaches to theology that were both ecumenical and interdisciplinary.

These general sessions answered some questions but raised others at the same time. For whom is this theology? Is the exhaustive evaluation of social structures leading to nothing but a "social theology" because the personal factor was either played down or ignored? These two questions were also raised later in the Conference at Wennappuwa. Reports of the meetings and related documents were published in dossiers after each session and were shared with the preparatory committees of the other countries. Two of these documents, one by Tissa Balasuriya entitled "Towards the Liberation of Theology in Asia" and another by Bishop Lakshman Wickremesinghe entitled "Christianity in the Context of Other Faiths," appear in Part One of this book.[19]

The preparatory committee in the Philippines held two consultations in Cebu and Malaybalay, respectively. The participants were all religious and lay people either from the grassroots themselves or working directly in grassroots situations. Their first significant question was: Who are the real theologians? Another: How can theological reflection be facilitated among the grassroots Christians? Participants for the ATC were nominated from among those who attended either the Cebu or the Malaybalay consultations and were committed to continue the process. Because of their corporate experience, the Philippine group presented a solid position at the consultation and saw the value of meeting after the Conference to plan a follow-up.

The preparation in India consisted of working on a series of case studies of oppressive situations in that country. Several theological and research centers cooperated in this project. The Slum Development Department of the Tamilnadu Theological Seminary in Madurai wrote up a forty-nine-page case study of the social structure of slumdwellers in their city. Other case studies dealt with the problem of untouchability in a rural area, with the fishing industry on the Madras Coast, with rickshaw pullers in Habalpur, and with the landlords, tenants, and landless laborers of an agrarian village outside

Bangalore City. The case studies, all products of collective investigation and reflection, were made available to the participants at the ATC.

The second stage of the ATC was the live-in in Sri Lanka, the site of the Conference itself. The live-in was a three- or four-day immersion into the actual life situation of different depressed and marginated sectors of Sri Lankan society. Neither the importance of the live-in, nor its impact or effects, can be captured in words, but attempts to do so appear in Part II of this book. This part gives (1) a brief overview of the purpose and plan of the live-in, (2) a report prepared by the coconut plantation group, and (3) some reflections written by Samuel Rayan, S.J., from Delhi, who describes his exposure to the Colombo slums and the challenge and questions posed by this experience to him as a professional theologian.[20]

The third stage of the ATC was the consultation itself. The live-in reports marked the initial phase of the consultation and were followed by three others: the input by the resource persons, the surfacing of issues based on the live-in reports and resource people's presentations, and finally, the work towards a relevant theology culminating in the final statement.

It was during the reporting session on the live-in experience that the first sign of conflict and tension surfaced in the Conference. Opposing views and sympathies regarding the struggling groups became evident at this point. This was not the only tension: there were others during the course of the consultation. Though these did present difficult and frustrating moments, they prompted concrete action and exciting interchanges that have continued beyond the Conference.[21]

The input from resource persons followed. Several had been invited to share their insights and to help in the accomplishment of the conference aim. Part III of this book contains the papers which they prepared for the Conference. Their papers were presented in summary form so as to allow more time for questions and comments from the participants.

Dr. K. Matthew Kurian, director of the Indian Institute for Regional Development Studies in Kerala, India, supplemented the social analysis contained in the live-in reports by a more scientific analysis of the socio-economic and political power structures in the Asian countries and their nexus with international developments, particularly the crisis which international capitalism is facing today.[22] In response to Dr. Kurian, Dr. Feliciano Cariño of Philippine Christian University gave a counter-analysis claiming that, instead of a decline or downfall of international capitalism, he found the system stronger than it had ever been. He supported this contention with evidence from the rise of the new political phenomenon of military technocracy. Unfortunately Cariño's response is not available for publication.

Also invited to supplement the participants' reports on the Asian reality were representatives from the Asian world religions and Aloysius Pieris, S.J., a Sri Lankan and a scholar of Buddhism, who presented a paper entitled

"Towards an Asian Theology of Liberation: Some Religio-Cultural Guidelines." Because Pieris' paper provoked not only much discussion but also moments of polarization among the participants, it is included in this book. It gives an excellent insight into the poverty and religiosity of Asia: "Two inseparable realities which in their interpenetration constitute what might be designated as the Asian context and which is the matrix of any theology that is truly Asian."[23] Another paper dealing with Asian world religions, Lynn de Silva's "Christian Reflection in a Buddhist Context," which was the basis of a pre-conference dialogue with a group of Buddhist monks and laity, is also included in this book.[24]

To facilitate theological reflection on the Asian reality, three Asian theologians were invited. Sebastian Kappen, S.J., one of India's foremost Catholic theologians spoke within the Asian context of religious pluralism, Marxism, and the prevailing socio-political situation in the continent. Within this context, he developed what he considered the fundamental notion: theology as a critical reflection on one's primordial encounter with God.[25]

Carlos Abesamis, another Jesuit, who had coordinated the preparatory sessions in the Philippines, suggested a methodology for theologizing in Asia which grew out of his experience with Christians involved in the struggles against the current oppressive situation in his country. His participation in the Cebu-Malaybalay meetings with the grassroots Christians and those committed to their struggles led him to the firm conclusion that only "the conscientized grassroots poor" can produce a relevant theology for Asia. Appropriately, the original subtitle of his paper was "Towards a Theology from the Grassroots."[26]

As a Protestant and feminine theologian from Indonesia, Henriette Katoppo's participation in, and contribution to the ecumenical consultation in Wennappuwa was doubly valuable. Her paper on "an Asian woman's perspective" starts with her personal experience as a woman and a Protestant in Jakarta. Her reflections about "the other" support her assertion that Asians must claim their right to be "the other" vis-à-vis First World Christians, who have thus far rejected independent Asian thinking.[27]

Equipped with their live-in accounts, national group reports,[28] and the supplementary input of the resource persons, the participants were then ready to identify and classify the issues for theological reflection. But it was now January 17 and there were only three more days of the consultation to go and one day had been reserved for a visit to the nation's Buddhist center, Kandy. But no debate was necessary to decide the next move. It was for theological reflection that the participants came and this they wanted to do. The trip to Kandy was cancelled and the remaining days were re-scheduled for collective theological reflection.

However, underlying the issues that surfaced for reflection based on the social, political, economic, cultural, and religious realities of Asia were some unresolved and more basic questions and concerns which kept coming up. It became evident that they needed to be answered first. Professional theologian, church person, social activist: Who is the subject of theology? And for whom is this theology? Whom does it serve?

A further concern: It was recognized that a meaningful theology could only emerge from the life struggle of the people in their given context. But in a continent as vast and as complex as Asia, which one was the basic context that must be taken seriously: the social-political context which contains the root causes of the injustices against which the people are struggling? Or the religio-cultural context in which their "Asian-ness" is rooted? It began to seem that there were two basic Asias: the Asia of the vast subcontinent of India and other countries immersed in their indigenous culture and the religious traditions of Buddhism, Hinduism, and Islam, and the Asia of the Philippines, Hong Kong, and other countries dominated by the neo-colonialism of technology, modernization, and the transnational corporations, with their dehumanizing and impoverishing effect upon the people. For these latter countries, religious traditions did not seem to be a determining factor in their struggles against their common enemy. The Philippines is predominantly Christian while Hong Kong, for example, is predominantly "non-Christian."

Still a further concern was expressed. Has the nature of the Asian struggle been really examined from the perspective of the struggling grassroots poor and the oppressed or from an academic/ecclesiastical point of view? It became clear to the participants that one's experience, history, and situation heavily conditioned one's theology.

Though some of the participants felt uncomfortable and frustrated that with all the concerns and controversies very little "theologizing" was being done, many others found the tensions creative and the confrontations healthy; they considered conflict an integral part of the quest for a relevant theology in Asia.

Tensions and shortcomings notwithstanding, the participants decided that the Conference was an experience that had to be shared with fellow Asians as well as with people of good will who want to find meaning in their life struggle. A Draft Committee was therefore formed to prepare a final statement. Drawing from all consultation materials, discussions, and small group reports, the Committee prepared and presented its first draft at a plenary session on January 19. There was no doubt about the importance of the final statement. On the last morning, the participants willingly sat through almost five hours of discussion, even postponing dinner and condensing the closing liturgical celebration so that a statement could be articulated and then turned over to an Editorial Committee for its final redaction. Without doubt, the participants wanted to share their conference. Although their final statement is in this book, in no way does it tell the total story.

Post-Conference Reflections

What did these two weeks together mean for the seventy-two Asian participants and for their future? Part IV of this book begins with the assessment of the ATC by a Sri Lankan delegate.[29] In general, the experience of the Conference taught Asians that theology in Asia must be an ecumenical effort, and a collective and ongoing process. In a very concrete way, they realized their fellowship and faith-sharing with their Asian brothers and sisters and other Third World Christians. They came to understand that their theologizing is conditioned by their history, cultural background, ideological convictions, and class values as well as their present commitment. In analyzing their context, they found that the cultural-religious dimensions must go hand-in-hand with the socio-economic ones. They learned that liberation must be both personal and societal and that the resources for human fulfilment are present, though often latent, in other Asian religions and cultures. They saw that their relation with other world religions must go beyond dialogue to the level of collaborative action for a more just society. They learned the creative force of tensions and honest confrontations. Above all, their experience convinced them that their theology, to be relevant, must spring from their faith in Jesus lived out in the service of Asia's poor, who aspire to live as human persons.

But the Conference had its shortcomings. The use of English as the common language of the Conference was decidedly one of these. Many of the participants did not feel comfortable with English. Possibly more serious was the underlying question: Can any authentic "Asian theology" be done in a Western language?

On the other hand, perhaps the ATC hoped to accomplish too much in a short time. Were all the participants really ready for the inductive approach in a theological conference? Faced with the various levels of preparation and experience of the participants, the ATC tried to compromise, swerving back and forth between the inductive and deductive approaches, between drawing from experience and depending on expertise. To some the theological input from the "experts" still remained highly theoretical. The two factory workers felt that it hardly touched their actual life situation in the Hong Kong factories.

A further shortcoming was the uneven representation of the participants themselves. They were mostly Catholic and religious, with relatively few Protestants and only one member of the Orthodox Church. The lay people who comprised one-third of the group felt that the Conference hardly addressed them. Furthermore, it is to be regretted that there were very few women.[30] Finally there was insufficient input from other world religions, as well as a total lack of representation from the socialist countries, such as China and Vietnam.

The Conference had its disappointments, too. The Korean delegation was missed. Not one of the five persons invited to the Conference was permitted to leave Korea. Fortunately, the Korean input will not be entirely absent from this Conference record. Among the assessments in Part IV are the reflections by some Protestant theologians from Korea on the Final Statement, which they submitted after the Statement was shared with them.[31]

What did these two weeks mean for the delegates from the other continents? Three of these delegates share their evaluation of the Asian Conference in Part IV.[32] With the other non-Asian participants, they helped the Asian delegates to clarify their Asian identity and to extend their vision to global dimensions. Moreover, the non-Asians were able to pose challenges to the Asians on their emerging theology, for they too are on a similar search.

In conclusion, while the ATC did not come up with a "relevant theology" or even define "full humanity," it did accomplish the "towards" of the total task. The importance of the Conference is that the participants went through a theological learning experience and have become part of the on-going search for a relevant and dynamic theology in Asia.

This Introduction would be incomplete without acknowledging the efforts and contribution of key persons and groups.

The members of the Organizing Committee deserve gratitude for their work in planning this Conference, in particular for the active role played by Dr. Preman Niles, who represented the Commission on Theological Concerns of the CCA, Bishop Julio X. Labayen, who represented the Office of Human Development of the FABC, Dr. J. R. Chandran, who represented EATWOT, and above all, Rev. Tissa Balasuriya, who accepted the responsibilities of Convenor and Organizing Secretary.

The Centre for Society and Religion also played an indispensable part in the preparation of the Conference in its work of coordination, communication, and documentation. Furthermore, special mention must be made of the Local Preparatory Committee in Sri Lanka under the co-chairmanship of Bishop Leo Nanayakkara and Bishop Lakshman Wickremesinghe, of the Live-in Coordinators, and of all the Sri Lankans who contributed to making the ATC a reality.

Thanks are also expressed to all who were part of the Conference, as resource persons, delegates, or staff, and to all who gave their support from afar: the churches, organizations, agencies, and Support Committees in Europe, the United States, and Canada.

Deep appreciation goes to John Eagleson and Elizabeth Higgins of Orbis Books and to Sergio Torres, Executive Secretary of EATWOT, for their generous help and advice in editing this book.

Finally special praise and gratitude are given to the Lord of history, who is actively present in the midst of all struggle for full humanity.

NOTES

1. See List of Participants for members of the Organizing Committee.

2. EATWOT was formed at the conclusion of the Dar Es Salaam Conference in 1976. This meeting was followed by the Pan-African Theological Conference held in Accra, Ghana in December 1977. The papers from both conferences have been published by Orbis Books. See Sergio Torres and Virginia Fabella, eds., *The Emergent Gospel: Theology from the Underside of History* (Maryknoll, N.Y.: Orbis Books, 1978) and Kofi Appiah-Kubi and Sergio Torres, eds., *African Theology en Route* (Maryknoll, N.Y.: Orbis Books, 1979).

3. Theological Education Fund, *Ministry in Context* (London: TEF, 1972), p. 20. The TEF stance continues: "Contextualization, while it stresses our local and situational concerns, draws its basic power from the Gospel which is for all people. Thus contextualization contributes ultimately to the solidarity of all people in obedience to a common Lord."

4. Ibid. For further explanation of contextualization, see Sheki Coe, "Contextualizing Theology," in *Mission Trends No. 3: Third World Theologies,* ed., G. H. Anderson and T. F. Stransky (New York: Paulist Press, 1976), pp. 19–24.

5. Chairman Mao had just come into power in China, establishing the People's Republic.

6. M. M. Thomas, "Christian Action in the Asian Struggle," Christian Conference of Asia. *Christian Action in the Asian Struggle* (Singapore: CCA), p. 2. This article is actually M. M. Thomas's opening address before the Fifth Assembly of the EACC (later CCA) in 1973. M. M. Thomas is one of the leading Asian theologians. His *Christian Concern for the Social Revolution* (Calcutta: YMCA Publishing House) dates back to 1953.

7. The European Renaissance and Reformation, the American War of Independence, the French Revolution, the Industrial Revolution, and the Proletarian Revolution. M. M. Thomas, *Christian Action in the Asian Struggle,"* p. 3.

8. The CCA program of "theology in action" has called together people who have been engaged in Asian struggles to reflect theologically. Cf. for example, Oh Jae Shik and John England, eds. *Theology in Action, A Workshop Report* (EACC, 1972).

9. EACC, "Confessional Families and the Churches in Asia" (Report of the EACC Consultation held at Kandy, Sri Lanka, in December 1965), as quoted in Douglas J. Elwood, ed., *What Asian Christians Are Thinking: A Theological Sourcebook* (Quezon City, Philippines: New Day Publishers, 1976), p. xxii.

10. Elwood, ibid., and G. H. Anderson, ed., *Asian Voices in Christian Theology* (Maryknoll, N.Y.: Orbis Books, 1976).

11. Emerito P. Nacpil, "The Critical Asian Principle," in Elwood, op. cit., pp. 3–6.

12. "Living Theologies in Asia" (A CCA Statement), reprinted in *Center for Society and Religion Dossier 39* (Colombo, Sri Lanka, July 1978):8–9.

13. Cf., for example, D. Preman Niles, "Toward a Framework of Doing Theology in Asia," in *Asian Theological Reflections on Suffering and Hope,* ed. Yap Kim Heo (Singapore: CCA, 1977).

14. Cf. Raymond Fung, "On Doing Theology in Asia—An Industrial Missioner's Reflections on the Manila Theological Consultation," *Ching Feng* 20 (1977):148–152. The addresses, workshop reports, and papers of the Consultation on Theological Education for Christian Ministry in Asia held in Manila in May 1977 are published in Emerito P. Nacpil and Douglas J. Edwood, eds. *The Human and the Holy* (Quezon City, Philippines: New Day Publishers, 1978). The book also includes the background material for the Consultation. For a brief survey of the development of Asian theology up to the Manila Consultation from a Protestant perspective, see Ching-fen Hsiao, "Asian Theology—in Retrospect and Prospect," *The South East Asia Journal of Theology* 19 (1978):1–6.

15. The seminal book in this field dates back to 1964. See Raimundo Panikkar, *The Unknown Christ of Hinduism* (London: Dalton, Longman and Todd, 1964), but most of the works have been written since 1971.

16. J. Dupuis, "Five Years of Theological Reflection in India," *Indian Theological Studies* 14 (March 1977):91–114. Among these institutes actively engaged in working towards an Indian theology in a Hindu context are the Theology Center in Kettayam and the Centre for the Study of World Religions of Dharmaran College in Bangalore. In 1978, the conference "Theologizing in India" was held in Puna in October. For the most recent development, see the issue on Indian theology, *Jeevadhara* 9 (January–February 1979).

17. Cf. Tissa Balasuriya, "Emerging Theologies of Asian Liberation," in Kofi Appiah-Kubi and V. J. Asumin, comp., "Third World Theology en Route, from Dar Es Salaam to Accra," Part II (mimeographed).

18. Quoted from the minutes of the Organizing Committee meeting held in Colombo, Sri Lanka, February 10–12, 1978.

19. See Documents 2 and 3.

20. See Document 6.

21. See *Voices of the Third World* (Semi-Annual Bulletin of EATWOT) 2 (June 1979).

22. See Document 7. Dr. Gamani Corea, Secretary General of UNCTAD, was also invited to speak on the Asian reality at the Conference. However, since his talk focused on the history and development of UNCTAD and especially on UNCTAD V, held in Manila in May, 1979, it is not included in this book.

23. See Document 8.

24. See Document 9.

25. See Document 10.

26. See Document 11.

27. See Document 12.

28. After the sessions with the resource persons, the participants formed national groups to bring up issues to backtrack at this point: this work was supposed to have been accomplished prior to the Conference.

29. *Voices of the Third World*, op. cit., pp. 4–7. See also Document 14.

30. It is the writer's conviction that any emergent theology which does not take woman's perspective seriously cannot be truly relevant.

31. *Voices of the Third World*, op. cit., pp. 16–18. See also Document 15.

32. See Documents 16, 17, and 18.

2

Towards the Liberation of Theology in Asia

Tissa Balasuriya (Sri Lanka)

In the course of our own preparations for the Conference in Sri Lanka, some general insights have emerged which may prove helpful to the participants in situating the task of this Conference.

The Subject of Theology

Theology flows from a conscious reflection on the Faith as lived in a given context. Its scientific systematization and critique can depend much on full-time professional theologians.

However, not only professional, scientifically trained theologians but also others more directly engaged in the effort to transform their lives and society motivated by the Christian Faith can make valuable contributions to the elaboration of a theology relevant to our situations. In this, both groups need to listen to, learn from, and creatively challenge each other to an ever more faithful response to the demands of the teaching of Jesus Christ.

But there are inevitable problems in this collaboration process. Academic

Tissa Balasuriya, O.M.I., is director of the Centre for Society and Religion, Colombo, Sri Lanka.

theologians in general do not usually question the social conditioning of their own theology, or the centuries of theological tradition that lie behind it. They are more mindful of the years of effort that have been put into their own training, and they can tend to be rather wary of a theology drawn from mere experience and reflection by "lay persons." They may even see the fallacies in such efforts, since "lay persons" who are not well versed in Scripture may use sacred texts without understanding them in their original context.

On the other hand the "lay person" in theology may think that the academic theologians seldom—if ever—come to the heart of the matter, to the real gut issues of human existence, with regard to both interpersonal relations and societal injustices. The committed "lay person" in theology thus suspects that the academic theologians may really be finding in their scientific method an escape from the exigencies of the gospel in the real circumstances of our time.

There is thus a need to build mutual confidence and respect among persons of these two levels of orientation in theology or Christian reflection and to learn to benefit from each other's expertise in their common endeavor towards a relevant theology. Committed persons from action groups can bring the sensitivity of lived experience and struggle, while professional or technical theologians can contribute a more scientific understanding, especially of the Scriptures, in the light of advances in modern knowledge.

In all this we must have the widest ecumenical approach of openness to all others of different religions, Christian denominations, ideologies, and cultures. At the same time we must see ourselves and all others under the critical light of conscience, both individual and collective.

The ATC is thus to be a multidimensional encounter of persons from different disciplines, countries, experiences, and age groups.

The formation of new attitudes is necessary if we are to contribute to the creation of a relevant theology in Asia. Rethinking our definition of "theologian" is necessary, but a prior necessity is to remove from our minds any fears we may have about theology or doing theology.

The Fear of Theology

Most people tend to think that "theology" is something beyond their competence. They think of it as a highly sophisticated discipline or as demanding an ecclesiastical appointment for "doing theology" or as needing a direct communication line with God.

But the fact is that all of us do theology in some form or other, even if it be in negating the existence of a God. When we reflect on the meaning of our lives in relation to its ultimate values, it source, and destiny, we are theologizing. When we consider the good and bad of an action we are making a theological reflection. Our conscience, the inner light and voice within us, places us before such values, and in relation to the deepest insights and instructions within us. Theology relates to the act of righteous living and reflection concerning it in relation to the light we receive from God in different ways. God can manifest himself (or herself) to us in many ways: e.g., by his revelations through other persons, or his voice within us, through events, through religious leaders, etc. The believer in God believes that God is in direct and indirect relationship to every person. This is the first source of our knowledge of and union with God. From it can flow the science or wisdom about God, or theology. Therefore in some way or other all believers in God are doing theology.

The professional science of theology relates to the systematic study of its sources in the Bible, in history, and in the present situation. Professional theology tries to make a systematic analysis of faith in God. It uses human reason and scientific skills in doing so. It presents an organized body of knowledge that tries to interpret belief in God and its consequences, in a scientific manner.

However, theology is also an art, in that it is to be lived in a given situation. Experiencing God in prayer and contemplation often gives a richer awareness of the divine than the scientific analysis of God in a theological study. Likewise active commitment in trying to live the message of Christ is a deep experience of the meaning of the gospel that cannot be attained by mere academic study.

While appreciating the role of the specialist in theology as a help to others, we can all reflect theologically and try to live our beliefs. We can also contribute to the development of a theology relevant to our times and situation. Liberation from the fear of doing "theology" is then a condition for our creative contribution to theological reflection.

All this is more easily said or written than realized or lived. However, if our encounter genuinely brings together these different experiences, then we can expect deep and even difficult sessions both inside the conference halls and in and around the entire experience of the Conference. To draw maximum fruit from it, there must be a profound listening and contribution from each one and an attentiveness to the Spirit present amidst the encounter.

Towards the Liberation of Theology in Asia

As we reflect from an Asian point of view on the Christian message and activities present and manifest today, we are struck by the extent to which they have been molded by the experience and interests of the Western peoples, especially of Europe and North America. While the Christian Faith is presented as universal, valid for all times and meant for all peoples, the content of its dogma, moral teachings, and pastoral orientations has been largely related to the needs, concerns, and interests of the Western peoples. It is as if Christianity, having converted Europe, had in turn been made European.

A Methodological Problem

This raises a methodological problem for an approach to theology by non-Westerners, especially by Asians. If we do not accept the Euro-American worldview of history, geography, economics, technology, and culture, we find that many elements in the Christian teaching are not relevant to us. Many issues that have agitated the minds of Christians are not really our major concerns. They are peripheral to us; they are imports to Asia. A clear example is the division of Christianity into denominations and sects. These have been largely fashioned by European history and American concerns. They are not a central issue for us. Having first created the problem for believers in Christ, Western Christians then present us with an ecumenical movement and guidelines for contact between Christians; e.g., Roman Catholics and Anglicans. This is an example of the irrelevancies passed on to us. Europeans fought their politico-religious battles in the sixteenth century, and we as a result are divided into separate Christian churches today in Asia; plus we need their permission for greater communion among us.

A similar situation can be seen in attitudes towards other religions. Christians began by defining their self-importance in God's plan of salvation as expounded by them. "Outside the Church, there is no salvation" was a theological axiom. Into this the so-called "pagans," "non-Christians," and "nonbelievers" had to be fitted. Christian theology opened itself to a less indecent consideration of the position of these "outsiders" only after the latter became politically independent and intolerant of the attitude of Christian missioners who wanted to save the pagans.

For us in Asia, though, the problem poses itself the other way round. As an Asian I cannot accept as divine and true any teaching which begins with the presupposition that all my ancestors for innumerable generations are eternally damned by God unless they had been baptized in or were related to one of the Christian institutional churches. It is no use beginning by burdening ourselves and God with such a vision and then trying to elaborate theories of how the "pagans" might have been related to the church even prior to the birth of Christ. Such theological gymnastics do not do honor to God or to us. God is surely not an unfair God; God is no acceptor of persons; God loves all. Theology must honestly respect these millions upon millions of my ancestors and future human beings, before I can accept theology as a true interpretation of revelation from a loving God, Father of all.

The problem poses itself for us, even if we do not accept the premise of "no salvation outside the Church" and the theological method of poring over centuries of Christian writings. We get buried in a mass of irrelevancies on which we do not wish to waste our lives. In discussions with Westerners we spend time and energy (as I did in the early 1960s) trying to disabuse them of their holy convictions and learned prejudices. When I present to them the only view which they can accept, namely, that God is just and fair to all persons of all times and ages, they say, "Then of what use is the church?" or "Why should my uncle have gone to Indonesia as a missionary to save the natives?" Their point of departure is different.

For an Asian theology to evolve with genuine respect for the other religions there must be a fundamental change in the mental attitudes of Christians towards others. So long as we have an attitude of superiority and self-justification we cannot meet others in frank dialogue. We need to disabuse ourselves of many views and prejudices which we have held and harbored over generations. This means we have to rethink basically our "conversion mentality." We have to rid ourselves of a competitive mentality with regard to other religions; suspicions need to be replaced by warmth and a desire for understanding. In this manner our own theology must be requestioned; our reading of Scripture undertaken with a universal vision of humankind. These things cannot be done with mere declarations and patchwork reforms; we need a total reorientation of mentalities and practices. We have to begin from other premises, such as: God loves all persons; all are called to his kingdom; this kingdom has to be understood in a manner consonant with the aspirations of all human beings.

We find a similar viewpoint on other issues, such as: the teaching and practice of international affairs, the right of colonization, capitalism and socialism, the relationship between church and politics, and local cultures and liturgy. Capitalism and colonialism were acceptable to the churches; socialism and communism were anathema to them irrespective of their impact on our people.

Thus we see that we cannot accept many of the conclusions, premises, and even issues which concern theology in the West as necessary, true, or relevant. We see further that these have, in many instances, been damaging to our own self-respect and creative inquiry. They have also been harmful to us economically, politically, and socially. They help domesticate our peoples. They inhibit meaningful theological reflection by Christians in Asia. For Asian Christians to be able to relate meaningfully to the aspirations of our people and the vast changes taking place in our countries we need a freeing of our theology from many categories imposed from abroad and by the past. For theology to be helpfully connected with struggle for liberation, theology itself needs to be liberated.

Culture-Bound

Theology in recent centuries has in fact been profoundly culture-bound in almost the totality of its human elaboration. It has been, at least implicitly, ethnocentric—meaning what concerns the West. It has been a handmaid of Western expansion; an ally, at least, in the centennial exploitation of the peoples of other continents by the North Americans. The combination of the "sacred" duty of civilizing, baptizing, and saving the pagans with the military, economic, political, and cultural domination by Europe over our countries has been disastrous for Christianity itself. It has not only made Christian theology unacceptable in many aspects to the rest of humankind, it has even dehumanized the content of theology and, as it were, culturally blindfolded theologians themselves.

These statements are made very briefly and badly in order to explain some of the reasons for the need of a liberation of theology, and hence also for a different methodology in theology. There is a need for a critique of the way in which theology is elaborated. We cannot assume that theology is not limited by the cultural limitations of those who have elaborated it. Naturally this will be said of our present work, and rightly so. Hence from the beginning it is accepted that what I can present is only a point of view, some aspects of the overall human problem. Similarly Euro-American theology has to be relativized in its human elements. It goes without saying that the substance of divine revelation meant for all is universally valid. The problem is to get to this core message without its human limitations; this concerns not only Asians but all others.

Church-Centered

Theology has been very largely church-centered. It has tended to equate the universal kingdom of God and the common good of humanity with the progress of the church. The church was regarded as so divine that all else was faulty and in need of submission to and remedying by the church. The church was in fact made an ultimate value. The church was regarded as the necessary vehicle of salvation, with many distinctions about belonging to it. The focus of interest of theology has been the life within the institutional church; and among Roman Catholics, very much dominated by the more powerful European churches, with their focus on the Church in Rome. A heavier accent was placed on this juridical belonging than on living a life of love and service.

Male Clerical

That the churches are so taken with themselves is due in part to the near monopoly of theology by the clergy, especially as teachers in seminaries and universities. Hence theological preoccupations have been very much those of persons within the church institution and administration, or dependent on them. Incidentally, in the Roman Catholic Church, they are almost all males and mainly celibates. Thus theology has given much attention to issues which concern adult, male, celibate clerics. Theologians have tended to read the Scriptures with culture-bound eyes. They naturally were inclined to find in revelation many texts which reinforced their power, self-importance, and indispensability even for God.

An obvious example of the blind spots in theological reflection concerns the rights of women. Here too the method seems to be to start by attributing all rights a priori to the males, beginning with the garden of Eden, and then let the women fight for their rights when they can. During the many centuries of male domination, churchmen—in particular those in the Roman Catholic Church—have placed God on the side of the dominating male. Whatever changes are accepted are still mere reforms and tranquilizers. Thus women are to be accepted as deaconesses, to be given functions such as the distribution of communion under exceptional circumstances. But there is no acceptance of the fundamental equality of men and women in the life of the church—and this in an age when there have been women heads of states including elected Prime Ministers. Real power in matters both spiritual and temporal within the church is kept in the hands of the males. The same is true of the laity-clergy relationship. The theology of marriage is such that it is considered a bar to certain positions within the Roman Catholic Church. These may be purely disciplinary norms, but they are also the reigning pattern of thought, in spite of the practice of the early church.

Theology is also adult-dominated. It is still rather unthinkable that youth could be theologians. A theologian is supposed to be someone who has spent many years in reading hoary volumes of the past, whereas the contribution which youth can make is essentially in their vitality, sense of justice, dynamism, freshness of approach, openness to the future, and preparedness to face risks. The whole apparatus of church life is adult-dominated. The higher the echelon of authority, the higher is the average age of those exercising it. Hence youth are practically excluded from an impact on the thought and action in the churches. Here too, as yet, even the most forward looking changes give youth only a subsidiary role. There is little acceptance that persons of eighteen to twenty-five or thirty years of age can be mature human beings capable of making a significant contribution to the community, precisely as youth.

Capitalistic

In its social orientation theology has for many centuries been pro-capitalist. Theology and church action have been influenced by the class composition of church personnel. The lifestyle of most theologians has been within the framework of Western capitalism and benefiting from it. This is also true of church leaders, particularly in the higher echelons. Hence, consciously or unconsciously, they do not deal with issues that threaten their interests and positions. Thus theology has had little to do with the condition of the working class. It has been rather unrelated to the issues which concern the peasantry, who form the bulk of the people in the poorer countries of the world.

Where theology or church social teachings were concerned with these issues, the remedies proposed were in the nature of palliatives rather than of a fundamental reform of the social structure itself. Economic power was to remain with the owners of capital, with a certain softening of the exploitative process through sedatives such as recreational facilities for workers, labor laws, profit sharing, diffusion of shares, workers' councils, and trade unions. These are good in themselves; but there was no intention of fundamentally altering the social system so that the benefits of work would accrue principally to the workers themselves. There was to be no basic change of the social order to end exploitation of one person by another. The practical impact of the church was even more conservative than the official church teachings.

Another wide area of theological blindness, up to recent years, has been concerning Communist regimes. Our problem is that the church first condemns them, but now that the rest of the world is coming to a co-existence with the Soviet Union, Eastern Europe, and China, Christian thinkers are beginning to open their eyes. Even here, openness to China is still only beginning. On the other hand, Communist regimes have not harmed Asians in the same manner as Western imperialistic capitalist ones have done over the past four to five centuries. Hence we find it rather awkward to begin our theological search with the attributing of positive values to our known enemy and negative ones to Communist regimes which have been to some extent the liberators of Asian peoples. Once again culture-bound preferences of the West pass for Christian theological positions with, of course, many references to the recent teachings of churchmen. There is here an implicit identification of the interests of the world order dominated by the West with the good of all humankind and the cause of God himself. Asians are thus in a dilemma which is more profound than the assimilation of Christianity with its Western languages, rituals, and even culture and mentality.

A similar evaluation can be made of the thinking among church leaders concerning development, justice, and peace. Development within the present world order, with the technology of the West and its financial and economic institutions, is thought to be normal. At most, it is thought that some adjustments have to be made. As yet the churches have not opted for a world system other than the prevailing capitalist, Western-dominated one. As within society, the remedies suggested are palliatives—except for one or two references in Pope Paul's encyclical *Populorum progressio.* The churches recommend reforms within the world system such as economic cooperation through "aid," commodity agreements, reform of the currency, reduction of the arms race, and peace. These are good things in themselves, but utterly inadequate to transform the system in which 80 percent of the population of the world has only 20 percent of the resources. Poverty thus continues in the midst of plenty. Peace is understood as the preservation of the present world order.

Yet from an Asian point of view totally different approaches are necessary. We need a revolutionary change in the world system. Revolutionary does not mean necessarily violent. It does mean a radical and rapid change in the world system; the change has to be not merely marginal, or quantitative, but rather throughout the whole system and qualitative. The world is meant for all humanity; and a qualitative change in the relationships among peoples and resources is required to ensure basic human rights to all persons in the world. The churches lack a theology that is revolutionary in the content of change advocated—be it within countries or among nations. In this sense, while the world requires revolutionary changes, theology is still fundamentally conservative, capitalist, and pro-Western.

Lack of a Socio-Economic Analysis

There are other characteristics of the theology of recent centuries that are gradually being questioned all over the world and yet are still prevalent as the major orientations of Christian thinking. Thus analysis of society has not been accepted and incorporated as a basic element in theological reflection. Theology tends to be deduced directly from the scriptural sources and church traditions. Since there is an absence of the data of the world, it is influenced more by the prejudices, myths, and preoccupations of the theologizers. This is a further point of methodology that needs to be remedied radically if there is to be any worthwhile consensus in the churches concerning Christian action in society. The absence of socio-political power analysis makes the churches complacent about the consequences of the dominance of some over others, especially of the Western powers and the local elites in Asian countries. They even become implicit legitimizers of such domination. Since a good deal of theological thinking is individualistic in orientation, the social aspects of the kingdom of God, sin, conversion, and salvation are neglected. Sometimes these social aspects are considered merely human, humanitarian, horizontal, and natural as if they were not related to the spiritual, to God. Here too the basic presuppositions have to be overhauled if we are to meet the aspirations of modern human beings, and be honest to reality with its absurdities, such as immense poverty in the midst of unprecedented affluence.

Absence of Action-Orientation

Closely related to this is the absence of action-orientation in theology. When theology is only theoretical, it fails to take into account the exigencies of the real situation, and of the effort to change it. It is only in action that the many discussions of a problem become clear. When action is absent from reflection, the thought tends to be sterile; and hence, in fact, status quo-oriented and conservative. It is possible to elaborate theology merely academically, but with little relevance to the actual conjuncture of events and forces as they develop in the world. An action-oriented theology, on the other hand, would have to assess the forces operative in a situation, think of goals, strategies, and tactics, of timing, and groupings of persons. All these require skills different from those of the merely academic theologians. It will also have to develop a different spirituality, including active participation in social change even in conflictual situations.

The church has been action-oriented, even though theology may have been speculative. But this action has been church-centered in its missionary approach, and conservative in its social impact. We need a theology that is more human-centered, and oriented towards justice in society. This requires an option in favor of the oppressed. Such a theology would also be more God-centered, as God is present and active in human history. There has been a neglect of the dynamic nature of the kingdom of God being realized through history.

A theology that is action-oriented must take into account the time dimension. Timing is of the essence of the matter. The pace of events has to be an input for decision making. Today it is not much use to condemn the old colonialism (except Macao, Hong Kong, etc.). Today we have to deal with new colonialism and new forms of exploitation as in some nations in Asia and in Czechoslovakia. The church has had a knack for siding with the prevailing oppressors, but then trying to make up with the liberators, once these are successful. This is opportunism. Prophetic timing is to be with the oppressed in their struggles—while they are engaged in them.

Such a theology would be one which would be continually in process rather than static. It would have to meet the problems posed by a fast-changing world. A theology that is action-oriented would be largely lay—unlike at present; the ministerial clergy, as such, would not necessarily be leaders in such a theology requiring the skills of socio-political analysis, decision making, and risk bearing. The youth too would have a significant role in the growth of such a theology, for youth are more present where the action is than are the adults, especially the aging academics and clerics. It would also be a theology that is concerned with real issues and events as they occur in time and in different places and environments. Hence theology would be more practical than merely speculative.

Action orientation will mean that theology is to be concerned with strategies of action. Theology over the past few centuries has been concerned largely with intra-church strategies and methods: conversion to Christianity, fight against personal sin, spiritual combat within oneself and inside cloisters, ecclesiastical sanctions and controls, rewards and punishments. Today action is very much in the field of public life. Hence the conjuncture of events, forces, and obstacles has to be evaluated, different strategies weighed and adopted. Risk taking in these areas is quite a different phenomenon from the risks inside cloisters.

The spirituality of conflict situations requires a different evaluation of virtues and of progress in the spiritual search. Ascetical practice and mystical experience can and will have to evolve within such a context of a struggle against the sinfulness of socio-political structures and consequent sacrifice and joy. All these elements are only beginning to be brought into Christian theology. They are essential elements for the building of the kingdom of God in our world.

These considerations together point to the need for a new orientation in theology, a fundamental break from a theology which was, in fact, the ideological support for the Western hegemony of the world, for capitalist domination over the poor, and for adult, male clerical domination within the church which was in the service of the prevailing world order. We need a theology and an action that will help rid the world of the enormous injustices that are a planetary evil. Theology must counteract this global madness masquerading as civilization blessed by God.

How Can Asian Christians Help Such a Reorientation?

Some of the approaches required are already being developed in the "political theology" in Europe, the practical action-oriented theology in North America, and especially in the theology of liberation in Latin America. We can help in broadening this reflection by relating to Asia more consciously. This will not only widen the scope of these approaches but also intensify the issues. The Asian contribution can include a certain understanding of the human person which the Asian religions and philosophical traditions can contribute, as well as a sharpening of the strategies due to the demands of the Asian revolutionary processes. In this sense, our reflection relates to the tradition of Western theology at the point which it has reached today in the more future-oriented thinkers and persons in the "movement" for freedom and justice in the world.

Yet if we wish to try to meet the problems faced by Asian reality or the Asian religions, we cannot begin with a consideration of the issues that are dealt with in traditional European theology. For this unnecessarily involves us in a mass of less relevant material that merely takes up time and energy and mystifies the issues. The major thrust for us cannot come from the Euro-American worldview. We have to think about how we view the world from our context.

We have to take a fresh look at the central core of the Christian message. This requires a direct return to the sources of revelation, especially to the person of Jesus Christ in the Gospels. In this too we have to bypass many less relevant debates and get as much as possible to the core of his message. We even have to purify our minds of merely Christendom-centered theologies which have missed the universality of Jesus Christ. We need a deeper awareness of the historical Jesus of Nazareth. We have to ask ourselves how we understand the Gospels today in our times. Here again modern Euro-American thought can help us, but we need to go further than they have gone hitherto.

Another point of departure has to be a socio-economic and political reflection on the world of our times, and on the Asian scene. This can be a partial view—one aspect of a contribution to a theological inquiry. We should try to relate reflections to the basic yearnings of the human person for freedom and personal fulfillment.

Fulfillment and liberation struggles are being sought in Asian countries at different levels and with different means. Persons seek meaning and peoples want a chance to be, and be themselves. In sincerely relating to this Asian quest for full humanity, Asian Christians can evolve a theology relevant to our aspirations, needs, and struggles.

A consideration of the situation of the church in Asia can help us see what its impact in Asia has been in the past. From a reassessment of this position in the light of our understanding of Christ and the Christian mission in the world we can see what directions the church should take in Asia and elsewhere—at least in relation to the Asian problems.

The overall considerations indicate to us that a fundamental reorientation of the thinking of Christians is required to meet the challenges of our times. It requires a liberation of our own thought processes to know the issues and respond to them. What we need amounts to a veritable cultural revolution within the church, including its theology.

3

Christianity in the Context
of Other Faiths

Bishop Lakshman Wickremesinghe (Sri Lanka)

This topic has assumed fresh importance because Christians have begun to assimilate the significance of radical changes in their midst. Though it is gathering momentum elsewhere, this process is most evident in Asia. It is primarily in terms of Asian experience, therefore, that this article is written.

Christian enterprise was undertaken in the context of imperial expansion within stagnant societies and moribund cultures. It was accompanied by an urban lifestyle, a plantation capitalist economy, liberal democratic polity, an individualist ethic, and the outlook of a sophisticated and racially conscious Western civilization. It led to the growth of local churches, the fostering of Christian family traditions along with the anglicizing of manners, the translation of the Bible into the vernacular languages, the opening of social-service institutions for the sick and the destitute, and the transmission of values, knowledge, and skills required for living in a modernized society. The world was viewed as a state prepared by Providence for church expansion and the spread of civilizing influences, in which the agents of change were mainly Christians.[1]

Lakshman Wickremesinghe is the Anglican bishop of Kurunegala.

The radical changes which have gathered momentum in Asia signify the reversal of this situation. There has been a resurgence of ancient societies under the impact of imperial expansion and missionary enterprise. Indigenous leaders of other religions have replaced Christians as agents of change in refashioning their societies to revitalize their co-religionists and to establish a sense of national self-identity. The rural masses with their educated but unemployed children have been affected by these changes and have begun to seek ways to emancipate themselves. The ancient religions have re-emerged in the wake of modernization to offer both religious vision and social ideology as a basis for personal fulfillment, cultural renaissance, and social reconstruction. They also make the claim that they alone have the resources to cure the ills of modern man and to resolve the conflicts between nations.

This changed situation led to fresh insights emerging among Asian Christians. Like the exilic prophets they sat dazed, reflected with penitence, and received a wider vision of God's activity in the world and their own role within it.

First, they realized the cultural particularity of the Christianity that had been transmitted to them in the era of Western dominance. Christians had been isolated from their cultural inheritance, which they now viewed in fresh perspective.

Second, new attitudes emerged among them, regarding the status of other religions in relation to Christianity. They were totally committed to Jesus Christ, but they also appreciated the positive elements in other religions for their own worth; and they saw how these could enrich historical Christianity.

New Responses by Christians

The responses made by Christians to the new situation can be described in three stages.

First, there was the process of adaptation. This could be likened to the transplantation of a potted plant brought from abroad. Transplantation exposes it to the local environment and begins the process of rooting it in the local soil. Likewise, Christians began to adapt features from local temple architecture in building their churches, elements from local arts and crafts, painting and sculpture to adorn them, styles of music and types of devotional practice associated with the offering of flowers and lights, dance and drums to enrich the liturgy and other rites.[2] Ashram buildings with their ceremonies and styles of dress are other examples.

Second, there was the process of naturalization. This is akin to the shoot of a traditional local plant being grafted on to the pruned stalk of the transplanted foreign plant. Similarly, Christians began to relate the insights and values of other religions to their Christ-centered vision. This has been done quite often in consultation with persons of other faiths with expertise. Some examples are these: The creative use of words with technical meaning in the traditional culture to convey the meaning of the person and work of Christ in the new version of the Sinhala New Testament; murals in churches which make creative use of traditional and contemporary artistic imagery to communicate the meaning of the crucifixion of Jesus;[3] and the use of readings from other Scriptures on particular occasions followed by Christian readings in the liturgy and daily office.

Third, there is the process described as dialogue. Though last in point of time, it is the most mature response made by Christians. The kind of adaptation and naturalization arising from dialogue has greater depth than previous attempts.

Dialogue describes the response of sharing and cooperating with persons of other faiths in a spirit of love, openness, and the desire for mutual enrichment. A person's faith is engaged by the faith of others. This guards against both fanaticism and also indifference to basic convictions; it also enables persons and groups to discover their specific identity in a community with a plurality of religions.[4]

At the intellectual level, dialogue enables participants to view their basic convictions through the thought forms of other religionists, reconceive them with fresh insight, and communicate them to others with better understanding.[5] However, there are those who ask whether assimilating insights from other religions to enrich the apprehension of truth based on one's own religion is sufficient. They desire also the discussion of the truth and validity of each other's religions as part of the dialogue.[6]

At the experimental level, participants learn to incorporate the spiritual experiences and vision of other religionists into their own religious vision and experience. The creative incorporation of Yoga and Zen into Christian contemplative experiences is an obvious example.[7]

At the level of working together to achieve justice, peace, and development in society on the basis of common human values, more progress has been made. In Sri Lanka, there has been fruitful collaboration in producing suitable syllabuses for religious instruction. In the Sarvodaya movement, there is acceptance of common values, shared work, and joint meditation over a wide range of rural development ventures. Churches have also released money and personnel to interreligious groups managing joint ventures.

A further development of such collaboration is found in interreligious groups working for the liberation of the oppressed. They manifest a more secularized and interiorized spirituality, directed to social struggle. Liberation ideology unites them, while they also acknowledge religion as an important dimension in their common life. Their devotional acts symbolize their common values and shared activities as seen in a transcendental perspective. In one such commune, there is a para-liturgy in which acts of thanksgiving, confession, and commitment are shared in the context of chanted readings from various Scriptures and radical writings. It takes place after shared labor or discussion, and is followed by a symbolic partaking of ordinary food and drink.[8]

Dialogue, whether intellectual, experiential, or social activist, is limited at present to small groups, as only a minority in Asian societies share in this concern for pro-existence. In practice also, collaboration is effective in a society only where there is prior acceptance of one's respective majority or minority status among the participants. However, in the midst of the tensions and potential divisions of pluralist societies, they bear witness to a more excellent way.

Dialogue must be understood in its proper perspective; it need not undermine the communication of the full gospel message. In the past, the discerning Emperor Dharmāśoka of India promoted what was best in our faiths and encouraged mutual understanding and respect among diverse religionists.[9] He also combined this with missionary endeavors on behalf of Buddhism all over Asia. In the present, dialogue has yielded greater reciprocity and enrichment than was possible then. To the discerning Christian, it is a decisive way of receiving and communicating divine revelation at its appropriate levels.

Basic Perspectives for Dialogue

There is a basic attitude underlying the dialogic process as understood by Christians. It represents a tradition of thought within the historical Church from the time of Irenaeus,[10] through Cardinal de Lugo, to Baron von Hügel.[11] But contemporary Asian experience has given it new directions.

It is an attitude of Christ-centered reciprocity towards other religions and their adherents. It yields insights which guide Christians in appreciating and assessing the value and efficiency of other faiths, within God's creating, saving, and transfiguring purpose. Initial insights reflect experiences of the Christian verities arising from initial dialogue both with the experience of other religionists and also with the experience testified to authoritatively in Scripture. They provide an "interpretive model" which has to be tested further in the face of new insights emerging from the ongoing dialogue. Interpretation and the evidence of experience have to be continuously correlated.[12]

Present insights can be summarized in this way. God's prevenient love operates everywhere, at all times, in each person and group, but uniquely in biblical history centered in Jesus Christ. He is unique not merely because, in the Nazarene, God is expressed from within a human nature brought to moral perfection, but also because the Son of God was embodied in him to the fullest extent possible to the receptive capacity of human nature. His work is unique not only because it is fully effective to secure salvation for us personally, but also because God has set him in the world and among us, as the inescapable saving Presence before whom all persons and situations are accountable. The Scriptures which testify to him are unique because they record the normative, though not sole, interpretation of God's dealings with humankind. The church which derives from him is unique because it is the appointed, though not sole, sphere which expresses and makes effectual the kingdom of God.

In other words, the particular salvation history centered in Jesus Christ provides the unique model. The other salvation histories are prologues, but with their own range of effectiveness and autonomous contribution to the salvation history of mankind. Their saviors and saints are worthy of recognition and honor; their Scriptures and their community life have insights, values, and spiritual authenticity available for enriching the thought and life of the visible church. Though not the appointed sacrament, other religions are effective sacramentals, made available in the providence of God.

For example, in Christianity there is a covenant relationship between God and his people mediated through Jesus Christ. In other world religions there is a Transphenomenal Beyond (Yahweh, Allah, Brahma, Nirvana), and the humanward relationship (love of neighbor, brotherhood, *ahiṁsā, mettā*) mediated through saviors; and these are analogical ways of expressing this covenant relationship. In Christianity, the covenant people are a community of disciples who share in the experience of the covenant relationship, and who celebrate events and persons representing various aspects of it, through liturgy and calendar. Likewise, other religionists are communities of adherents who share in their experience of this dual relationship, and who give socio-cultural embodiment to it, through celebration of its various aspects (Passover, Ramazan, Mahā Sivarthi, Wesak). In Christianity, the covenant people are conscious of a covenant history initiated by God and leading to a goal in which they and their Scriptures have a decisive role to play. In like fashion, communities of other religionists have, in varying degree, an analogous kind of consciousness (Kingdom of God/Torah/Jewry; Kingdom of God/Koran/Islam; Brahman-Atman/Śruti-Smriti/"Saṁpradāya"; Nirvana/Tripiṭaka/Saṅgha.).[13]

In what ways are Christians to testify to the ultimacy of Christ while appreciating other religions?[14] Should a Christian offer flowers before the Buddha statue if occasion requires—is it an act of veneration or an act of worship? Should Christians managing institutions catering to all religionists permit them separate places of worship on the premises, or should they permit only acts of worship as occasion requires? Does the former policy imitate the uniqueness of Jesus in his self-effacing humility for the good of others, or reveal an indifference to the basic Christian affirmation that Jesus alone is worthy of worship? Does the latter policy testify to this affirmation or reveal a crude and petty way of asserting his uniqueness?

Furthermore, what are the specific tasks of the church in the context of dialogue? Other religions have their relative autonomy; in the providence of God they are not meant to be absorbed simply into the visible church. At the end-time, they will bring their special gifts into the kingdom of God. On the other hand, the church is required to draw others into its unifying membership from all religio-cultures, as a foretaste of and a testimony before all nations, to the kingdom of God.

The Mission of the Church

What then is the mission of the Church? First, it commits Christians to live alongside religionists, and to share life with them both in their search for salvation, and in their resistance to God seeking to save them. This is the way of Jesus.

Second, it obliges Christians to commend the values and insights of the kingdom of God revealed in Jesus Christ, for other religions to absorb and manifest. For example, Christians have been able to transmit in Asia commitment to an historical purpose, social service, and community reconstruction to religions preoccupied with an other-worldly orientation, for incorporation into their total vision of life.

Third, it involves helping persons of other faiths to accept Christ-like values as Zacchaeus did. These values stem from Jesus, but those who absorb them can remain in their own faith with a higher quality of life. It is a form of conversion. People are attracted to and altered by a challenging lifestyle, as many testimonies have indicated.

Last, there is the obligation to evangelical witness. It requires a Christian to present to others the claims of Jesus, as the one who alone can save us from ourselves and lead us in love to the Father and to our fellow human beings. It may be giving testimony to the hidden meanings of a particular religious inheritance, as Paul did with the Athenians; or evoking a deep response within the personal longing for deliverance, as Jesus did with the woman of Samaria. It is essential evangelism in the context of dialogue with persons in their situations.

Christ-centered reciprocity with other religionists means relating to them as persons at different levels. In deciding how particular aspects of the gospel message are to be affirmed or commended in particular situations, Christians will differ in emphasis. The modernist and the fundamentalist, the proclaimer and the evoker of hidden depths are ever with us and perhaps within us. In any particular situation, the mind of Christ who indwells us, remains incognito in other religionists, and interprets Scripture, will have to be discerned in the response of personal faith.[15]

Scriptural Testimony and Contemporary Testimony

During the period of Western missionary enterprise, and even now, many Christians have understood the testimony of Scripture regarding the relationship of Christianity to other religions in this way: other nations and their religious cultures or histories serve as a preparatory background for the establishment of the kingdom of Christ through the expansion of his church.[16] Adherents of other religions were reckoned as those living under the wrath of God and as stiflers of the truth they perceived, under the influence of the Prince of Darkness.[17] The duty of the Christian was to preach the gospel message of salvation to them all so as to seek their conversion to Christ as their Savior and Lord.[18]

But there are other strands of scriptural testimony whose weight needs to be recognized. Other nations with their religious cultures are viewed as guided by God, and in the end they share in the inheritance of his kingdom without the intervention of Israel or the Christian church.[19] Adherents of other religions are seen as illuminated by God, who indwells them within their religious commitments.[20] There are also those who finally find a share in his Kingdom even though not members of the visible church.[21]

Jesus reveals diverse ways of ministering to others, especially in the Synoptic Gospels. Sometimes the emphasis is on the values of supernormal powers of the kingdom; sometimes it is on himself. He heals and forgives a paralytic without indicating who he was, or asking him to become a disciple; as a Rabbi, he changed radically the values of Zacchaeus and left him in his situation; he exorcises the Gerasene demoniac who cried out to him as the "Son of the Most High God" and asks him to witness among his own people to this God and his mercy; he reveals himself as the "Son of Man" to the man born blind who worshiped him, but does not ask him to become a disciple; yet he calls others to join his company of disciples and trains them to recognize who he is. He remains incognito or reveals himself with a sensitive appreciation of the occasion. From this it can be seen that scriptural testimony has other strands which provide a proper basis for the new attitudes emerging among Asian Christians. We must appreciate the diversity of emphasis in scriptural testimony for its own worth.

Asian Christians accept scriptural testimony as authoritative because of its divine inspiration. This is attested in the Scriptures, confirmed in the variegated tradition of the church, and authenticated in their own experience. But this testimony must be seen in its proper perspective, especially in regard to the relation of Christianity to other religions.

The testimony in the New Testament records the realized experience of Christians in that era, arising from their many-sided engagement with surrounding cultures, under the guidance of the Spirit. For example, the church realized the cultural partiality of some of its Jewish practices, such as circumcision, when it spread among the Gentiles. These were no longer imposed on them after the Council of Jerusalem. The term "Messiah" with its Jewish associations was replaced by the term "Logos" borrowed from Greek thought, and by the word "Christus" associated with cult titles and saviors of the Greco-Roman world.[22] The early Christians received fresh perspectives as they encountered other religions, which enriched their understanding of their own faith and helped them to present the gospel message more effectively.

The new perspectives emerging among Asian Christians record their experience as they have been engaged with other religions, seeking the guidance of the Spirit. Contemporary testimony is revealed in their specific insights. This testimony has to be scrutinized in relation to scriptural testimony, being the testimony of those uniquely placed in regard to the events concerning Jesus Christ. Such testing needs to take place in each era as the church journeys to the end, awaiting the full manifestation of the kingdom of Christ. The authority of scriptural testimony is exercised through the guidance it provides in the face of new developments, in the ongoing history of the church.

In other words, a dialogue takes place between contemporary testimony and scriptural testimony, until the Spirit provides a discernment for faith in the present situation. When contemporary testimony is discerned as the development or rediscovery of scriptural insight for new contexts, it is affirmed as arising from the inspiration of the Spirit;[23] as a result, what is culturally conditioned in scriptural testimony is also recognized. Where contemporary testimony is discerned as clearly undermining scriptural insights, it is not affirmed as inspired by the Spirit and its cultural conditioning is thereby discerned. At the present time, for example, this dialogue is taking place with regard to such issues as the ordination of women, the relation of Christianity to other religions, the interpretation of the person and work of Jesus Christ in Asiatic cultures, in secularized societies, and in the face of liberation movements.[24] Recognized discernments of the Spirit have yet to be received in faith by the universal church.

Such discernment is facilitated when dialogue takes place between particular regions and branches of the universal church. It is in such mutual openness that the universal elements or permanent insights belonging to Christianity will be discerned. It is church leaders who must make this possible, as in the early church.[25]

Conclusion

While the universal church searches for the "tradition" that should be handed down to the next era, the mission of the regional churches must continue. Local churches have their relative significance and autonomy.[26] Their task is to lay hold in obedient faith on those insights that will help renew the church, and also communicate the gospel with effectiveness to others in their contemporary setting. Jesus Christ, to whom we give our final allegiance, comes to us not only through Scripture and tradition, but also as the Living One who is saving and renewing life in our midst. It is as we are centered on him with fresh vision that we shall discover our unity in diversity.

NOTES

1. This summary makes no reflection on heroic missionary endeavor.

2. Some ventures in the Diocese of Kurunegala.

3. Masao Takenaka, *Christian Art in Asia* (Kyoto, 1975).

4. Lynn de Silva, "The Understanding and Goal of Dialogue," *Dialogue* (New Series) 4 (January-August 1977): 3–8.

5. Lynn de Silva, *Why Believe in God?* (Colombo, 1967); *The Problem of the Self in Buddhism and Christianity* (Colombo, 1975).

6. Dr. G. Dharmasiri, *Buddhist Critique of the Christian Concept of God* (Colombo, 1974), pp. ix–xi.

7. Abhishitkananda, *Prayer* (Delhi, 1967); *Saccidānanda* (Delhi, 1974).

8. Devasarana Collective Farm, *New World Liturgy* (Ibbagamuva, 1976).

9. Rock Edict 12.

10. Iraeneus, *Adversus omnes haereses,* Book 3, ch. 11, 8; and Book 4, ch. 28, 2.

11. Cf. E. C. Dewick, *The Christian Attitude to Other Religions* (Cambridge: The University Press, 1953), pp. 120–125.

12. Ian G. Barbour, ed., *Science and Secularity* (New York: Harper & Row, 1970), pp. 11–32.

13. Aloysius Pieris, S.J., "The Church, the Kingdom, and the Other Religions," *Dialogue* (Old Series), No. 22 (October 1970): 3–7. "Maoism is a secular faith to be faced in the Asian context. ... It can also be likened, as can the religious faith, to an 'analogue', i.e., 'Phenomenal Beyond' = universal love for humanity; 'manward relationship' = love and service for the people in the present order; 'celebrations' of events like the Long March or the Chinese Revolution = liturgy; the 'end' = classless society; 'Scriptures' = Marxist-Leninist-Mao's Thought/Writings; 'covenant people' = Communist Party/Cadres."

14. M. M. Thomas, *The Acknowledged Christ of the Indian Renaissance* (Naperville, Ill.: Allenson, 1968; Madras, 1970), pp. 246–288.

15. Acts 16:6–10.

16. Acts 17:22–30; Matt. 28:19–20.

17. Rom. 1:18; 2 Cor. 4:4; Eph. 2:2; 2 Tim. 2:26; John 3:19–20.

18. Mark 16:15–16; 1 Cor. 9:16; Rom. 10:1.

19. Isa. 19:19–25; Rev. 21:22–26; Mal. 1:11.

20. Mark 12:28–34; Matt. 8:5–10; John 1:47–51; Acts 10:30–35; Acts 18:24–28; John 3:21.

21. Luke 13:29; Rom. 2:13–16.

22. Kenneth Cragg, *Christianity in World Perspective* (London: Oxford University Press, 1968), pp. 55–62.

23. John 15:21–26.

24. Kosuke Koyama, "Jesus the Buddha" (cyclostyled manuscript); Tissa Balasuriya, O.M.I., *Christ and Human Liberation* (Colombo, 1976); John Hick, ed., *The Myth of God Incarnate* (London: SCM Press, 1977).

25. C. F. D. Moule, *The Birth of the New Testament* (London, 1977), pp. 174–177.

26. Acts 11:19–20.

Part Two

The Live-In Experience

4

The Live-In Plan

Virginia Fabella (Philippines) and
Sergio Torres (Chile)

The live-in experience was a vital part of the ATC. Without it, the Conference would have been incomplete, for deriving help from actual life situations and issues for theological reflection is basic to a contextual and relevant theology.

The success of the live-ins was due to a large extent to the preliminary work of the Preparatory Committee in Sri Lanka. An organizer was appointed for each of the nine live-ins with (1) village folk; (2) fisherfolk along the Indian Ocean coastline; (3) tea plantation workers; (4) coconut plantation workers; (5) industrial workers and trade-union personnel; (6) women in Baddegama, where a special training project for women is located; (7) youth and students on a collective farm; (8) minority groups in Paranthan; and (9) slumdwellers in Colombo.

When the participants arrived in Sri Lanka for the ATC on January 7, they were immediately ushered to a small retreat center in Negombo, conveniently located near the airport on the outskirts of Colombo, the capital city. As each participant registered for the Conference, she or he was given a choice of the live-ins, and equipped with a short introduction to that particular live-in and a detailed schedule for the next three days, together with a map and a general survey of Sri Lanka.

The live-ins were well organized, giving the participants opportunity to visit local groups and lay people working for the liberation of the oppressed

39

sectors, as well as time to do collective reflection on their experience. The live-in organizers had been cautioned not to cushion any of the difficulties of life in these sectors so that the participants could know at first hand what it meant to queue for transportation, to sleep on mats on bare floors, to be without any running water or modern hygienic facilities, and to do without privacy.

The three-day experience had a great impact on all the participants. It was an eye-opener even to the Asians themselves. It was one thing to see a slum from a passing automobile, another to be immersed in its squalor and dejection. Some of the participants were shocked to see the outright contradiction between the living conditions of the poor, and the witness of the church. The dehumanizing situation is far from the claims of liberation of the gospel of Jesus Christ!

All these experiences and reactions were apparent in the reports that each group was asked to present in both written and audiovisual form to the rest of the ATC participants when they convened in Wennappuwa for the Conference proper.

The audiovisual presentations were either in drama, song, or pantomime. In ten to fifteen minutes, each group captured for the assembly the core of their three-days experience. The presentations depicted the attitudes, questions, and struggles of the different marginalized sectors as the participants had observed them. In most cases, the assembly could easily empathize with the portrayals, but the depiction of the minority situation of the Tamil-speaking people of Paranthan provoked such controversy among the Sri Lankan participants right in the process of the presentation that it was never completed. The opposing views and sympathies regarding the situation of the Tamil-speaking flowed from both emotion and conviction. At this first indication of conflict and tension, one participant stood up and announced: "Now our conference has really begun."

The written reports did not evoke the same reactions. The questions they raised were more factual and intellectual.

The general format for the written report consisted of a brief description of the situation, an analysis of it, a comparison with similar situations in other Asian countries, and a short theological reflection on the experience or on relevant issues that surfaced in their particular live-in.

One of these reports follows. It is a description of the live-in at the coconut plantation prepared by Cynnyc Cheng from Hong Kong and Eunice Santana de Velez from Puerto Rico.

It was recognized that the live-in made a difference in the shape of the conference. Most of the participants agreed that it was an excellent preparation for the sessions that followed. It imparted both the dynamics of the group and the depth and sensitivity of the reflection. Perhaps not enough was utilized from the live-in experience, but it helped to relativize a lot of things.

It made the simple Holy Family retreat-house dormitories and facilities seem like First World accommodations; it made clearing the tables and helping with the dishes seem part and parcel of theological conferences. It confirmed the conviction that no theology or talk about God can be separated from the life of the people, especially from the struggle of the poor and the marginated.

5

The Coconut Plantation Live-In Report

Cynnyc Cheng (Hong Kong)
and Eunice Santana de Velez (Puerto Rico)

Description of the Situation

Importance of the Coconut Industry

- as important as the tea and rubber plantations in this country
- 25% of cultivated land areas are coconut plantations, just second to the rice paddy fields
- involves one million workers in the industry directly or indirectly
- 65% of the product is for local consumption; 35% exported, mainly to Western countries
- virtually every part of the plant is useful; enormous potential to further derive more products for foodstuffs, drinks, construction materials,

Cynnyc Cheng was the Asian secretary of the International Movement of Catholic Students (IMCS). He died in a plane crash October 31, 1979. Eunice Santana de Velez is an ordained minister of the Christian Church (Disciples of Christ) and member of the coordinating committee of the national ecumenical movement of Puerto Rico, PRISA.

house utensils, medicine, and chemicals from the industry (more than 150 products)

- intercrops possible in the plantation; it can also provide pasture for animal raising as well as provide living space within the plantation
- in short, it is a blessed richness of the tropical countries with very promising potential for greater self-reliance

Area of the Live-in

- located at Nainamadama, a few miles south of Wennappuwa; it is the central coastal part of the coconut triangle
- the area's economic life revolves around the coconut plantation and related industry and services
- the religion of the people in this particular area is predominantly Catholic, thus the church plays an influential role

Places We Visited

Church compound // planters' residences // mill workers' huts // tappers' houses // factory owners' residences // managers' residences // coconut plantation // dehydration factory // fiber mill // combing factory // vinegar factory // timber production workshop // side industry factories // Coconut Research Institute (CRI) // fishing village // cemetery

People We Met

Parish priests and nuns // workers of different sectors // middle men and managers // mill owners and planters // CRI director and researchers // self-employed workers // young people and students in the area // children and child laborers // mothers and women workers

Categorization of the People into Sectors

1. *Upper wealthy:* planters, landlords, industrial plant owners. They constitute a small minority of the population. In many cases, they are co-owners of many different plantations, factories, and mills. Many of them hold honorable positions in the community and in the government sector. They are well organized among themselves.

2. *Management:* managers, professionals, and supervisors. They are employed by the upper sector to take charge of the daily routines of the plantations and factories. Quite a number of them are relatives or associates of the upper sector. They also constitute a small minority in the community.

3. *The poor:* the contract workers in plantations, mills, factories, and trans-

port. They descend from poor families and constitute a majority of the population in the area. This sector is practically unorganized.

4. *The auxiliaries*: the middlemen, small landholders, independent tappers, small workshop owners, and craftsmen. They earn enough for a moderate lifestyle through their holdings or skills. Most of them can afford to provide education for their children. They also constitute a minority of the population in the area.

5. *The religious*: parish priests, nuns, and church employees. They cater to the religious needs in the community, run schools, and provide humble services. Some derive their income from plantations owned by the church and donations from the upper sector. Basically they have a middle-class lifestyle. They also constitute a minority of the population, but enjoy high social prestige among the common people.

Some Observations on the Economic Relationships in the Area

Despite the enormous amount of wealth that coconut industries have brought to the nation, in the area we observed there is a stark contrast between the upper class and the contract laborers under them. While those who live on profits enjoy an affluent lifestyle and look towards a bright future, those who have no choice but to sell their cheap labor are struggling for survival in abject poverty. The continual accumulation of wealth by a few does not benefit the majority.

We are aware that all of the workers are exploited as usual by the multinational traders who buy the products of their hard labor and determine the low prices for them.

Some Observations on the Upper Sector

From the information we gathered, they are originally from the traditional planters' families who live in luxurious mansions with nice gardens. They have house servants and new private cars. Most of them are well educated and many have children studying in Western countries or working overseas. They have many plans for their future. Many of them are Catholics and regular churchgoers who hold responsible positions in lay organizations of the church, as well as do charitable works during the Christmas and Easter seasons. Businesswise they control most of the means of production as well as the products. Their basic source of income is from profits. They form cooperatives and associations among themselves to secure their social status and guarantee continuous profits.

When we asked why their workers were living in very miserable conditions, they explained that the workers were uneducated. Besides, they did not know how to save and they spent whatever money they had on alcoholic drinks, so they were always in debt. If the workers cannot afford to pay back their loans and interest, they escape and shift to other mills. Since workers have never complained about their working conditions, the patrons conclude that they really have treated their workers fairly.

Some Observations on the Poor Sector

We talked with some of the contract workers and visited their homes. Although they may come from different places, their ancestors had also been workers in plantations or mills. Many of them live in small huts in the plantations without electricity or hygienic facilities; there is no furniture, no beds, so they sleep on muddy or sandy floors. Whenever it rains the floor becomes wet and they cannot sleep. They also suffer from insect bites.

The workers in the mills ranged from 11-year-old children to 59-year-old women. Since they are paid only on a piecework basis, they have no job security. Many do not even have work everyday. Most of them work very fast and hard to earn as much as possible to cover family needs. Many of the mill and combing factory workers and some workers in the dehydrations factory are women, but in many cases the whole family is mobilized to work for survival. Workers earn from four rupees* a day (i.e., women in the fiber mills) to twenty-five rupees a day (i.e., skilled machine operators in dangerous situations). They cannot afford to send their children to school. In fact, most of the workers had hardly more than a few years' education.

The hygienic conditions and the pollution in the mills are quite bad. We observed that quite a number of the workers coughed as if they had lung diseases. Since they have very unnutritious food, many of them are in poor health. A woman explained that when their children are sick, they have no means of sending them to doctors, though sometimes the planters will come and give them some medicines.

They are basically unorganized and are not aware of the legal rights they should enjoy. In one mill, the workers have asked the owner to cement the floor of their huts. Although the owner had promised it for years, this has not yet been done. They said they could only ask the owner again and hoped that one day their wish would be granted.

Many of the workers are Catholics who go to church regularly on Sundays. The most memorable and valuable thing they have in their house is the photograph taken on their first communion. In the church they tell God their sorrows and sufferings. Somehow they receive consolation from God. They pray, but feel that they are powerless to change the situation; it is their fate. They hope their children will lead a better life than theirs, but do not know how these hopes can be realized. They hope that the owners will one day treat them better and that they can enter heaven after they die.

They are friendly to strangers. Their simple huts have no doors to close.

*Fifteen rupees=one U.S. dollar.

They have shared with us their warm friendship and deepest sincerity. We have learned a lot from them.

Reflections on the Situation

Despite the local nature of the coconut plantation, the situation we saw was to a large extent very similar to the situation in many of the other Third World countries in Asia.

Key Problems We Felt

1. Abject poverty of the majority as a consequence of large accumulation of wealth by a few.
2. The poor suffer from inadequate income, malnutrition, subhuman living conditions, harsh labor, and exploitation of child labor and old women.
3. There is a chain of exploitation:
   - contract laborers by local elites
   - small plantation holders by middlemen
   - laborers and local elites by multinationals and world capitalists
4. General atmosphere of submissiveness and hopelessness.
5. Silence of the church at large, despite the fact that members in the church sector are aware of the situation and that the area is mostly Catholic.

Causes We Felt That Lead to These Problems

1. The structure of the social setup:
   - semi-feudal relationships
   - ownership of means of production concentrated in the hands of a few and carried down through the family relationship
   - workers are deprived of knowledge of their own legal and human rights, and there are also threats against any organization among themselves into unions
   - control of local and international markets not in the hands of the people
2. The superstructure that perpetuates the social setup:
   - profit-making motive dominates among the planters and owners; they regard laborers as tools rather than as persons
   - the middle sector is also dominated by the ideology of the rich and aspire to be exploiters
   - the poor are too oppressed to realize their potential and capacity for changing the setup, thus resorting to fatalism
   - religion preaches the message of resignation, of consolation to the poor and blessings to the rich

Potential and Forces We Felt That Can Change This Situation

Not all the potential and forces for change mentioned below were observed in this particular situation. However, some of these do exist in similar situations in other Asian countries.

1. We feel that there is a need for radical change in the economic and social structure as well as in the superstructure.

2. Conscientization process among the workers is essential: so that they can become gradually aware of their own rights, dignity, capacity, and responsibility to change the existing unjust situation.

3. Continual impoverishment of the workers and the widening gap between them and the owners make the situation more clear to the people, favoring the work of conscientization.

4. Some attempts have been made to organize the workers but are not yet widespread in this area.

5. To protect and to promote the legal rights of the workers, there should be increased efforts to introduce legislation and reinforce implementation of the legislation.

6. Individual church members have expressed their concern to commit themselves to live among the poor and serve their righteous struggle for their fundamental human dignity and rights.

7. Some church members have already started efforts to dialogue with the rich and are listening to the grievances of the poor.

8. There should be increased opportunity for education of the younger generation to build the potential force for change.

9. There is increasing awareness in some of the local elites for a more equitable share of the wealth from the raw materials exported, thus some work towards establishing a more just international economic order against the domination of multinational traders.

10. Some intellectuals return to the villages and help in the struggle of the people.

Theological Reflections in Christian Perspective

Our Impressions of the Role of the Church at the Present Time

1. The church is influential in the coconut area and parish priests and bishops are highly esteemed local authority to the people.

2. The local church has not taken a clear stand in favor of the contract laborers.

3. The local church has not exercised its healing power by pointing out to the upper sector that they are acting unjustly towards their brothers and

sisters; or to the oppressed that it is not God's will for them to remain miserable.

4. The local church supports the side of the rich by accepting their donations and in commending their works of charity. This eases their conscience and blurs their very exploitation of their own workers.

5. Consequently, the church continues to enjoy its social status and is not threatened by the established order.

6. The church limits its service to the poor to charity.

7. There is a minority group among the church members who recognize the immensity of the problems and see the gospel challenge to take a stand in this situation; however, there is also an attitude of fear of exclusion for those who are beginning to understand the situation of injustice and wish to begin a meaningful ministry among the poor.

8. Some individuals also feel that the institutional church structure limits their capacity to really serve the needs of the poor.

The Challenge of the Gospel for This Situation

Questions for reflection: We can perhaps begin by asking ourselves:

1. What is the relationship between salvation and the historical process of the liberation of humankind?

The biblical message is clear in presenting God as acting and therefore saving, within a concrete historical context. God acts in history. His presence and actions point to breaking away from situations of oppression and misery. The Exodus God acts in favor of the oppressed and protests against injustices regardless of their origins. He clearly sides with the oppressed (Micah 6: 10–11; Isaiah 3:12–15; Amos 5:10–11; Luke 20:46–47; Luke 16:19–31). Poverty and other states of misery and exploitation are an unnatural state, since they result from humankind's inability or irresponsibility to be good stewards of God's gifts. This is an affront to God, who means for his creatures to be happy and have plenty (Genesis 1–3; Psalm 8).

Situations of misery and exploitation do not happen by accident or by God's plan, but are a result of both personal or collective will that rejects God's will. God's plan for humankind to have dominion over the whole of his creation becomes meaningless when it is utilized only for the good of some. The relationship between God and one's neighbor is so clearly stated that to have little regard for one's neighbor is to offend God. "He who mocks the poor insults his Maker," so the person who shows no compassion and lives affluently while others have little or nothing insults God (Proverbs 14:21; Deuteronomy 24:14–15; Exodus 22–23; Proverbs 17:5). The law therefore is summarized in terms of love for one's neighbor (Galatians 5:14; Mark 12:28–31; Matthew 22:34).

2. What is the concrete meaning of love for one's neighbor (Isaiah 1:17; Matthew 18:21; Luke 2:27–36; Ephesians 4:23–32)?

3. What is our role as we try to respond to the challenge presented by the gospel?

4. What does it mean for Christians to be salt of the earth and light of the world?

5. The prophet announces God's will and denounces unjust situations; what is our prophetic voice?

6. What is real worship? (Isaiah 58:6–7; 1:10–17).

7. For followers of Christ what is the meaning of this life and teachings for this situation? *In defiance of the Law* he moved, acted, and lived among the poor, outcasts, persecuted. He said he came to save and find those people (the sick and lost) and not those who were well (upright and religious).

8. He purified the temple of Jerusalem by whipping and throwing out of it the exploiters of the people (Matthew 21:12–13; Mark 11:15–17; Luke 19:45–48; John 2:13–22). What is the meaning of this for us: "To know God is to do justice"?

9. Matthew 25 (the Judgment of the Nations) confronts us with: "As you did it to the least of these you did it unto me."

10. What is the meaning of the Parable of the Rich Man for us—the church? (Matthew 19:20–24; Mark 10: 17–27; Luke 18:18–22; 12:15–21).

11. What is the meaning of the following for the church today? The condemnation of poverty (Amos 2:6–7; Isaiah 10:1, 2) and exploitation (Amos 8:4–7; Micah 6:10–12, 15; James 2:5–13). The condemnation of both the violence and the complacency of the dominant classes (Amos 4:1; Micah 3:1–2; Jeremiah 22:13–17; Luke 2:14; James 5:1–6).

How should we (as persons and as the church) relate with "the least of our brothers/sisters"?

What is God's message to us for action within our nations where unjust conditions exist and internationally where unjust relationships between nations exist?

How does this influence our preaching, our role—our Christian responsibility?

6

Reflections on a Live-In Experience: Slumdwellers

Samuel Rayan (India)

Options

Live-in experience made up the first phase of our theological conference. We were going in small groups to live three or four days in close touch with people and their problems in the actual places and conditions in which they lived. We had several options. Did we wish to live among peasants in a village? Or among workers in tea estates and coconut plantations? Or among industrial workers in the city, or the dwellers in city slums? Did we wish to contact women, or young people and students, or racial minorities in order to sense and register the dire realities of their life?

I had not made my choice as many participants had before arriving at Negombo. My instinct was to opt for the youth and student group. I thought I could understand their language, I could sympathize with their quest, their nonconformity, and their radicalism. Had I not moved and worked with youth for many years? But then a gently nagging voice within me kept saying,

Samuel Rayan, S.J., is both professor and dean of theology at the Vidyajyoti Institute in Delhi and a member of the Faith and Order Commission of the WCC.

"You are playing safe. You choose to stay within the familiar. Are you afraid of what is strange, what might challenge and shock you? And don't you wish to learn something new?" I therefore began to ask myself what fear was lurking within me, from what possible inconvenience I was shying away, and what middle-class sensitivity was ruling my moves. In that mood my option could only be the city slums. I had never lived in any. I knew the disgust with which I had seen them and the swiftness with which I had passed them by. I knew there was compassion somewhere in my soul which yearned to be with those discarded people and to lift them out of the filth and the stench. It is the stench I cannot stand, and the filth. I am middle class, bourgeois, clerical. But I guess I care for people. I knew the anger in my heart's depths against whatever was responsible for messing up our world with slums and shacks and hunger and squalor, and women in rags and children with thin limbs and bloated bellies, and men broken under the weight of failure and hopelessness. I let this mood and its memories revive and wander freely over all the hills and valleys of my soul. For me the Asian Theological Conference had already started. I had yet another day to study myself and debate with my thoughts before having to give my name to one or another live-in group.

What decided my final choice was something much smaller than all this. It was the eve of the day we were going for the live-in; most delegates had made their choice, and I found to my surprise that the slum live-in was the lowest in demand. I put my name down, third on the list. The day of the live-in itself, we had become eight in number. To side with the weakest and opt for the neglected is perhaps a common human trait. On reading plays and novels, does not innocence and powerlessness sway us and win our sympathies? Is that some instinctive passion for justice? Remember reading *Child of the Dark* by Carolina Maria de Jesus of the slums of São Paulo, Brazil? She wins our heart. Did not her diary become a bestseller? And she had only two years' schooling, was unmarried, had three children to rear, earned a tiny bit of money by picking trash, and lived in a *favela* full of filth and crime and hunger.

Remember the translator of her book telling us in a preface how Carolina, now become famous as a writer, and rich, left the *favela* in a truck, and how the miserable *favelado* rabble cursed her and threw stones at the children? I found that at that moment my sympathies were with the rabble. That, to be sure, is a Brazilian reality and won't fit into Asian theology. Or? But hunger and human degradation are strangely similar in São Paulo and in Delhi where I live and in the slums of Calcutta. There are numerous slums in Delhi in the squalor of which, in the shadow of big, beautiful houses and government offices with extensive grounds and gardens, live huddled together tens of thousands of men and women and children. Some of the *bastis,* built on low-lying land, get flooded in the rainy season, and the floods come carrying into the shacks visible and tangible filth from the drains and latrines of the neighborhood.

Summits and Slums

The eight of us, from six different nations, regrouped ourselves in twos and threes and lived in three different slum areas not far from each other. We also visited a fourth one. These four are only a fraction of the slums and shanties of the great city of Colombo. We were told that perhaps 52 percent of the population of the city were slumdwellers. We are not going to describe here the poverty and suffering of these people. It is known that the conditions in which they are forced to live are subhuman; they lack the most elementary amenities of life, such as water and latrine facilities. These are often denied them by municipalities and governments in order to make their eventual eviction easier. The people will have to go when landlords and authorities think fit. They cannot therefore build anything decent even if they had the means. They cannot plant a fruit-tree even when there is an inch of earth. They may have to move before the fruits are ripe or the new mud-wall is dry.

The most miserable of the slums we saw bore the name Summitpura. The name is written large on a board by the roadside for all passersby to see. The 800 distraught families existing in this slum area were removed by the government's police from Colombo Centre on the occasion of the Summit Conference of Non-Aligned Nations held in the city in 1976. The poor were removed from the city and their work-place, and their shanties demolished lest they offend the eyes and the noses of the honorable delegates to the Conference, lest they haunt their sleep, lest the ugly truths about Sri Lanka be noticed by them along with the beautiful truths about Sri Lanka, lest they remind them of the uglier slums of their homeland. No delegate from any Non-Aligned Slum was attending that Conference. The poor were removed from the city and dumped here.

That is why this slum has the name Summitpura. A fitting memorial for a great event. A tell-tale name. A story that bares with trenchant simplicity the real nature of the economic and political system represented by the Summit Conference. All over Asia summits rise by digging hells. It is the same economic and cultural process that creates wealth for the few and misery for the many. Can theology fight shy of the implications of the Summitpuras, or are they necessary grist to any theological mill?

Where Does Relevant Theology Come From?

This was not the first time most of us were having a live-in experience as preparation for and as part of a conference. But the procedure is comparatively recent. Formerly we came to conferences armed with concepts and systems of thought. Our preparation began and ended in the library. Our contribution was already neatly dressed and tucked away between files in a briefcase. It had only to be produced at the right moment according to schedule to the delight and applause of the house. But today oftener than not professors and bishops start conferences and deliberations by touching and smelling the earth and its people, and tasting though but for a few brief days the tears and frustrations of the hungry and the dispossessed. And we were now in the slums.

The roots of this new practice seem to lie deep in the new awareness of a close link between life and thought. There is an intimate dialectical relationship between objective reality and subjective consciousness, between existence and ideas. A dialectical relationship also exists between the experience and struggle of the masses and the analysis and reflection of intellectuals. For this rich view of the theory and process of human knowledge we are thankful to Marx and Mao. "Where do correct ideas come from?" asked Mao in a speech made in May 1963. They do not drop from the skies. They are not born with the mind. "They come from social practice, and from it alone." At first knowledge is perceptual. When sufficient perceptual knowledge is accumulated there occurs a leap of the mind to conceptual knowledge and ideas. Then comes the second stage that leads from ideas back to existence, which by now will be exhibiting new features it has developed from within. The first stage is here applied to social practice, and its correctness tested. And social practice is of three kinds: the struggle for production, the class struggle, and scientific experiment. Live-in experience would normally belong with the first stage of the process of accumulating perceptual knowledge. Live-in is a humble reality, though occasionally when we are slightly bored with its lowliness, we give it a louder name and call it Exposure Program or Research Encounter Live-In.

Four days of slum life for bishops, professors, and university students is not much of an accumulation of perceptual knowledge, is it? It can only be an immediate stimulus of reflection. It can sharpen our awareness of the plight of the people, focus our attention and clarify and deepen our commitment. We were in the slum not to make an accurate survey, not to count carefully, not to put classroom questions. We were there to look and listen and sense; to touch and take in the reality of the slum as much as possible with our whole skin; to let the shapes and smells of the place and the expressions in people's faces and eyes and the ways of welcoming or not welcoming register themselves upon our soul. Occasionally we communicated in words; that was good. Most of the time the communication was wordless; that was better, so I thought. We listened to things and to people, to unspoken words, to silences, to tears both shed and unshed.

The People

Philo said: "I was not rich enough to learn English. When we heard two foreigners were coming to this place I never thought they would know our language. Now God has sent one who understands at least a few words of our language. I am so happy." The language in question is Tamil, which I can follow somewhat, in which I can respond haltingly. Philo is a teenager, one of three girls who have acceptance and influence in the slum because of the training they have had in various local services from a devoted social worker. Her colleagues are Navamani Devi and Soma. What do Philo's words reveal? What inner world of dreams and disappointments, of self-understanding and pride, of sensitivities and loyalties?

A young mother explained how her boy could not join school in their new neighborhood for want of a certificate from his old school, which would not give it unless the family went back to the old place and lived there for some months to prove domicile, and paid a small fee, and gave "presents" in addition. As a shift to the old place was not possible, the family arranged for tuition for the boy. He is intelligent, and can already read and write. But now that wages have fallen, the tuition cannot continue. The mother was sad. "How do you see his future?" We asked. "We are hopeful," she said; "we must find a way." In the evening we reflected on the spark of life that refuses to be completely quenched; that mother and her child are the seed of a great fire and the promise of the future. Meanwhile the rules, the laws, and the insensitivity of the ruling classes are becoming a Moloch devouring the children of the poor and denying the oppressed a future.

Three middle-aged men of the slum wanted us to talk to a young man who had taken to drinking because, we discovered, of some misunderstanding with his wife. What struck us was the mature combination of concern, understanding, and gentleness the three men showed. And we had the feeling that the young man himself felt accepted and helped, not accused or corrected.

Many more instances of human riches as well as of practical initiative and resourcefulness could be cited. Examples could also be given of obstacles to the solution of problems and to meaningful struggle. When Philo got girls together for a first-aid seminar, one of the girls refused to join; her family had a house of their own; her sense of class superiority would not let her sit with the rest! Individual ambition is the rule despite a great deal of sharing among the families. Young men feel they should fend for themselves, and are not easily organized. Due to lack of analytical understanding of their situation, the people are often divided in terms of caste, religion, and political parties. Many have come to believe in their own complete worthlessness. "I am nothing" is the terrible phrase in which they are accustomed to express their identity and self-understanding: the fruit of generations and centuries of oppression and the seed of total resignation and accepted dependence. It is important to look into the role the religions have played in the emergence and consolidation of resignation and the sense of worthlessness, or in dealing with these basic evils and rebuilding each person's pride and creative confidence.

Experience of such realities and challenges is part of the process of change we intellectuals—as distinct from the masses with little or no formal schooling or training—are willing to undergo in order to be able to think and work with the people for the transformation of the social order. We know that "only a long process of practice, living and working integrated with the laboring people" can change us. That is why intellectuals should be encouraged to go among the masses. "They should seize every opportunity . . . even if they just go for a walk, to look around the countryside, like looking at flowers while on horseback." (That word is from Mao as cited by Han Suyin in her book *Wind in the Tower*, 1978).

Slums and Theology

Our live-in was a not-too-long walk as we took in the lives of neglected and discarded people in the suburbs of a big city. It enabled us to touch people's problems in the raw and look at them straight as they throb in the eyes and hands of the downtrodden. That should save our thinking from academic impersonality and bland generalizations. It should add urgency and warmth to our quest for a relevant theology. Our ideas should thereby begin to be transformed into knowledge which, whenever it is genuine, originates always in direct experience.

But did we really think that our live-in experience was an adequate basis for theology? Hardly. This immediate, on-the-spot stimulus made us keenly aware of the need for a global analysis and understanding of the political, economic, and cultural reality of Asia as a whole. Theology cannot be built on discrete data. It calls for a comprehensive picture of society and for critical reflection on that picture with the aid of concepts and theories forged within concrete struggles in our actual situations. Admittedly, theology is a process, always hard, and sometimes long; we cannot be unaware of this, nor of the temptation to an instant theology.

One of the convictions the live-in deepens is that truth is not words and books. Truth is people, their lives, their minds, their self-understanding. If the gospel is directly addressed to the poor, they are the ones likely to have the best grasp of its intent and meaning. It is in their praxis that the gospel becomes an historical force for transformation, and thus acquires historical truth. We do well in going to them to encounter the revelation that is being made in their midst. There we may meet him "where his feet rest among the poorest, the lowliest, and the lost"; for "he walks in the clothes of the humble," and "keeps company with the companionless"; "he is there where the tiller is tilling the hard ground and where the pathmaker is breaking stones," "with them in sun and in shower, his garments covered with dust" (Tagore).

There were moments in our reflection when the suggestion was made that the real point of the live-ins lay in the shift from a deductive method of theologizing to an inductive approach to theology. But we proceeded to ask ourselves if these two models were mutually exclusive; if there is need to carry this Western dichotomy into Asian theology; if the one approach has ever been or could ever do without the other; and if they are not related dialectically. We asked whether inductive and deductive are at all adequate methodological words for use in theology. Coming from the mathematical and physical sciences they seem to ill fit Asian theology, which will be less a science than an art, seeking not merely to understand the world but to transform it into something deeply human. Live-in was, in this perspective, a symbolic action having its own suggestive richness of meaning, transcending all categories of induction and deduction.

On arrival at the venue of the Conference after our slum experience, the sight of extensive grounds, beautiful gardens, a spacious complex of buildings and long clean corridors made one of us exclaim, "This now is paradise." What happened at that moment to the symbol of the live-in experience? Was it being substituted by a different symbol? And did not the two come into severe conflict in our minds as the Conference progressed? Some at least had the feeling that the first symbol was crucified at the center of our souls. At that center they experienced a tearing apart. Of this pain and unease were born questions which kept coming back in the days that followed: Have we been using the people of slums and plantations and factories as guinea pigs or launching pads? Who has benefited by the live-in? The people or we? We surely have benefited: we now have the raw material for a relevant theology! But what becomes of the poor?

Valid concerns, these, and integral to the theological method we were struggling to clear for ourselves. Two things were, we felt, required to meet these questions with some measure of adequacy. One was to make sure that the live-in experience was not left behind but taken up into the vital fabric of theological processes. Live-in was to be no mere overture or aperitif, but an opening chapter which defined the terms and purposes of the Conference and was therefore present and influential throughout. Here perhaps our success was small, and the reason for it may well be that our reflections did not take off immediately from brief, concrete visual presentations of live-in experiences; instead we fell back on paper work. Paper has a fascination for us; it is our worship of paper that prevented the potent experience of live-in from fecundating the theological process that followed. But we are in a learning process, and mistakes and failures are not without their point. The other requirement is that we justify our live-in by making of the theology we create a theology of the poor and the struggle of the poor, till the day dawns when we can celebrate their victory over all that oppresses people, over all principalities, powers, thrones, and dominations. That is a project with which we must keep faith. That faith will coincide with the faith we should keep with the people we have met in the villages, estates, plantations, and slums.

Part Three

The Consultation

7

Socio-Economic and Political Reality in Asia

K. Matthew Kurian (India)

The participants of the Asian Theological Conference have already presented their reports giving valuable insights into various problems of working people of Sri Lanka, which they gained through their live-in experiences. The reports prepared by the participants after their live-ins contain not only information regarding the miserable and dehumanizing conditions in which the majority of the people live in Sri Lanka but also reflections on the situations in which the participants find themselves in their own countries all over Asia.

The reports prepared by various groups did throw some light on the total socio-economic and political reality of Asia. However, a comprehension of Asian reality cannot be completed without a detailed structural analysis of the socio-economic and political power structure in the Asian countries and their relationship with international developments, particularly the crisis which international capitalism is facing today.

K. Matthew Kurian is director of the Institute for Regional Development Studies in Kerala, India.

The Socio-Economic Reality

Countries in Asia are passing through an epoch of great significance—an epoch in which the people of these countries are increasingly asserting their rights for a fuller human existence and for self-determination and the self-creation of their own destinies. The character of the present historical epoch for Asia, and indeed for the whole world, is the decline of capitalism and imperialism and the rise of socialism and socialist social formations.

Socio-economic and political reality in Asia cannot be understood by a mere narration of discrete data on poverty, unemployment, rising prices of commodities of common consumption, degradation in terms of social and political existence, and so on. Nor can it be comprehended by a purely "emotional" approach to the problem; that is, an approach based exclusively on sentiments of identification with and charity to the poorest of the poor.

A comprehension of reality, of course, is not possible without an emotional identification with the poor and oppressed. But it must be emphasized that without a detailed scientific analysis of the dynamics of socio-economic and political systems as they operate in each country in Asia, we can never hope to understand reality. This involves the process of making valid generalizations about discrete data, reflections arising from experiences, and the conceptualization and formulation of theoretical or ideological positions.

Asian reality, again, cannot be considered in isolation from the changes that are taking place in the socio-economic and political arena the world over.

International Capitalist Crisis

The international capitalist system is passing through the worst crisis it has ever faced in its history—worse than even the Great Depression of 1929–32. By the middle of 1973 most of the capitalist countries, particularly the advanced among them, faced a severe depression in their economic activities. Prices rose substantially. Unemployment swelled, and the living conditions of the people below the so-called poverty line worsened. The crisis was not limited to the urban and rural poor but it affected all sections of the capitalist class itself. Many banks had to be closed. There was panic in the stock markets of the capitalist world; the market prices of ordinary stocks showed a fantastic decline of U.S. $300 billion in 20 months. The *Financial Times Industrial Index* for the United Kingdom declined below 200 for the first time during the last sixteen years.

Unemployment rates in the advanced capitalistic countries rose as a direct consequence of the world economic crisis. The rate of unemployment (as percentage of labor force) was 8.7 percent in Belgium, 5.5 percent in Denmark, 4.1 percent in West Germany, 5.6 percent in France, and 5.7 percent in

Italy and Britain. In the United States, the jobless, who were 7.9 percent of the work force in October 1976 rose to 8.1 percent in the next month. If we take five countries: U.S.A., Canada, Britain, France, and Italy, the total unemployment figure, which was 4.7 million in 1969, rose to 7.5 million in 1972. According to the *U.S. News and World Report* of May 15, 1978, in Britain alone the figures increased from 0.61 million in 1973 to 1.5 million in 1978.

It is estimated that in the U.S.A. alone about 15 million people live on the doles (unemployment benefits) given by the government. On the one hand unemployment rose; on the other, managements of factories increased the work load.

The inflationary spiral of prices coupled with economic stagnation has been a special feature of the world economic crisis since 1973. The prices of food during July 1975–August 1976 increased by 16.8 percent in Italy, 16.2 percent in the U.K., 10.1 percent in France, 11.6 percent in Sweden, and 8.4 percent in Denmark.

The crisis was marked by serious problems in international payments. The monetary system built by the Bretton Woods Agreements, that is, a system based on the strength of the U.S. dollar, collapsed. From 1960 onwards there was a gold drain from the U.S.A. Excess dollars generated by heavy U.S. spending under Lyndon Johnson and Richard Nixon flooded the markets of Western Europe. With successive devaluation of the dollar, the system of fixed parity of exchange of other currencies with the dollar collapsed. The supremacy of the Almighty Dollar as the reserve currency of the world ended. The International Monetary Fund had to introduce a new system based on Special Drawing Rights (SDRs).

Gone are the days when Japan and West Germany could be described as exceptions in the capitalistic world so far as rates of growth in GNP and other indicators are concerned. According to *Asahi Shimbun,* the Japanese newspaper, 90 percent of the 100 big industrial establishments which it surveyed were in a state of complete stagnation. Workers suffered: as admitted by the Japanese government there was a decline of 2.8 percent in the real wages of the workers.

The economic crisis of 1973 and after has a number of special features. First, there has been a synchronization of the trade cycles of all the capitalist countries. Second, there has been an absolute decline in industrial production in the capitalist world. This never happened before except in 1958. Third, the new crisis is a crisis of inflation plus stagnation—a phenomenon which could be characterized only by coining a new word in the English language, "stagflation." Fourth, the economic crisis in the advanced capitalist countries has had a direct and more penetrating impact on the economies of the less developed countries. Thus, the International Monetary Fund in their report had to come to the conclusion that:

At mid-1974, the world economy was in the throes of a virulent and widespread inflation, a declination of economic growth in reaction to the preceding high rate of expansion and a massive disequilibrium in international payments. This situation constitutes the most complex and serious set of economic problems to confront national governments, and the international community, since World War II.

Keynesian solutions which helped world capitalism to perpetuate itself for a number of years since the slumbering thirties have now proved to be totally ineffective. The economic experts of capitalist countries are no longer in a position to offer effective remedies for the serious ills of world capitalism. Moreover, there is no prophet like Keynes to inject new life in the decaying capitalism. The Special Economic Consultant to former U.S. President Ford had this to say:

The conventional wisdom was that unemployment was usually worse than a little inflation, and that inflation can be curbed by mildly restrictive policies where necessary. We studied the ways and arts of economic stimulation. We forgot we were stimulating a lazy relaxed animal. But most important we had no idea how sensitive the economy had become to stimulus.

Response of the Working Class

The working class in the capitalist countries have not remained idle during the period of the new economic crisis. The workers have boldly resisted attempts by big capitalists to reduce their wages during periods of recession. The capitalist class has been stopped in its tracks to even partially solve the crisis by a direct attack on wages. In the first nine months of 1973 about 43 million workers participated in strikes and other mass labor actions. In the United States alone the average number of person-days lost by labor struggles during 1971–74 was 7,018 per struggle. In 1974–75 it increased to 7,804. If we examine the average number of workers who participated in each struggle we find a substantial increase in many countries. In the EEC (European Economic Community) countries the average number of workers per struggle during 1971–74 was 829; this increased to 1,250 by 1974. In Japan there was an increase from 600 to 664 during the same period. There was not only a quantitative increase in the number of workers' struggles and the number of workers who participated in strikes and other forms of agitations, but there was also a qualitative growth in the intensity of the struggles. Apart from a rising trade-union consciousness in industrial workers, government servants, and other white-collar employees, women and peasants entered the arena of struggles against the system. Teachers, municipal employees, transport workers, and many other sections of the toiling masses joined forces with greater vigor than ever before.

As the intensity of the worker's struggles increased there were changes in the form of struggles as well. Strikes, go-slow methods, sympathy strikes, picketing, and taking over of factories were forms of struggle resorted to by the workers in many countries.

An important feature of the resurgence of trade-union consciousness in the capitalist world is the increased number of nationwide struggles. In 1974 alone in the U.S.A., Britain, West Germany, Japan, France, and Italy there were twenty nationwide struggles.

It is true that the working class in most of the advanced capitalist countries which waged heroic struggles against all forms of exploitation in the early competitive stage of capitalism, unfortunately got bogged down in "economism" in the stage of monopoly capitalism, and even got domesticated to the point where many revolutionary youth and other sections of the people lost all hopes about the revolutionary potential and the leading role of the working class. But in the new phase of the decline, decay, and final destruction of imperialism, in the epoch of an acute general crisis of international capitalism, the working class in the advanced capitalist countries has risen again from the grave. Based on available evidence, we can state with a high degree of confidence that the workers will play their historic role.

The crisis of capitalism and the working-class response to it are of immense interest for us in the less developed countries of Asia. Our economies are still tied to strings that are controlled from London, Paris, and Wall Street.

Colonialism and Neocolonialism: Heritage of the Past

Though colonialism in its overt form ended in Asia, its roots are deep. Imperialism and neocolonialism continue to operate in disguised forms. The new methods used by them are subtle and cover all aspects of life.

Neocolonialism refers to the covert forms of dominance exercised by the ex-colonial and imperialist powers—an indirect version of colonialism wherein "the metropolitan power exercises control within the context of the nominal independence of the people affected rather than by an outright colonial administration imposed on them." [1]

The rise and fall of colonialism in Asia have to be studied in terms of the specific features of each region or country. The transformation of the Malayan states into a number of British colonies during the second half of the nineteenth century[2] and the independence granted to the Malaysian Government on the basis of an acceptance of the traditional economic relationship with the United Kingdom form a familiar pattern. Even in countries where the revolutionary class participated actively in the national movement for independence, the colonial government took great care to ensure that power was transferred only to a combination of dominant classes on whom they could rely, at least partially, in the post-independence period. No wonder that in 1969, foreign private companies were controlling 62.1 percent of the total share capital in companies in Malaysia.[3]

In the Philippines, where the national movement succeeded in destroying

Spanish control over Luzon, the United States of America established its absolute control through occupation following the Spanish-American War and during the presidency of William McKinley. Though formal power was transferred to local people, American business had reached a deal with the United States government to help establish favorable relationships. The Bell Trade Act and the Philippines Rehabilitation Act passed by Congress were the products of the private monopoly lobbies in the U.S.A.

By 1970 the Philippines had a total foreign debt of 1.96 billion U.S. dollars to be repaid to about 25 governments and international institutions. If the rescheduling of the debts had not occurred, the Philippines would have paid 480 million U.S. dollars by way of interest and amortization in 1970, accounting for 33 percent of the estimated earnings from exports of commodities and services.[4]

India, Indonesia, and China, which had more advanced material cultures than Europe in the seventeenth century,[5] were relegated to a backward situation through imperialist rule. "Consequent plunder, forced labour, taxation, and enforced specialization in an export monoculture reversed the relative position; and Asia was progressively reduced to underdevelopment."[6]

The total wealth transferred from India by British imperialism has been variously estimated at between 500 million and 1,000 million pounds. The fantastic material contribution (deprivations) made by the ex-colonial underdeveloped part of the world to the coffers of the colonial or imperialist countries at different periods of time should be calculated with "compound interest" to arrive at a fair value in today's terms.[7]

The dependence of some of the Asian countries for so-called developmental assistance poses a serious threat to their economic independence and self-reliance. In the case of Indonesia, for example, 40.3 percent of official international assistance in 1970 was from the U.S.A. The Philippines relied on the U.S.A. for 34.9 percent of total external assistance. Sri Lanka and Singapore depended upon the United Kingdom for 21.4 percent and 39.4 percent respectively. The assistance received by Sri Lanka from the U.S.A. in the same year was 20.7 percent of the total assistance received by them from official sources abroad. Despite various appeals by world bodies to the developed capitalist countries to soften the terms and conditions of loans advanced by them to the underdeveloped countries, no tangible results have been forthcoming.[8]

Imperialist Penetration and the Multinationals

Export of capital has been one of the powerful means by which imperialist countries have exploited the people of Asia. Multinational corporations with annual sales turnover higher than the national incomes of some countries of

Asia, Africa, and Latin America have proliferated, threatening the economic and political independence of these countries.

Moreover, the imperialist countries have been imposing a very heavy burden on the underdeveloped recipient countries, in terms of exorbitant payments for the so-called "transfer of technology," payments for patents, licenses, know-how, trademarks, and managerial technical services. Such payments made by the ESCAP countries in 1968 amounted to 1.5 billion U.S. dollars. On the basis of past trends, it has been estimated that the direct costs of "transfer technology" to these countries during the 1970s will increase by 20 percent per annum.[9]

Private foreign companies, particularly multinationals, still continue to have a substantial control over the foreign trade of most of the Asian countries, both imports and exports. Three important factors are responsible for this development. First, the foreign firms, which are either subsidiaries or branches of parent companies abroad, have intimate connections with export markets. The worldwide connections of the present companies are directly utilized to the advantage of the subsidiary companies and branch firms. The already established export outlets of the parent companies give a definite superior advantage to the foreign firms as compared to the indigenous firms in Asia. Second, the growth of monopoly power in the foreign sector and the organization of the industrial and trade associations among foreign companies have further strengthened the power of the foreign firms to keep local industries from a considerable portion of the country's export trade. Third, the products in which multinationals have come to specialize in Asia are mostly those which can command an increasing demand in the world market.

In direct contrast are the beneficial terms and conditions of aid from the Socialist countries. The cumulative money value of bilateral aid commitments made by the U.S.S.R. to the ESCAP countries during 1954–70 is estimated at 6.6 billion U.S. dollars and that from the East European countries at 3.6 billion dollars equivalent.[10] Aid from the Socialist countries is strongly project-oriented and is utilized mainly for strengthening the key productive sectors, particularly in the public industrial sector, of the developing countries. As the U.N. has admitted in one of its reports:

The bulk of the U.S.S.R. and East European countries' assistance to developing countries is extended in the form of government long-term development loans, usually at 2.5 percent interest with maturity of 10 to 15 years. Grace periods vary according to the nature of the project financed.[11]

All the costs of colonialist and imperialist "aid" cannot be quantified. Some have to be assessed in terms of deprivation of health and education and in terms of cultural domination. Eduardo de Sousa Ferreira stresses the need for understanding the problem of decolonization and the cost of colonization in the scientific, educational, and cultural fields.[12] A lot of classified information of U.S. government agencies is collected through social scientists, anthropologists, and other scientists.[13] It was not accidental that there was "a great increase of research interest in povery-stricken and minority group areas of Thailand since the beginning of guerrilla activity there."[14] The imperialist designs of Project Camelot are now fairly well known — a project in which social scientists and anthropologists were asked to undertake studies to make

. . . it possible to predict and influence politically significant aspects of social change in the developing nations of the world. . . The U.S. Army has an important mission in the positive and constructive aspects of nation-building in less developed countries as well as a responsibility to assist friendly governments dealing with active insurgency problems.[15]

U.S. imperialism—functioning directly through both government agencies and multinational corporations—also functions indirectly through apparently nongovernmental institutions such as the National Science Foundation (NSF), the National Institute of Mental Health, and the Ford, Carnegie, and Rockefeller Foundations.

How apparently innocuous small beginnings in financial and technical support by the U.S.A. to military governments in Asia can end in disaster can be seen from the experiences of the Vietnam War. From 1961, when the first military advisors were sent to Vietnam, until 1965, when a full escalation of U.S. military involvement came about, many observers apparently did not see how dangerous the implications of involvement were. American monopoly companies apparently did not play a front-line role. But "there is no doubt that they were interested parties. In fact the U.S. Government appealed to foreign investors to assist the Vietnamization, on grounds that saving the Thieu government would keep it within the Western economic network."[16]

Role of Japan

The most significant development in the post-Vietnam war period is the emergence of Japan as an integral part of the U.S. military war machine in Asia. As the U.S. makes agonizing reappraisals of its position in Asia, Japan has been prompted to get involved in the U.S. global strategy in confrontation with other Asian countries. Japan is expected to cover South Korea's territorial air space with its Air-Self-Defense Force. The Nixon doctrine also called for greater Japanese and European involvement with men and materials to fight Asian wars.

After the stunning defeat of American imperialism in Indochina, Thailand remains the major outpost of U.S. war apparatus in Southeast Asia and the "linch pin of continuing U.S. involvement in Indochina."[17] The image of the Thai ruling classes has been blackened by their American connections.

Japan is getting involved in the U.S. defense strategy in Asia in a bigger way at the wrong time: U.S. imperialism has had its crushing defeat in Indochina, and Japan suffers from increased "economic dependence on recession-torn U.S. economy."[18]

Integration of economic policy of the U.S.A. and Japan is not new. For more than a decade now, Japan has been playing the assigned role of supplier of capital and technology to other Asian countries; U.S. economic strategy has been the promotion of Japan as the country trying to marry its scarce capital resources with the abundant cheap labor of "fellow Asian" countries. In addition to open involvement in Asian countries, U.S. imperialism has maneuvered to get indirect entry, via Japan. In the realm of export trade, the Japanese Ministry of Trade and Industry expects Japan to control 40 to 45 percent of Asian exports by 1980.[19]

Poverty and Unemployment: The Struggle of Peasants and Workers

The problems of mass poverty and unemployment are two key questions in the underdeveloped countries in Asia.[20] Famine and starvation and deaths loom large.

There is no agreed standard definition of poverty. Statistical method may not reveal much more than even a cursory visual or photographic view of poverty-stricken people in the Asian countries. Most people in Asia and the Pacific have seen such abject poverty, at levels of living worse than those of animals, that they have developed a kind of psychological defense mechanism, enabling them to be indifferent to and blissfully oblivious of the actual reality. The legitimation involved in such a process of formation of social consciousness adds insult to injury.

According to World Bank statistics (if statistics have to be relied on after all), about 85 percent of the 750 million poor in the underdeveloped world are considered to be "in absolute poverty" — absolute poverty being defined arbitrarily on the basis of an annual per capita income of 50 U.S. dollars—but those below one-third of the national average per capita income are defined as people in "relative poverty."

The significant point to be noted is that more than 80 percent of the population in the underdeveloped countries considered to be in absolute or relative poverty live in the rural areas.[21] Since the principal occupation of about four-fifths of the rural poor is agriculture, it is clear that the core problem of poverty is linked with the question of land and the mode and relations of production in agriculture.

All available data about the agrarian situation in Asia show that the peasants, particularly the poor peasants, in most countries are facing ruination and getting more indebted to landlords and moneylenders. Many of them get alienated from their land and join the ranks of landless agricultural workers. The percentage of landless workers to active population in agriculture is 32 in India, 20 in Indonesia, and 29 in Pakistan. The agonizing fact is that the number of landless or near landless workers is growing in the Asian countries, with consequent decline in the average number of days of work available to them in a year, as well as its dampening effect on the level of agricultural wages. Since they have to depend on seasonal work, part of which is being taken away by tractorization or mechanization implicit in the so-called "Green Revolution" strategy, landless laborers are among the poorest of the working community. The ruination and decay of traditional rural industries, handicrafts, and cottage-level productions have accentuated the level of poverty in the rural areas.

Thailand can be taken as a case study. With an increase in population and the consequent pressures on land, there has been a process of fragmentation of holdings and increasing indebtedness. As rice production became more and more commercialized and as the government started introducing restrictive laws regarding acquisition and registration of land, many ordinary peasants have been alienated from their land. In the village of Banoi in the central plains, about 60 percent of rural families are in the category of landless laborers, compared to 36 percent back in 1930.[22] Traditional squatting has become increasingly difficult in view of the new restrictions and land laws. Some studies indicate that the practice of tenancy has increased in Thailand, particularly in the central plains. About 21 percent of the agriculturists' loans in the north, 31 percent in the northeast, and 66 percent in the central plains are reported to be borrowed from moneylenders at "staggering" rates of interest.[23]

The consequence of food shortages in Asian countries is the increasing dependency of the subsistence population of this region upon the imperialist nations, particularly the U.S.A., for food supplies.[24] The dependency rate has steadily increased in the case of grain, animal food, and oilseeds. About half of the food exports of the U.S.A. are directed towards the target markets in the Third World. The political significance of the growing stranglehold of American imperialism over food supplies of the underdeveloped countries in Asia can be gauged from the frank statement of former U.S. Secretary for Agriculture, Earl Butz:

Before people can do anything they have got to eat. And if you are looking for a way to get people to lean on you and to be dependent on you, in terms of their cooperation with you, it seems to me that food dependence would be terrific.[25]

In the perception of world power by U.S. imperialism, "Food is power."[26]

The low level of income of the rural and urban poor results in low intake of calories and proteins, leading to the perpetuation and widening of the vicious circle of low income/low consumption/lower capacities for work/lower income, and so on. In Sri Lanka, people in the rural areas had a total daily caloric intake per capita (1961–1966) of only 1,864 while the upper classes in Colombo (1957) had an intake of 3,271 calories per day per capita. A study in Maharashtra, India, showed that in 1958 about 23 percent of the families with income below Rs 11 per capita had a daily calorie intake of 1,340 per capita. In the case of 39.1 percent of the families with per capita incomes of Rs 34 and above, the daily intake was 3,340 calories per capita.

The specter of unemployment haunts the youth of Asian nations and millions in the upper age groups of the working population. The so-called "crash programs" initiated by some governments in the region have the aim of preventing the anger of the wretched from breaking out into struggles and militant action. Here again, the contractors, bureaucrats, and the landlord classes more than anybody else are the beneficiaries of the "crash programs," which have been described sometimes as "relief work for the rich."

One of the "fondly-held economic theories" is that economic growth is followed by increasing employment. How fallacious such a theory can be is demonstrated by the experience of both developing and developed countries.

Government spokesmen in many Asian and Pacific countries have made pathetic attempts to explain away the massive inflationary spiral by describing it as a "global phenomenon" or "passing-phase." The fact is that the incidence and depth of mass poverty increased as a result of a steep rise in prices, particularly food prices.

Industrial workers have had a raw deal. While the net output per worker in India, for example, increased by 49.5 percent in 1969 compared to 1949, wages increased by only 24.5 percent. The increase in share of the income created by workers has been amassed by the owners of big property.

Failure of Power–Elite Planning

The non-socialist Asian countries, being part of the international capitalist system, are governed by laws of motion characteristic of the capitalist countries, with the important qualification that the capitalist mode of production still remains superimposed on feudal, semi-feudal, tribal, and other pre-capitalist formations.

Apart from the lack of adequate industrial development, agriculture, which is the mainstay of the vast majority of the population, remains feudal and semi-feudal, although in many parts of Asia, capitalist farming is expanding. Land monopoly and tenancies restrict the possibilities of unleashing the productive energies of the peasantry. The "Green Revolution" and other technological innovations, instead of helping the rural poor, have acted against their interests. The lesson to be drawn from the failure of the "New Agricultural Strategy," designed with the blessings of American experts, is that it does not pose the central problem of agriculture—the problem of ownership of land, production relations, and radical land reform. Only through a consistent struggle by peasants and agricultural laborers can the fetters on the agricultural sector, namely feudalism, semi-feudalism, and land monopoly, be abolished and the productive forces unleashed.

This brings us to the whole question of national economic planning and the experience of Asian countries. It is obvious that the philosophy of planning which has guided the development process in the non-socialist countries of Asia has been borrowed mainly from the Western capitalist countries, though the vocabulary of socialist planning has been cleverly used as a political tactic by some governments.

One of the ingredients of the Western philosophy of planning is the unquestioned presumption that planning is a purely "economic" phenomenon. A discussion of socio-political phenomena is invariably discounted as "politics" beyond the scope of discussion of the "planner," who is defined basically as an economist, an econometrician, a statistician, or a technocrat.

Another ingredient of the Western philosophy of planning is what may be called the GNP-biased concept of economic growth. A given investment of resources is expected to produce a particular income and output, given the capital-output ratio, capital intensities, a broad picture of inter-industry balances, and a few other coefficients and relationships. Using a mathematical model, the planner feels confident to "plan" for the nation.

The Political Reality

Human Rights and Political Repression

If poverty, unemployment, and gross economic exploitation are the material realities of social life in most Asian countries, the most agonizing fact of life is that a pernicious and all-pervading darkness has been shed on the people by governments which have given a go-by to parliamentary democracy, constitutionalism, and the rule of law. Suppression of human rights, political repression, and authoritarian semi-fascism have become the order of the day. Possibly the most distressing fact is that some countries where similar tendencies were only dormant (with an apparent tradition of inherited parliamentary values) have recently removed their camouflage and have decided to tread the path of political suppression of all dissent.

Asia has an impressive array of authoritarian and military regimes. South Korea had a military coup d'etat in 1962. President Sukarno of Indonesia was overthrown in 1965 in a military operation which was accompanied by a bloodbath and the massacre of thousands of revolutionaries and democrats. After the demise of democracy in Pakistan and the period of instability intermixed with successive military regimes, and the butchery of the people of Bangladesh fighting for liberation, the present civil government there has relapsed into a tyrannical one. A military regime was established in Thailand in 1972. Though this military regime was toppled by the coalition of students-workers-citizens in 1973, another military coup was staged October 6, 1976. Taiwan had the misfortune of a superimposed, harsh military and police regime for twenty-five years. Lee Kuan Yew of Singapore, using the monopoly of power of his People's Action Party, imposed exceptional laws in violation of all norms of freedom and democracy. We witnessed in 1973 a sliding back from whatever modicum of democracy that existed in Malaysia and Bangladesh.

The people of Asia rejoiced when the military puppet governments in Indochina were ousted from their last hideouts in 1975. But the humiliation of the U.S.A. did not mark the end of the dark forces of domestic repression. In fact, after the fall of the puppet regime in Indochina, the dominant power cliques in South Korea, the Philippines, and Malaysia have unleashed harsher repressive measures in a desperate move to stem the tide of history.

The authoritarian political rule of President Marcos in the Philippines is virtually the result of a coup, "a seizure of power (by using the armed forces to eliminate the mass media, the Supreme Court, and Congress from the national decision making) sufficiently drastic to warrant the use of the term 'coup' to describe the event."[27] This came about against the backdrop of increasing penetration of the Philippines economy by American private investments (50 of the 750 American corporations working in the Philippines in 1969 had 2 billion U.S. dollars of investments accounting for 42 percent of the total equity of 1,000 top companies), the Marcos government policy of terror against the Muslim population of Mindanao to make room for the expanding logging industry and other plantation interests, the rising tide of popular discontent against such policies, and the militant anti-imperialist struggles of the people against the U.S. war in Vietnam and against American domination of the Philippines through private investments, official loans, and grants.

The National Question and the Problem of Minorities

Many states in the Asian region are multinational/multilingual/multiracial in character. India, Sri Lanka, Malaysia, and most of the other countries in Asia pose problems relating to the diversity or plurality of national, linguistic, and racial groupings. The contradictions between the people belonging to these diverse groupings are being effectively utilized by the ruling classes to impose their hegemony, using the tactics of divide and rule.

The ruling classes are more or less unitedly operating at the state/national level. It is the duty of the people, therefore, to unite against their common enemies. But such a unity can be self-sustaining only if it is based on the principle of "unity in diversity." National or linguistic minorities should be given maximum opportunities for their indigenous development based on their cultural tradition; at the same time these minority groups must make a conscious effort to march together with the mainstream of national life and foster unity among all peoples for a united attack on the ruling classes. Minority questions can be effectively tackled only through such a dialectical approach.

Socialist Countries in Asia

While the capitalist countries are in serious crisis with mounting unemployment, poverty, and an inflationary rise in prices, the socialist countries present a picture of full employment, stable prices, and continuously rising standards of living of the working people. This is true of the Soviet Union, China, East European countries, Cuba, North Korea, Vietnam and so on. It does not mean, however, that the socialist world is without all problems. Border disputes and clashes, mainly the heritages of the past, continue complicating differences of an ideological-political nature. Despite mistakes committed by many socialist countries, both in their domestic policies and international positions, the fact remains that the socialist world as a whole has witnessed unprecedented progress in the material, cultural, and spiritual life of the people.

Tasks of the Working People

Against the backdrop of deepening world capitalist crisis and the worsening conditions of working people in Asia (and indeed, on other continents) what are the tasks facing the working people?

It is clear from the analysis made above that working people have an important stake in the present crisis. Indeed, they have to play an historic role in solving the crisis by overthrowing the rule of capital and establishing a new social order based on equality, freedom, socialist production relations, and new cultural values.

The working people have to make a thoroughly scientific analysis of the socio-economic and political power structures in their own countries and formulate clear-cut strategies for the advance of the progressive social forces.

It is obviously not possible to make prescriptions for each country in Asia. This task can be effectively undertaken only by the people's organizations in each country struggling for a new social order. But some broad generalizations may be attempted, knowing very well the limitations of such an exercise. In general, it may be stated that the three main obstacles to socio-economic and cultural advancement of Asian working people are monopoly capitalism, landlordism, and imperialism (which refers to all overt and covert forms of imperialist penetration, the role of multinational corporations, and so on). Only by a consistent struggle against these three enemies of the people can the working people play the historic role of emancipating themselves.

The struggles against monopoly capitalism, landlordism, and imperialism can be successful only if the workers are fully organized and armed with the most modern scientific ideas about society and social transformation. Without strong and united trade-union movements the workers will remain powerless before the mighty sway of capital.

The formation and growth of trade unions can be achieved only by taking up the economic problems which the workers face at a given moment of time. Struggle for economic demands is necessary for the flowering of trade-union consciousness. But, if leaders of the trade-union movement get bogged down in "economism"—that is, the style of trade-union functioning which focuses attention on economic demands only and refuses to go beyond into the area of political consciousness—it will be a tragic development. The main task before the trade-union movement, therefore, is to organize the workers on the basis of their economic demands, but at the same time enabling the workers (in the area of struggles for economic demands) to see the more fundamental or basic task of changing the whole structure of society and creating a new social order.

The development of the workers' movement away from "economism" to political consciousness cannot be achieved in isolation. Since the workers are numerically a minority in most of the Asian countries, and since peasants form the bulk of the toiling population, the workers' movement for total and radical transformation of society can be successful only by unity with the peasantry, particularly the poor and middle peasantry. *Worker-peasant alliance, thus, becomes a key issue.* On the basis of such a unity, it will be possible to bring into the mainstream of people's struggles all other toiling people, artisans, petty traders, middle-class, small and household manufacturers, women, youth, and students. Workers, particularly in the key industrial sectors, have a leading role in this process.

An analysis of the present socio-economic and political reality has meaning only if it leads us to ideological-political positions which enable us to change the present unjust system and create a new order. Our duty is not merely to analyze the world, but to change it.

NOTES

1. D. Boone Schirmer, "The Philippine Conception and Gestation of a Neo-Colony," *Journal of Contemporary Asia* 5 (1975): 53.

2. George Lee, "Commodity Production and Reproduction among the Malayan Peasantry," *Journal of Contemporary Asia* 3 (1973): 441.

3. M. R. Stenson, *Industrial Conflict in Malaysia* (London: Oxford University Press, 1970), pp. 148–180.

4. *Manila Times,* Banking Supplement, October 29, 1971.

5. For a good summary of the destructive effects of the European impact on underdeveloped countries, see Keith Griffin, *Underdevelopment in Spanish America* (Cambridge, Mass.: MIT Press, 1970).

6. Norman Girvan, "The Question of Compensation: A Third World Perspective," *Race* 16 (July 1974): 56.

7. For an interesting proposal for calculating compensation for the Third World countries, see the article by Norman Girvan, in *Race* 16 (July 1974): 53–82.

8. At one of the conferences initiated by the U.N., a resolution (Resolution 60-III) invited the developed countries to take into consideration the views expressed that "(a) on average, interest rates on official development loans should not exceed 2 percent per annum; (b) maturity periods of such loans should be at least 25 to 40 years and grace periods should be not less than 7 to 10 years; (c) the proportion of grants in total assistance of each developed country should be progressively increased, and countries contributing less than the 1970 Development Assistance Committee average of 63 percent of their total assistance in the form of grants should reach that level not later than 1975." See United Nations, *The Second United Nations Development Decade: Trends and Policies in the First Two Years,* 1974, p. 24.

9. Direct costs to the ESCAP countries from transfer of technology in 1968 constituted 37 percent of their public debt service payments and 50 percent of the annual flow of direct private investments. See United Nations, *The Second United Nations Development Decade: Trends and Policies in the First Two Years,* 1974, p. 36.

10. United Nations, *Economic Survey of Asia and the Far East,* 1972, p. 42.

11. Ibid.

12. Eduardo de Sousa Ferreira, *Portuguese Colonialism in Africa: The End of an Era,* UNESCO Press, Paris.

13. For the rare appearance of titles of classified projects, see U.S. *Congressional Record:* Study by M. L. Thomas, "Rural Value Systems, Republic of Vietnam," sponsored by the Defense Department's Advance Research Projects Agency (ARPA).

14. Jack Satuder, "The Relevance of Anthropology to Colonialism and Imperialism," *Race* 14 (July 1974): 14.

15. Quoted from the recruiting letter for Project Camelot in I. L. Horowitz, ed., *The Rise and Fall of Project Camelot: Studies in the Relationship Between Science and Practical Politics,* rev. ed. (Cambridge, Mass.: MIT Press, 1974), pp. 47–49.

16. Mare Lindenberg, "The Politics of Foreign Investment in South East Asia from 1945–1973," *Journal of Contemporary Asia* 5 (1975): 11.

17. Arnold Abrams, "Back in Business," *Far Eastern Economic Review,* August 26, 1972.

18. Yamakawa Akio, "Post-Vietnam Japan–U.S. Relations: Greater Cooperation and Growing Contradictions," *AMPO* (Japan-Asia Quarterly Review) 7 (July-September, 1975): 2.

19. T. Kawata, "The Asian Situation and Japan's Economic Relations with Developing Countries," Quaker Seminar on the Impacts of Foreign Investment, Penang, Malaysia, September 1–3, 1971.

20. United Nations, *Economic Survey of Asia and the Far East,* 1972, Part I.

21. World Bank, *Rural Development* (Sector Policy Paper), February 1975, p. 4.

22. S. Picker, "Sources of Stability and Instability in Rural Thai Society," *Journal of Asian Studies* 27 (August 1968): 789.

23. J. C. Ingram, *Economic Change in Thailand, 1850–1970,* rev. ed. (Stanford, Calif.: Stanford University Press, 1971), p. 268.

24. Documents of the World Food Conference, Rome, 1974.

25. Cited in Harry Cleaver, "The Contradictions of the Green Revolution," *Monthly Review* (June 1973).

26. An expression used by Hubert Humphrey.

27. Explanations by Robert B. Stauffer in his article, "The Marcos Coup in the Philippines," *Monthly Review* (April 1973): 19.

8

Towards an Asian Theology of Liberation: Some Religio-Cultural Guidelines

Aloysius Pieris (Sri Lanka)

Part I
Towards a Definition of the Religio-Cultural Dimension

This being a *Third World* theologians' *Asian* Consultation, I presume that the theological axis of our deliberations should have, as its two poles, the *Third Worldness* of our continent and its peculiarly *Asian* character: two points of reference we must never lose sight of. Spelt out in more realistic terms, the common denominator between Asia and the rest of the Third World is its overwhelming poverty; the specific character which defines Asia within the other poor countries is its multifaceted religiosity. These are two inseparable realities which in their interpenetration constitute what might be

Aloysius Pieris, S.J., is founder and director of the Centre for Research and Dialogue at Kelaniya, Sri Lanka.

designated as the Asian context and which is the matrix of any theology that is truly Asian.

We must immediately warn ourselves that Asian poverty cannot be reduced to purely "economic" categories just as Asian religiosity cannot be defined merely in "cultural" terms. They are both interwoven culturally and economically to constitute the vast socio-political reality that Asia is. Hence an Asian theologican can hardly ignore Roy Preiswerk's appeal[1] that the "dependency theories" of the Latin Americans (Cardoso, Frank, Furtado, etc.) which offer valid explanations of and useful strategies against the increasing poverty in the Third World, ought to be complemented (and I would add, even corrected) by the "cultural approach" of social scientists.

This is nowhere more applicable than in Asia, for there is in our cultural ethos "a yet-undiscovered point" at which *poverty* and *religiosity* seem to coalesce in order to procreate the Asian character of this continent. In fact history attests, as we shall indicate later, that the *theological* attempts to encounter Asian religions with no radical concern for Asia's poor and the *ideological* programs that would eradicate Asia's poverty with naive disregard for its religiosity, have both proved to be a misdirected zeal. Hence the theologies now prevalent in the Asian church and the secular ideologies presently operating on this continent have all to be judged in the light of this axiom, as will be done in the course of our discussion.

Without, therefore, diluting or de-emphasizing the economic features that define the "Third-Worldness" of Asia, I am compelled here, by the organizers, to concentrate on the "religio-cultural" dimension of the Asian context. As it might be objected that such a dimension exists also in all other poor countries, let me straightaway name three distinctive features which clearly demarcate the "religio-cultural" boundaries of Asia within the Third World. They are:

    (a) linguistic heterogeneity;
    (b) the integration of the cosmic and the metacosmic elements in Asian religions;
    (c) the overwhelming presence of non-Christian soteriologies.

Linguistic Heterogeneity

Asia is diversified into at least seven major linguistic zones, the highest that any continent can boast of. There is, first of all, the *Semitic* zone concentrated on the Western margin of Asia. The *Ural-Altaic* group is spread all over Asiatic Russia and Northwest Asia. The *Indo-Iranian* stock alongside the *Dravidian* races have their cultural habitat in Southern Asia. The *Sino-Tibetan* region, by far the largest, extends from Central Asia to the Far East. The *Malayo-Polynesian* wing opens out to the southeast. Last but not least, is the uncatalogable *Japanese*, forming a self-contained linguistic unit in the northeastern tip of Asia.

The first theological implication of this linguistic heterogeneity derives from the very understanding of "language." According to a nominalist view, a truth is apprehended intuitively and is *then* expressed outwardly through a language. If this were true, communal disturbances between linguistic groups—such as those in Sri Lanka, Cambodia, or Burma—would have to be explained purely in terms of political and economic factors, which is not the case. The fact, however, is that each language is a *distinctly new way* of "experiencing" the truth, implying that linguistic pluralism is an index of religious, cultural, and socio-political diversity. Zaehner seems to be implying this when he, too easily perhaps, typifies the whole Western religiosity as Semitic and the Eastern religiosity as Indian.[2] I think it is only partially true to say that religion is an "experience" of reality and language is its "expression"; the converse is closer to the truth: *Language is the "experience" of reality and religion is its "expression."* Religion begins with language. Would it be wrong to say that language is a *theologia incoativa*, an incipient theology?

And what is the fundamental reality that a particular culture grasps through its own language and symbols? Read what the Asian proletariat has produced over the centuries, not merely the sophisticated writings such as the Vedas and Upanishads, the Tripiṭaka, the Torah, or the Taò Té Chīng. Learn, first, the folk-language; assist at their rites and rituals; hear their songs; vibrate with their rhythms; keep step with their dance; taste their poems; grasp their myths; reach them through their legends. You will find that the language they speak puts them in touch with the basic truths that every religion grapples with, but *each in a new way*: the meaning and destiny of human existence; crippling human limitations and our infinite capacity to break through them; liberation both human and cosmic; in short, *the struggle for a full humanity*.

Every Asian culture, therefore, has grown around a soteriological nucleus which has not yet been assimilated into the Christian conscience. The Asian theology of liberation lies hidden there, waiting to be discovered by whoever is ready to "sell all things." For a recovery of an ancient revelation is indeed a new creation. This means that the task of Asian theologians is more complex than that of their colleagues in the North Atlantic region and the southern hemisphere. After all, do not the European theologians communicate in the same Indo-Germanic languages? Even liberation theologians think, act, and speak in a common Latin idiom. They are all within reach of one another by means of a European medium of communication. Such is not the case here.

It is therefore regrettable that Asians (like the Africans at the Conference in Ghana) are not able to consult each other's hidden theologies except in a *non-Asian idiom, thus neutralizing the most promising feature in our methodology*. We Asians professionally theologize in English, the language in which most of us think, read, and pray. The theological role of language on a "continent of languages" has been grossly underestimated, and our stubborn refusal to consult each other's treasures directly in each other's linguistic idioms, or even to be familiar with *one's own cultural heritage*, will remain one major obstacle to the discovery of a truly Asian theology. This is not an appeal for chauvinism but a plea for authenticity imposed on us by what we have defined as the Asian context. The foundation for a genuinely *Asian* consultation must be laid here at this Conference.

Integration of the Cosmic and the Metacosmic in Asian Religiosity

The institutional framework within which Asian religiosity operates is composed of two complementary elements: a *cosmic religion* functioning as the foundation, and a *metacosmic soteriology* constituting the main edifice. By the term "cosmic religion" I wish to designate that species of religion which is found in Africa and Oceania and has been *pejoratively* referred to as "animism" by certain Western authors. Actually it represents the basic psychological posture that the *homo religiosus* (residing in each one of us) adopts subconsciously towards the mysteries of life; a sane attitude which an unwise use of technology can disturb. They relate to the cosmic forces—heat, fire, winds and cyclones, earth and its quakes, oceans, rains and floods— which we need and yet fear. They serve as ambivalent symbols of our own subconscious powers, symbols freely employed in ordinary speech and in sacred rites, as expressive of our deepest yearnings. Even in the West where these natural elements serve humanity through technology, can the Christian celebrate the Paschal Mystery without using fire and water? After all, if the theory of evolution is really true, we were all once a mountain, the crust of the earth, the water and the fire and all that we now carry with us as our material substratum, by which we become sacramentally present to others and to ourselves. We cannot be fully human without them.

In our cultures these natural elements and forces merge into the mysterious world of invisible powers which maintain the cosmic balance. They may appear in various guises in various regions: *devas* in the Indianized cultures of Southeast Asia; *Nats* in Burma; *Phis* in Thailand, Laos, and Cambodia; *Bons* in Tibet; *Kamis* in Japan; and of course, in the Confucianist worldview, the departed *ancestors* belong to this invisible sphere. Rites, rituals, and a class of mediators form the constitutive elements of this religiosity.

The characteristic feature of Asian religiosity is that, unlike in Africa or in Oceania, this cosmic religion does not appear in its pure and primordial form except in certain isolated pockets which anthropologists frequent. It has practically been domesticated and integrated into one or the other of the three *metacosmic soteriologies*, namely, Hinduism, Buddhism, and to some extent Taoism. The Summum Bonum they present is a "Transphenomenal Beyond" which is to be realized here and now through *gnosis*. This justifies the existence of a certain spiritual elite, the wisemen, who become the personal embodiments of the *mystico-monastic* idealism held out as the climax of human perfection. They serve as models and the symbols of "liberated persons."

Hence it is also true that the metacosmic soteriologies mentioned above are never found in abstract "textual" form but always "contextualized" within the worldview of the "cosmic religion" of a given culture, creating a twofold level of religious experience well integrated into each other. Here the Asian context differs from the African because, due to this superimposition, cosmic religions, unlike in Africa, are not *regarded as salvific*. This is of great consequence for Asian theology. Let me mention in passing that it is invariably at the cosmic level that both technological and socio-political activities affect the major religions; we shall discuss this later. (One might say, parenthetically, that the establishment of biblical religions such as Islam in Indonesia and Catholicism in the Philippines, was easier partly because "cosmic religions" were found there in domesticated or mildly domesticated forms at that time; whereas in Sri Lanka, India, Burma, and other countries, neither Islam nor Christianity could sweep over these cultures because the aforesaid gnostic soteriologies had already domesticated cosmic religions into a well-integrated cultural system.)

These facts have hardly engaged the attentions of Asian theologians but have been a major preoccupation of anthropologists doing field-work in Asia.[3] The terms cosmic and metacosmic used here, however, have not been borrowed directly from anthropologists, but are derived from a Buddhist self-understanding of the two levels: *Lokiya* (Sinh: *Laukika*) and *Lok'uttara* (Sinh: *Lokottara*). Buddhists recognize the two dimensions and explain their own religious experience in terms of this distinction. [See diagram on p. 83.]

My reference to Buddhism here is not accidental. To sharpen our focus on Asian religiosity, it is only reasonable that I should concentrate on one of the major religions. If my choice falls on Buddhism, it is not only because I would be traversing familiar grounds, but even more because it is the one religion which is *pan-Asian* in cultural integration, numerical strength, geographical extension, and political maturity. Though an integral part of Indian heritage, now preserved in its Indian form only here in Sri Lanka, it had penetrated practically every linguistic zone—even the Semitic, for a brief period.[4] In other words, Buddhism is not limited to one language or national group—as in the case of Hinduism and Taoism. By allowing itself to be shaped by the various "cosmic religions" of Asia, it has in turn molded several Asian cultures. Thus today there is an Asian Buddhist for every Roman Catholic in the world. There are at least twenty political territories in Asia where Buddhism is either the official religion or a culturally influential factor. It is the one religion that can boast of an Asia-wide ecumenical organization such as the World Fellowship of Buddhists (WFB) or the World Buddhist Sangha Council (WBSC) or the World Buddhist Social Service (WBSS), all of which look to Sri Lanka for leadership. It is also politically the most resilient of Asian religions with a major role to play in the development and liberation of Asia, for it has a rich experience of Western colonialism as well as of Marxism.

Hence no Asian theology of liberation can be construed without consulting Asian Buddhism.

While Buddhism, we grant, does not exhaust the whole phenomenon of Asian religiosity, it will nevertheless serve us as a paradigm to demonstrate how the interplay of the cosmic and the metacosmic levels of religious experience gives a new point of departure for politico-social change and technocratic advancement in the very process of Asia's liberation, something that neither Western technocracy nor scientific socialism has sufficiently appreciated and which Asian theologians cannot underestimate.

The Overwhelming Presence of Non-Christian Soteriologies

Asia is the cradle of all the Scriptural religions of the world, including Christianity, which, however, left Asia very early and forced its way back several centuries later as a stranger and an "intruder" whom Asia consistently refused to entertain. Thus with four centuries of missionary presence the Christians are numerically and qualitatively an insignificant minority: a mere 2 percent of the Asian masses. A good half of this Christian population is in the Philippines, which, in the process of becoming Christian, was forced to cut off its Asian roots. The Philippine church is only a magnified version of most Christian communities scattered in the Asian diaspora. Can a Christianity that has lost its "Asian sense" presume to create an Asian theology? Even the churches of the Eastern Rites have frozen their early openness to the Asian reality. However, this limitation is also the greatest potentiality the Asian church possesses of creating a Third World theology that will radically differ from the South American and the African theologies. The liberation theologians of Latin America can speak of Christ and his liberation as a national and continental concern because of their traditional Christian heritage. This is why they are able to offer us a relevant Christian theology in place of the classical one of the European churches. So can the Africans become soon, numerically and qualitatively, a powerful Christian voice within the Third World. But Asia, as circumstances clearly indicate, *will remain always a non-Christian continent.*

This situation is ambivalent. It creates enormous opportunities for more creative modes of Christian presence in Asia by humble participation in the non-Christian experience of liberation; or it can repeat past mistakes in radically new ways. Let me substantiate this immediately by signalling some salient features of a non-Christian soteriology with Buddhism as our sample—and disclosing thereby the worldview within which the Asian church is called to make its options. If our approach is basically positive and appreciative, it is because we wish to absorb from these religions the Asian style of being, thinking, and doing.

Part II
Non-Christian Soteriology:
Some Theological Perspectives

We must, first of all, recapture the picture of institutional Buddhism with its cosmic and metacosmic dimensions of religious experience. To the cosmic sphere must be relegated (a) all *socio-political activities* and (b) *technological and scientific progress;* to the metacosmic pertains all that is ordained towards *interior human liberation.* These elements are so well integrated that the equilibrium of the religious system could be disturbed by certain species of "cosmic" activities both political and scientific, as happens when Buddhism faces capitalist technocracy coming from the West or scientific socialism introduced by the Marxists. To this we shall return.

The *Sangha*, i.e., the monastic nucleus round which Buddhism evolves is, of course, the institutional center and the spiritual apex of a Buddhist society. It serves the cosmic level of human existence by directing its attention to the metacosmic goal, the ultimate perfection (*arahatta*) which consists of an absence of acquisitiveness and greed (*alobha*), absence of oppressiveness and hate (*adosa*), and perfect salvific knowledge (*amoha*). This is the classical description of Nirvana. The monastic community which embodies this ideal is also a symbol of religious communism, since they are called to share all things in common, "even the morsel of food falling into the begging bowl," as the Buddha has declared.[5]

The basis of such a community is *poverty*, voluntary renunciation of wealth and family life. But this poverty is sustained by the wealth-acquiring laity, who are entrusted with the task of advancing material (technological) progress and socio-political well-being. The mutuality implied in this system of cosmic and metacosmic religiosity can be best discussed in terms of the bipolarity that exists between (a) wealth and poverty, (b) state and church, and (c) scientific knowledge and spiritual wisdom.

Wealth and Poverty

In this system the one who renounces wealth is maintained by the wealth of the one who does not. Wealth is at the service of *poverty*, and poverty is the condition for liberation from acquisitiveness and greed (*tanhā, lobha, up-ādāna,* etc.). Hence all material progress is tempered by the ideal of *non-acquisitiveness and sharing*, of which monkhood is the symbol. This is, of course, the ideal; but it is open to abuse, as history shows. Hence in an Asian situation, the antonym of "wealth" is not "poverty" but *acquisitiveness* or *avarice*, which makes wealth antireligious. *The primary concern, therefore, is not eradication of poverty, but struggle against Mammon,* that undefinable force which organizes itself within every person and among people to make material wealth antihuman, antireligious, and oppressive.

In fact, one source of Christian failure in Asia was its association with Mammon (commercial and colonial exploitation) and its refusal to enter into the monastic spirit of non-Christian soteriologies. Today, this mistake is repeated through massive "development" programs with which the Asian churches (being minorities threatened by possible loss of identity) consolidate themselves into Western oases (big private educational, technological, or agricultural establishments run with foreign aid) thus forcing a non-Christian majority to depend on a Christian minority for material progress. This use of Mammon to be imposingly and manipulatively present in Asia is a continuation, albeit in a new way, of the missiology of conquest and power characteristic of the colonial era. When a revolution rises against such establishments, the churches speak of themselves as being persecuted—when in reality they are only trampled upon, as salt without flavor (Matthew 5:13).

On the other hand, Mammon has not left monks in peace either. For a monk poverty is the most difficult virtue, not celibacy. The paradox of monastic renunciation is this: The holier the monk appears to be, the more generous the people are towards him. The poorer he wants to be, the greater are the donations he receives. The more he runs away from riches, the closer he comes to it. The further he removes himself from society, the more crushing becomes people's devotion to him. Thus, dependence on the people for material sustenance is at once the most basic condition and the most vulnerable feature of monastic poverty. What is true of the individual monk is even more true of the monastery as a whole. Rich benefactors, and even rulers, show their appreciation by lavishing land and wealth on monasteries. Wealth-acquiring monasteries were not less frequently found in medieval Asia than in medieval Europe. In Tibet and Japan at one time, armies were maintained to protect the wealth of monasteries.[6] In fact, the monastic ideal of religious poverty which, by contrast, makes worldly happiness illusory, tends, under Mammon's influence, to become a "worldly structure" confirmative of Marx's opposite thesis that abolition of such a religion as an "illusory" happiness is required for their *real* happiness. In fact, it is here that Marxists and monks have collided in Asia.[7]

Theoretically, at least, Marxism is more consistently anti-Mammon than purely antipoverty, in contrast with capitalist technocracy. In fact no religious persecution under a Marxist regime can be compared to the subtle undermining of religious values which capitalist technocracy generates in our cultures. The former may purify institutional religion of its unholy alliances with the creators of poverty; the latter pollutes religion by betraying it to Mammon. Hence, the monastic spirit, healthy in itself, has always required as its complement a state machinery that could create a socio-political system conducive to its well-being. The reciprocity between religious and civil authority is an essential ingredient of the Buddhist worldview.

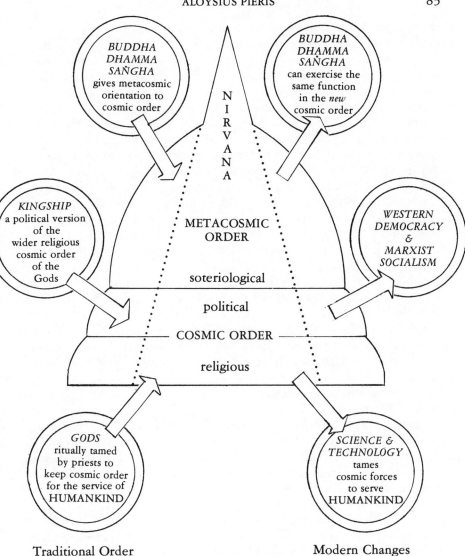

Traditional Order   Modern Changes

The State and the Saṅgha

The reciprocal dependence of the cosmic (*lakiya*) and the metacosmic (*lokuttara*) levels of existence is attested by the political history of Buddhist countries where the monastic institution has retained its spiritual status vis-à-vis the political authority. This is especially true of Southeast Asia, where the state's legitimization of the Saṅgha is reciprocated by the monks' moral sanction of the state.[8] The relationship is, therefore, not purely spiritual but political as well, because in the Buddhist scheme of things, the metacosmic is founded on the cosmic. Buddhist monasticism is, therefore, never neutral to the sociopolitical reality. This is why it has often suffered both persecution and purification at the hands of the state, but has also at other times initiated political revolutions against the state. In fact, one hears today of a military college in Thailand where monks prepare for an anti-Marxist war.[9] The anti-Christian and anticolonialist movements of Sri Lanka, Burma, and Indo-China were born in Buddhist monasteries. There have been several uprisings in China since the fifth century, which were messianic movements based on a desire to bring here and now the "era of justice and peace" foretold by the Buddha.[10] The Ming Dynasty in the middle ages sprang out of a Buddhist-inspired rebellion. Some of those political movements continued up to the middle of this century.[11] The dialectics between withdrawal from the world and involvement with the world—or contemplation and action—illustrative of the mutuality between the cosmic and the metacosmic, is nowhere so clearly attested as in the political role that spiritual men play in a Buddhist culture.

Let me illustrate this by referring to a lesson that Marxists learned about Buddhism. As Welch has shown in his ponderous treatise on how Buddhism fared in revolutionary China,[12] Mao Zedong did not at first insist on the eradication of Buddhism or any other religion in the beginning of his rule. His thesis was that religion springs from certain socio-economic structures which, when changed, would automatically make religion disappear. Instead of using time on eradicating a religion, he preferred to make use of it to change social structures, to expedite thus its own disappearance. This is the classical Marxist thesis.[13]

In this context we can understand the establishment of the Chinese-Buddhists Association (CBA) with its organ *Modern Buddhism*. Through this periodical the CBA tried to convince Buddhists that they could live meaningfully within a Marxist regime, by collaborating in the renewal of social structures. This is an understandable reaction. The CBA also organized goodwill missions to other Buddhist countries.

At the sixth session of the World Fellowship of Buddhists (WFB), the CBA tried to convince the Buddhist world that the Maoist vision of the new society was acceptable within the WFB. But at this session right-wing ideology prevailed and the failure of the Chinese delegation became all too evident. The Tibetan issue, misconstrued by the anti-Communist section of the Buddhists, became a setback for the CBA. On the other hand, one can never underestimate the active part that the Chinese-Buddhist Association played in the anti-Diem demonstrations in South Vietnam (1963–64), even though its success was of a temporary nature. In the period 1963–65 one is amazed at the debates conducted in mainland China about the "relevance of religions in the new society." *After all, religion did not die with the change of structures, but only adapted itself and regained its vitality.*

It is not surprising, therefore, that by 1965 we see a change in the Marxist theses. Religion is described, at this juncture, as a dying cobra who can sting before it dies. The need for killing it, therefore, was imperative. We see at this time that *Modern Buddhism* ceases to be published almost abruptly. The president of the CBA goes out of circulation and the Panchen Lama is demoted. These were the clouds that heralded the storm. Of course, the storm was the Cultural Revolution of 1966. There was a large-scale laicization and secularization of monks, not to speak of the destruction of statues and sacred articles. Since the persecutions of 644 A.D. and 845 A.D., Buddhism had never met a worse crisis than the Cultural Revolution of 1966.[14]

The Russian experience, on the other hand, moved in the opposite direction. It began with an intolerant attitude towards Buddhism and ended up dialoguing with it. The chief lamas' attempts, at the beginning of the October Revolution, to accommodate Buddhist thinking and behavior to the new Marxist environment were not taken seriously by the Russians. The Buddhists tried to accommodate their religion to the new ideology by appealing to atheism and humanism as the common ground they had with the Marxists, but at that time such overtures appeared naive to the new regime. Revolution was decidedly antireligious and anti-Buddhist. *Filosofikaya Entsiklopediya* (Moscow, 1960, Vol. I, *s.v.* Buddism) gives the classical Marxist explanation of Buddhism as ["opium"] pacifying the oppressed classes of Asia, making them submissive to the oppressive regimes. One need not tarry here to prove how convinced the Marxists were of their position. The ruthless elimination of the lamas, persistently accused of spying for the Japanese, was a proof of this.

But in recent times we see a sudden change in the Russian approach to Buddhism. One wonders what the reason could be. Is it a genuine appreciation of the religious content of Buddhism or is it a recognition of the social reality of the Buddhist masses, who did not give up their convictions; or is it the recognition of the potentialities that Buddhism has for social change? Or is it a search for political influence in Buddhist countries against Sino-American maneuvers?[15] We see for the first time since the Russian Revolution a world Buddhist conference organized in Ulan Bator in June 1970. It is significant that among the participants both Communist China and Taiwan were conspicuously absent. The official statement issued by the organizers made it clear that their intention was to save Buddhist countries against American aggression.[16] This meeting has had its follow-up since then.

Moreover, the *Bolshaiya-Sovetskaya Entsiklopediya* of 1971 (Moscow, 1971, Vol. IV, p. 89), seems to take a more lenient stand in its column on Buddhism and is clearly anti-Chinese in its evaluation of the Tibetan question, in contrast with the 1960 *Entsiklopediya*. This appreciation of Buddhism has been accounted for by Parfionovich, a Russian Marxist. He asks himself why Marxists should be so concerned about Buddhism; should not Marxists rather fight against Buddhism? His answer is enlightening:

Well, didn't Lenin say that Marxism, far from repudiating the past, should absorb and work on it as the only sure foundation of a proletarian culture?

Who can deny that Buddhism has been not simply a religion, but a way of life for millions? That its cultural and historical values have moulded the spiritual heritage of mankind? And still conscious of Lenin's precept that we should absorb all the achievements of the human spirit, we are acutely aware that our knowledge of the ancient and medieval world is largely concerned with Europe and the Middle East. We know far too little of the great civilisations of Asia.[17]

Both the Chinese experiment, which moved from accommodation to persecution, and the Russian experience, which started with intolerance and has ended up now with dialogue, show that Buddhism is a power to reckon with. This power is not merely in the sacred texts of a bygone era but in the culture of a people who have learned to integrate their cosmic concerns with a metacosmic vision, politics with spirituality.

Scientific Knowledge and Spiritual Wisdom

Technology tames the cosmic forces and puts them at the service of human beings. The "religious rites" by which such powers were earlier tamed may recede to insignificance as technology advances. There is, in a way, a desacralizing process which could be interpreted as a "liberation of human beings" from superstition. But this is not all there is to it. Technology is as ambivalent as the cosmic forces it claims to domesticate. Its unwise use, far from making cosmic forces really submissive to people, has only provoked them to retaliate and "enslave people" with pollution, consumerism, secularism, materialism, and a host of evils that a technocratic society has produced in the First World. Besides, it has deprived the human mind of the *myth* and the *rite*, two things by which human beings enact their deep yearnings and keep themselves sane in mind and body. Can technology liberate human beings? Certainly not in the form in which "Christian" nations have offered it to us. It takes away the cosmic religion from the masses, and substitutes it with neurosis. It takes away religious poverty and gives us Mammon.

One is annoyingly amused, therefore, to read a theological justification of this "development ideology" in the classical thesis put forward by Van Leeuwen: The scientific and industrial revolution with its modern secular culture is to be welcomed as the fruit of (Western) Christianity; hence Christianity should carry this mission to Asia and *liberate* its masses from its superstitious religiosity. The implication of this thesis seems to be that the church's mission is to use Western ideology and theology to eradicate at once the religiosity and the poverty of our continent! Ninian Smart of Lancaster University described this missiology beautifully when he called it "Western tribalism."[18]

It took a wise man in the West—Paul VI—to appeal for reciprocation between the *technician* busy with scientific progress and the *wise man* who could guide him from a contemplative distance.[19] Thus, the Patriarch of the Western church has recognized the need for a bi-polarity between secular knowledge and spiritual wisdom. Asia has taught this for centuries in its religious view on material progress.

Look at the ancient irrigation works of Sri Lanka. What a feat of engineering they uncover! How then has our technology failed to keep pace with the West? After all, was not technology—or *"ars mechanica,"* as the medieval Europeans called it—imported from the East after the Crusades?[20] Why are the skills of the past still hiding behind the facade of archaelogical remains? One thing is sure. The technician in our culture remained an illiterate artisan whose skills did not enter the ola-leaf manuscripts that the monks authored. The *literati* who knew the arts were also the wise men; cosmic sciences did not strictly enter into their domain. Thus technology as it started seems to have disappeared in the course of time. This could very well be a fundamental weakness in the Asian system.

But there is another side to it. In that system, the scientists could not create a class of "white-robed clerics" to officiate in the sanctum of the laboratory, preaching a dangerous brand of "neognosticism" which claims that the *power to liberate* humanity resides in the scientific *knowledge* of nature's secrets.[21] The Buddhist worldview has always preserved that orientation which Paul VI advocated; according to it true *gnosis* is spiritual wisdom guiding scientific knowledge to the "fullness of authentic development."[22] Technology is an induced cosmic process, which is a conscious continuation of the biological evolution and, like the latter, becomes humanized only by its metacosmic orientation.

The thesis that superstition has to be removed by technology must also be qualified by the fact that the cosmic religions in Asia are already being purified by the metacosmic orientation they receive at the hands of monastic religions—a fact that our own field work has amply demonstrated, and to which we cannot deviate here.[23]

The priest and journalist Piero Gheddo is also oversimplifying the case when he says that Western progress came from the Christian doctrine of the "dignity of man" and that underdevelopment among us is to be partially explained by a lack of such a perspective in our cultures.[24] *Contra*, a distinguished economist saw in our "slow progress" a certain wisdom which in the long run preserves human dignity. He called it "Buddhist economics" and epitomized it in a neat slogan: Small is Beautiful.[25] Which means, Mammon is Ugly.

"Freedom from poverty" which is the goal of Western technocracy, can be an enslaving pursuit ending up in hedonism, if not tempered by the "freedom that comes from poverty." This is not a glorification of poverty which is the "spirituality" that the exploiter usually imposes on the poor. I rather refer to the *religious understanding of poverty*, which forces the church to choose either

Marxist materialism or the hedonism of affluent societies! If "it is to the former that the Church turns its attention since it is potentially more renewing, closer to the call of justice and equality, even if to a lesser degree, a defender of formal liberties,"[26] it is equally true that Marxism has not appreciated fully the religious dimension that Asian cultures attribute to poverty and, consequently, the Latin American theology, *which is the only valid theology for the Third World today*, lacks a perceptive understanding of this monastic ideal. The Marxist embarrassment in the face of Asia's indestructible religiosity, as described above, may reappear in an Asian theopraxis too heavily dependent on the Latin American model.

The Asian religious attitude to poverty, even in the context of its march to economic progress, differs from the Latin American attitude as a *psychological* method differs from a *sociological* one. In the former, voluntary poverty is a spiritual antidote; in the latter it is a political strategy (see below p. 90). Mammon, which some Christian theologians have translated with the word "capital,"[27] needs to be vehemently opposed with both methods. To borrow Maoist jargon, a structural revolution can avoid much of its unnecessary violence if accompanied (not followed) by a cultural revolution. A "liberation theopraxis" in Asia which uses only the Marxist tools of *social* analysis will remain un-Asian and ineffective until it integrates the psychological tools of *introspection* which our sages have discovered. A new society evolves with the evolution of the new human being; and *vice versa*.

May I suggest a useful exercise that might illustrate what I am trying to say? Read theologically the revolutionary theory and praxis of Che Guevara in the light of a similar reading of Ho Chi Minh. Taste the distinct Christian flavor in the former. Then note the difference in the latter. What you notice would be the *Asian sense*.

The Asian Sense in Theology

To predispose ourselves to receive the *Asian sense* into our Christian consciousness, certain inhibitions inherited from the local churches of the West need first to be eliminated. Consistent with the methodology so far pursued in our investigation, this review of our theological past must also be made (*a*) from the *Third-World point of view* in general and (*b*) from the *Asian point of view* in particular. The contents of an Asian theology, however, does not concern us here. All we hope to achieve by this critique is to discover the *Asian style of doing theology*.

A Third World Critique of Our Theological Past

In the course of our discussion we met two "secular" movements engaged in liberating us from our "poverty"; both have originated in the West. The first is *Marxist socialism*; and the other is the *development ideology* associated with capitalist technocracy. The West is also "spiritually" present through the church which, for the most part, is an extension of Western Christianity. Thus the church too reflects, in its own *theological* self-understanding, the *ideological* conflicts of the West. Hence this inquiry into the theological equipment of the church.

The Asian church, for the moment, has no theology of its own, though the cultures that host it teem with them. It is today caught between two "theologies" which are as "Western" as the secular ideologies just mentioned. The first is the classical European theology which, in its various brands, is officially taught in all major institutions of the Asian church. The second is the Latin American theology which is also making itself felt in certain theological circles. These theologies, of course, are diametrically opposed to each other, as are the secular ideologies mentioned above.

Classical theology in the West, which went through the mill of renewal since the nineteenth century, is said to have made a major "breakthrough" in the middle of this century, climaxing in modern theology with its openness to the "world." The chief centers of this renewal were the French and German linguistic zones, according to Mark Schoof, because, to quote his own words, it was there that "the theologians seem to have the necessary scientific tradition and sufficient creative energy at their disposal."[28] One major source of inspiration for the Catholic renewal of European theology is traced back to Protestant Germany, according to the same author.[29]

This close-range view of European theology justifies Schoof's title of his thesis: *Breakthrough*. But an Asian looking from a critical distance sees quite another picture. The real breakthrough in Western theology came with the Latin American critique of that same "scientific tradition" which Schoof proudly alludes to. The openness to the world that European theologians achieved up to the 1960s by dialoguing with contemporary *philosophies*[30] is only a mild reform compared to what the Latin Americans achieved from the 1960s onwards. The latter effected a complete reversal of method. They seem to have done to European theology what Feuerbach did to Hegelian dialectics. They put theology back on its feet. They grounded it on theopraxis. What was formerly revolving in a Kantian orbit was made to rotate around a Marxian axis.[31]

For us Asians then, liberation theology is thoroughly Western, and yet, so radically renewed by the challenges of the Third World that it has a relevance for Asia, which the classical theology does not have. The Ecumenical Association of Third World Theologians (EATWOT), which is now holding its Asian Consultation here, is perhaps its first tangible fruit in Asia. In the churches of the East this *new method* has already begun to compete with the traditional theology. What the Latin Americans claim, and what we Asians must readily grant, is that it is not perhaps a new theology, but a theological *method*, indeed the *correct method* of doing theology.

The features of this methodology peculiarly relevant for us in Asia can be selected from Sobrino's presentation.[32] The first feature is that the Kantian attempt to "liberate reason from authority" paved the way to a theological preoccupation with harmonizing "faith with reason," while the Marxian attempt to "free reality from oppression" did not receive theological attention in Europe until the Latin Americans made an issue of it.[33] Thus the use of "philosophy" to explain away "suffering" rationally or to define God and his nature in such a way as to justify the existence of oppression and injustice, was understandable in a European socio-political context, while substitution of philosophical speculation with "sociological" analysis to *change* rather than explain the world of injustice has become the immediate concern of liberation theology. Such a concern cannot come within the "scientific" purview of European theology, whether Protestant[34] or Catholic.[35]

The second feature, quite important for Asians, is the primacy of praxis over theory. Spirituality, for instance, is not the practical conclusion of theology; the radical involvement with the poor and the oppressed is what creates theology. We know Jesus the *Truth* by following Jesus the *Way*.

Thirdly, this Way is the Way of the Cross, the basis of all knowledge. Thus, the growth of the world into God's kingdom is *not* a "progressive development," but a process punctuated by radical contradictions, violent transformations, and death-resurrection experiences—what Sobrino calls the *ruptura epistemologica*, "scripturally founded in the 'Transcendence of the Crucified God.' "[36]

Fourthly, we see that it is not a "development theology" such as would justify and perpetuate the values of an "acquisitive" culture, but a "liberation theology" demanding an asceticism of renunciation and a voluntary *poverty* that sneers at acquisitiveness. This resultant "spirituality" is not self-enclosed, motivated as it is by the desire to bring about the kingdom of God here on earth. What it inculcates is not merely a *passive solidarity* with the poor in their poverty and oppression, but also a *dynamic participation* in their struggle for full humanity. Indeed, a dynamic following of Christ![37]

Finally, the encounter of God and man, i.e., the interplay of grace and liberty, is seen as man's obligation to use all his *human potentialities* to anticipate the kingdom which, nevertheless, remains *God's gratuitous gift*. This explains the liberation theologian's political option for socialism, i.e., for a definite social order in which oppressive structures are changed radically, even violently, in order to allow every person to be fully human, the assumption being that no one is liberated unless everyone is.

This theology, and also its European predecessor, receive their contextual significance in Asia precisely in relationship to the aforesaid Western ideologies with which they are very closely connected. Our earlier criticism of how these ideologies operate in Asia has clearly situated the two theologies, too, in the context of Eastern religiosity. Hence our task is to complement the Latin American method with an Asian critique of classical theology.

The Asian Style as Asian Theology

Peking's recent prediction about the future of Buddhism runs as follows:

The Communists hold that, as a *religion* Buddhism will gradually die out, as history moves forward; but as a *philosophy* it merits careful study.[38]

This sort of apocalyptic optimism, which turns hopes into predictions, is not new in the history of Asian Buddhism. For instance, the Christian missionaries in Sri Lanka used to pronounce such prophecies in the last century[39] when the whole colonial state machinery was backing their missions against the Buddhists.[40] Buddhism, however, has lived to tell the tale. The analogy with the Chinese situation need not be labored here.

The Marxists seem to grant that it is "religion" that will die and not the "philosophy," which merits study. Here again, I cannot help drawing a parallel with the theologians of the West who, too, have detached religion from philosophy in their "theology of religions." In fact, the inherent incapacity of both classical Marxism and classical theology to grasp the Asian sense as revealed in the multifaceted religiosity of our people is ultimately rooted in this unhappy dichotomy, which both have inherited from a tradition which began perhaps with the early Western encounters with non-Christian cultures.[41]

Let me then put things back in focus. In the nonbiblical soteriologies of Asia, *religion* and *philosophy*, are inseparably interfused. Philosophy is a religious vision; and religion is a philosophy lived. Every metacosmic soteriology is at once a *darsana* and a *pratipadā*, to use Indian terms, i.e., an interpenetration of a "view" of life and a "way" of life. In fact, the oft-repeated question whether Buddhism is a philosophy or a religion was first formulated in the West, before it reached Peking by way of Marxism. For in the Buddha's formula, the fourfold salvific *truth* incorporates the Path as one of its constituents, while the Eight-fold *Path* coincides with the realization of the Truth.

Here let me refer to the current trend of *using* "Buddhist techniques" of meditation in "Christian prayer" without any reverence for the soteriological context of such techniques. For the naive presupposition is that the (Buddhist) *Way* could be had without the (Buddhist) *Truth*. It is time to impress on our theologians that in our culture the *method* cannot be severed from the *goal*. For the word "technique," now misused in task-oriented cultures to mean a mechanical action which, when done according to set rules, produces predictable results, must be traced back to its original Greek sense. *Technē* is not a mechanical action, but a skill, an art; in our traditions, the art of doing a thing is itself the thing done. The *goal* of life, in Buddhism, is the *art* of living it. The perfection to be achieved is the style of achieving it! The obvious corollary is that the Asian method of doing theology is itself Asian theology. *Theopraxis is already the formulation of theology.*

Thus the mutuality of praxis and theory which defines the Asian sense in theology is the missing ingredient in the theology of religions which we have uncritically accepted and this hampers our task of acquiring the Asian style. This inadequacy seems to have been introduced by the early Fathers of the church, who in their dialogue with the nonbiblical systems restricted their interest to the *philosophical* rather than the *religious* plane. They further impressed this dichotomy on the Western theological tradition when they took "pagan" philosophy out of its religious context and turned it into an intellectual weapon serving Christian apologetics against those very religions! Thus philosophy became the handmaid of Christian religions, *ancilla theologiae*, as already noticed in the writings of Clement of Alexandria and Peter Damien.[42] It is in this play of circumstances that one can understand the two permanent dents which the Western theology of religions received very early in history.

First, the use of philosophy minus religion imparted a *cerebral thrust* to the theology of religions. This emerged side by side with an abhorrence of "pagan" religious practices: an old Semitic intransigence continuing up to the apostolic era. Nevertheless, in the course of time these religious practices did influence Christian liturgy and ethics, even though theology held fast to its *ancilla!* Thus from the very inception, theology and theopraxis parted ways. The God-talk of theologians and the God-experience of the monks ran parallel. The former was working on "pagan" thought and the latter on "pagan" spirituality! The academicians and the mystics lived in mutual suspicion.

The second dent is even deeper. It is the apologetical technique of using a non-Christian religion against itself. This later became a missiological strategy, still resorted to in our theology of religions. It began with the way a "pagan" philosophy was removed from its original religious context and made to serve Christianity, not merely to enrich itself with an intellectual equipment but also to counteract the "pagan" religions. This process of "instrumentalization" is not absent even in De Nobili and Ricci, the missionary innovators of seventeenth-century Asia.[43] What the early Fathers did to nonbiblical philosophy, these men did to Asian *culture*. They truncated it from its religious context and turned it into a means of conversion. It was a step forward, no doubt, but in the same direction! To this category must be relegated also the Christian "guru" who, as we mentioned earlier, plucks Zen and Yoga from the religious stems which give them sap, and adorns Christian spirituality with sapless twigs!

This species of "theological vandalism" has been euphemistically expressed by a new Christian usage of the word "baptism." One hears of "baptizing" Asian cultures, and now after Vatican II, "baptizing Asian religiosity." Baptism, which in its scriptural usage expressed the most self-effacing act of Christ, first in the Jordan where he knelt before his precursor (Matthew 3:13–15) and then on the Cross (Mark 15:35; Luke 12:50) where, as the suffering servant he ended his earthly mission in apparent failure, has now come to mean Christian triumphalism, which turns everything it touches to its own advantage, with no reverence for the wholeness of another's religious experience.

Hence our conclusions:

1. Our theology is our way of sensing and doing things as revealed in our people's struggles for spiritual and social emancipation and expressed in the idioms and languages of the cultures such struggles have created.

2. Theology then is not mere God-talk; for, in our cultures, God-talk *in itself* is sheer "nonsense." As evidenced by the Buddha's refusal to talk of Nirvana, all words have *silence* as their source and destiny! God-talk is made relative to God-experience. The word-game about nature and person or the mathematics of one and three have only generated centuries of verbosity. It is word-less-ness that gives every word its meaning. This inner *harmony* between *word* and *silence* is the test of Asian authenticity, indeed it is the Spirit, the eternal energy which makes every word spring from silence and lead to silence, every engagement spring from renunciation, every struggle from a profound restfulness, every freedom from stern discipline, every action from stillness, every "development" from detachment, and every acquisition from nonaddiction. Since, however, silence is the *word unspoken* and the Word is *silence heard*, their "relationship" is not one of temporal priority but dialectical mutuality. It is the Spirit of Buddhist wisdom and Christian love. If there is harmony between our speech and our silence, whether in worship or service or conversation, the Spirit is among us.

3. The same *harmony* reigns between *God-experience* which is silence and the *human-concern* which makes it heard. One is not temporally prior to the other. It is, rather, the mutuality between wisdom and love, *gnosis* and *agape, pleroma* and *kenosis,* or as the Buddhists have put it, between "knowledge that directs us to Nirvana and the compassion that pins us down to the world."[44] For liberation-praxis is at once a withdrawal into the metacosmic and an immersion into the cosmic.

4. The most subtle point of this dialectic is between *authority and freedom.* The magisterial role in the Asian church has to be earned by the master's *competence to mediate liberation.* Authority makes no external claims. Authority is competence to communicate freedom. He who lacks competence uses power. "By what authority. . . ?" asked the power-thirsty clerics of the Son of Man, who submitted himself to that very power in order to vindicate his authority. His *authority was his freedom,* available to all who touched him. It is a self-authentication derived from a liberation-praxis; it is a human-concern testifying to a God-experience: the two prongs of a liberation struggle.

5. To regain its lost *authority,* therefore, the Asian church must abdicate its alliances with *power.* It must be humble enough to be baptized in the Jordan of

Asian *religiosity* and bold enough to be baptized on the cross of Asian *poverty*. Does not the fear of losing its identity make it lean on Mammon? Does not its refusal to die keep it from living? The theology of power-domination and instrumentalization must give way to a theology of humility, immersion, and *participation*.

6. Hence our desperate search for the Asian face of Christ can find fulfillment only if we participate in Asia's own search for it in the unfathomable abyss where religion and poverty seem to have the same common source: God, who has declared Mammon his enemy (Matthew 6:24).

7. What then is the locus of this praxis? Certainly not the "Christian life lived within the church in the presence of non-Christians"; rather, it is the God-experience (which is at once the human-concern) of God's own people living beyond the church and among whom the church is called to lose itself in total participation. That is to say, *theology in Asia is the Christian apocalypse of the non-Christian experiences of liberation.*

NOTES

1. Roy Preiswerk, "La rupture avec les conceptions actuelles du développement" in *Rélations interculturelles et développement* (Geneva, 1975), pp. 71–96.

2. R. C. Zaehner, *Foolishness to the Greeks. An Inaugural Lecture Delivered Before the University of Oxford on 2 November 1953* (Oxford University Press, 1953) p. 17.

3. For the most recent discussion on the matter, cf. H. Bechert, ed., *Buddhism in Ceylon and Studies on Religious Syncretism in Buddhist Countries* (Göttingen, 1978), especially Part III, pp. 146–339.

4. Rock Edict XIII of Aśoka speaks of Buddhist missions to Syria. A complement to this is the Aramaic inscription found in East Afghanistan in 1969.

5. Samagama Sutta of the Majjhima Nikaya.

6. Cf. Edward Conze, *Buddhism* (London: Allen and Unwin, 1956; New York: Harper & Row), pp. 64–65.

7. Cf. Dulamzhavyn Dashzhamts, "Non-Capitalist Development and Religion," *World Marxist Review* (December 1973): 27–29.

8. For an exhaustive historical illustration, see Bardwel L. Smith, ed., *Two Wheels of the Dhamma: Essays on Theravada Tradition in India and Ceylon* (Missoula: Scholars Press, University of Montana, 1972).

9. Cf. news item "Militant Monks" in *Far Eastern Economic Review* 97 (September 30, 1977).

10. In Cakkavattisīhanada Suttanta of the Dīgha Nikāya.

11. Cf. Daniel L. Overmyer, "Folk Buddhist Religion: Creation and Eschatology in Medieval China," *History of Religions* (University of Chicago) 12/1 (August 1972): 42–70.

12. Cf. Holmes Welch, *Buddhism Under Mao* (Cambridge, Mass.: Harvard University Press, 1972), pp. 1–41, 340–363.

13. Cf. Luciano Parinette, ed., *Karl Marx sulla Religione* (Milan, 1972), pp. 511 ff., referred to in Erich Weingärtner, ed., *Church within Socialism* (Rome: IDOC International, 1976), p. 9.

14. The CBA is once again in the news. Cf. *China Talk* (August 1978), quoted in Lutheran World Federation, *Marxism and China Study, Information Letter*, No. 23 (September 1978), p. 5.

15. Parallel to CBA activities, there was, on the pro-Western side, a world conference which called itself "World Buddhist Union," whose political leanings could be guessed from the nonparticipation of the People's Republic of China, North Vietnam, and North Korea and the presence of Taiwan and South Vietnam (cf. *World Buddhism* 19 [November 1970]:111). It regarded itself as the fourth world organization after the WFB, WBSS, and WBSC (ibid., 19 [December 1970]: 136).

16. Cf. *World Buddhism* 18 (July 1970): 325, and 19 (August 1970):17.

17. "Relevance of Buddhist Studies," *World Buddhism* 21 (October 1972): 67 ff.

18. Quoted in Charles Davis, *Christ and the World Religions* (London, 1970; New York: McGraw Hill, 1972), p. 21.

19. *Populorum progressio*, no. 20.

20. Cf. Edward Schillebeeckx, *God the Future of Man* (New York: Sheed & Ward, 1968), p. 54.

21. Cf. Langdon Gilkey, *Religion and the Scientific Future: Reflections on Myth, Science, and Theology* (London, 1970; New York: Harper & Row, 1970), pp. 76–77.

22. The quotation is from *Populorum progressio*, no. 20.

23. Our study of healing ceremonies shows that demons associated with sickness are brought to the open and then eliminated till the Buddha emerges as the Powerful One and his *doctrine well observed* is presented as the cure par excellence. The beliefs of the cosmic religions are constantly purified and made to align with the metacosmic goal of perfection.

24. Cf. Piero Gheddo, *Why Is the Third World Poor?* (Maryknoll, N.Y.: Orbis Books, 1973), pp. 30–37 and *passim*.

25. E. F. Schumacher, *Small Is Beautiful: Economics as if People Mattered* (London, 1973; New York: Harper & Row, 1973).

26. Cf. Weingärtner, ed., *Church within Socialism*, p. 3.

27. Cf. Robert B. Y. Scott and Gregory Vlastos, eds., *Towards the Christian Revolution* (Chicago and New York: Willett, Clark and Company, 1936).

28. Mark Schoof, O.P., *Breakthrough: Beginnings of the New Theology*, trans. N. D. Smith (Dublin: Gill and Macmillan, 1970), p. 17.

29. Ibid., pp. 22–30.

30. It is observed, ibid., p. 26, that the new theology began by making the "whole life of the Church" the locus of a theological reflection, especially "the *world in which this community* (of the church) *lived, especially the world of contemporary philosophy*" (emphasis and parenthesis mine). The way in which *the world in which the church lived* is filtered into "the world of philosophy" would not escape South American criticism.

31. For a lucid exposition of this Latin American breakthrough, cf. Jon Sobrino, "El conocimiento teológico en la teología europea y latinoamericana," in *Liberación y cautiverio: Debates en torno al método de la teología en America Latina* (Mexico City, 1975), pp. 177–207. For a neat summary of it, cf. Alfred T. Hennelly, S.J., "Theological Method: The Southern Exposure," *Theological Studies* 38 (December 1977):708–735.

32. Sobrino, "Conocimiento teológico," *passim*.

33. However, a relatively early example of a pioneering, and perhaps a premature but certainly praiseworthy attempt at a Christian assessment of the Marxist challenge, can be found in Robert B. Y. Scott and George Vlastos, eds., *Towards the Christian Revolution*.

34. According to the thesis put forward by Wolfhart Pannenberg (*Theology and the Philosophy of Science*, trans. Francis McDonagh [London, 1976; Philadelphia: Westminster, 1976]), the main task of theology is to establish rationally the truth of theological propositions.

35. For a self-understanding of Catholic theology as a "scientific pursuit," cf., Yves Congar, O. P., *A History of Theology*, trans. Hunter Guthrie (Garden City, N.Y.: Doubleday, 1968), pp. 221 ff.

36. Here Sobrino (Conocimiento teológico," p. 201) quotes Jürgen Moltmann. Cf. Hennelly, "Theological Method," p. 721.

37. Hennelly, "Theological Method," pp. 710–713.

38. *Peking Review*, No. 47 (November 24, 1978), p. 31. The emphasis is mine.

39. Cf. Kirsiri Malagoda, *Buddhism in Sinhalese Society, 1750–1900: A Study of Religious Revival and Change* (Berkeley; University of California Press, 1976), pp. 173–174.

40. Ibid., pp. 191–196.

41. Cf. Aloysius Pieris, S.J., "Western Christianity and Eastern Religions: A Theological Reading of Historical Encounters" (manuscript), a paper read at the German Theology Professors' Seminar, Bossey, Switzerland, September 27–30, 1978.

42. Cf. Pannenberg, *Theology and the Philosophy of Science*, p. 10.

43. For an illustration, cf. Pieris, "Western Christianity and Eastern Religions," p. 25.

44. *Nibbānābhimukhā paññā, samsārābhimukhā karuṇā*. For a lengthy excursus on the dialectics between *paññā* and *karuṇā*, see *Itv A* I 15–16, *Cp A* 289–290, *Pm* 192–193.

9

Christian Reflection
in a Buddhist Context

Lynn de Silva (Sri Lanka)

Theology is a living thing and has to do with our very existence as human beings in a particular situation and therefore must be related to the traditional beliefs, classical expressions of faith, and cultural forms. Theology is not an intellectual activity that takes place in the seclusion of a classroom, but a human activity that takes place in a culture; it is not a theoretical science with a fixed structure of thought applicable to all times and all places, but one that is dynamic and mobile and adaptable to changing circumstances. Of course there are elements of constancy and continuity and an unchanging content in any theology, but the form or the mode undergoes change in relation to the context. Although no theology is derived from the culture alone, it does take from and is shaped in the particular situation or context. Authentic, living theology arises from an interplay between the "Logos" and the culture in which it seeks to express itself. The theologian, being part of the culture, cannot but speak from its context and in its terms.

The need for restating Christian theology in relation to the faiths in Asia has been stressed over and over again. In this paper an attempt is made to restate briefly some fundamentals of Christian theology in relation to

Lynn de Silva is a member of the Ecumenical Institute for Study and Dialogue in Colombo.

Theravada Buddhist thought, speaking from its context and in its terms. An attempt is made to do this within the framework of the *Tilakkhana*.

Tilakkhana and the Human Predicament

Buddhism begins with an analysis of the human condition. This is the right starting point for theology, for a living theology must begin with living existential realities and not with metaphysical speculations. The Buddha in his diagnosis of the human predicament discovered three marks (*Tilakkhana*), or characteristics of all existence. They are *anicca, dukkha,* and *anatta.* These three terms indicate the fundamental "marks," or "characteristics," of all existence in the space-time order of reality. They are the hallmarks of existence which point to the fact that all existence in its absolute entirety is but a flux-in-process (*anicca*), having nothing permanent or enduring in the process of change (*anatta*), and hence inherently incapable of producing any lasting satisfaction (*dukkha*). *Anicca* means impermanence, *anatta* means soullessness, and *dukkha* means all aspects of suffering. *Dukkha* is a word that has varied shades of meaning and defies precise definition. Perhaps "existential anxiety" covers much of what *dukkha* means.

In my opinion, in the *Tilakkhana* analytic we have a comprehensive analysis of the human predicament, in which the anthropological, empirical, and experiential problems converge, embracing the whole breadth of human existence, which can provide a framework for an indigenous Christian theology.

It is important to note that the understanding of the human predicament in terms of the *Tilakkhana* arose, not from a theoretical interest but from an existential concern. This concern is reflected in Prince Siddhartha's experience of seeing the three sights—an old man, a sick man, and a corpse—signifying the fact of negativity, nihility, or mortality inherent in all existence. The three sights correspond to the three signs mentioned above. When he saw each sight he asked the question, "Will this happen to me?" That is the question "everyone" asks in silence or articulates in different ways. There was also a fourth sight which the Prince saw—that of a serene hermit. This signified to him that there was a transcendent state beyond conditioned existence. This experience of Prince Siddhartha is a paradigm for understanding the human predicament and finding a solution to it.

There is a striking parallel to this experience in Nietzsche's *Zarathustra* in the chapter "The Preacher of Death," in which he refers to three ways in which the threat of the possibility of nonbeing, or of ceasing to be, comes to a person: "They meet an invalid or an old man or a corpse and immediately say 'Life is refuted'."[1] It is significant that the distinguished theologian Paul Tillich refers to this and sees its existential significance.[2] We could relate this to what the father of modern existentialism, Sören Kierkegaard, said. He pointed out that a man who comes to realize that "all men are mortal" knows the universal essence of all existence, but what is needed is that he should apply this truth to himself and come to the conclusion in his own case, "I too must die." It is then that an individual will feel the need to find a purpose, a plan, and a destiny in life. Kierkegaard's aim was to help people to come to that conclusion and thus experience the truth—one might say the truth of *anicca, dukkha,* and *anatta*—in their own individual existences so that they will seek a rationale for true living. This was exactly the aim of the Buddha too—to help people to understand the real nature of existence and seek for a rationale of authentic living which can bring liberation from conditional existence.

Modern existentialist writers describe the human predicament in terms of anxiety. Paul Tillich describes the nature of anxiety as follows:

The assertion about the nature of anxiety is this: anxiety is the state in which a being is aware of its possible nonbeing. The same statement in a shorter form, would read: anxiety is the existential awareness of nonbeing. "Existential" in this sentence means that it is not the abstract knowledge of nonbeing which produces anxiety, but the awareness that nonbeing is part of one's own being. It is not the realization of universal transitoriness, not even the experience of the death of others, but the impression of these events on the always latent awareness of our own having to die that produces anxiety. Anxiety is finitude, experienced as one's own finitude. This is the natural anxiety of man as man, and in some way of all living things. It is the anxiety of nonbeing, the awareness of one's finitude as finitude.[3]

Based on this passage we could understand anxiety in terms of *Tilakkhana.* Anxiety is "the state in which a being is aware of its possible nonbeing" (i.e., the possibility of *anicca*). This awareness is due to the fact that "nonbeing is part of one's own being" (i.e., a person is *anatta.*) It is an "existential awareness" because "anxiety is finitude, experienced as one's own finitude" (i.e., the state of *dukkha*).[4]

If, as John Macquarrie says, "By 'existentialism' is meant the type of philosophy which concerns itself with human existence and which tries to understand this existence out of the concrete experience which, as existents, we all have," then we could speak of a Buddhist existentialism as some writers have done.[5] Christian theology should begin where Buddhism begins by trying "to understand this existence out of the concrete experience which, as existents, we all have."

Biblical Understanding of *Tilakkhana*

The polarity of conflict between being and the possibility of nonbeing that lies at the core of human existence, the mood of anxiety, the finitude and precariousness of life, is a familiar theme that runs through the Bible. There is no systematic exposition of this human condition in the Bible as is found in the Buddhist texts. The biblical writers were concerned only with stating facts of experience and not with systematization. The task of systematization belongs to the theologian. For this task of doing theology in the context of Buddhism the theologian could employ the *Tilakkhana* analysis of existence.

There should be no difficulty with regard to *anicca* and *dukkha*. There are a number of passages which speak of the transitoriness and suffering and anxiety of human life.[6] But *anatta* may present some difficulties, because the notion of an immortal soul is deeply embedded in Christian thinking. However, it is now seen that this notion is an alien infiltration from Greek philosophy into Christianity. Modern studies in biology, psychology, and physiology are all agreed in rendering incredible the doctrine of the immortality of the soul and modern biblical theologians are in agreement with this view.[7] For example, Karl Barth says, "We necessarily contradict the abstractly dualistic conception which so far we have summarily called Greek, but which unfortunately must also be described as the traditional Christian view. It was disastrous that this picture of man could assert and maintain itself for so long as the Christian picture. We must earnestly protest that this is not the Christian picture."[8]

There are two important passages in the Bible where the undertones of the terms *anicca*, *dukkha*, and *anatta* occur together.

The first is Psalm 90. Man is turned back into dust from whence he came (v.3). Man is *anatta*. His life is like a dream, like the grass that withers (v.5). He is *anicca*. Even the short span of life is full of toil, trouble, and anxiety (vv. 9–10; the Jerusalem Bible uses the word "anxiety"). Life is *dukkha*.[9]

The other passage is Romans 8:18–25. In describing the human predicament St. Paul uses three terms in this passage, namely, *mataiotes, pathemata,* and *phthora,* which have close approximations to the Pali terms *anicca, dukkha,* and *anatta* respectively. The Buddhist overtones of the Greek words are striking. There are three things that stand out in this passage:

1. The whole creation is subject to vanity (*mataiotes*). This means that all things are subject to corruption and decay; they are perishable since they are impermanent (*anicca*).

2. The whole creation is groaning in travail (*pathemata*). That is what *dukkha* means.

3. The creature is subject to corruption (*phthora*). Man is *anatta*.[10]

All in all, the *Tilakkhana* emphasizes man's non-egoity (*anatta*-ness). This concept is the bedrock of Buddhism. Man must realize his non-egoity and free himself from the false notions of I, me, and mine if he is to gain final liberation. Christian mystics also, as we shall see, stress this point. It has a deep significance in Christian spirituality which we have lost sight of.[11] It is in the Buddhist *nāma-rūpa* analysis that the fact of non-egoity is clearly shown. This is an analysis that Christian theology can assimilate.

According to the biblical view, man is a psycho-physical unity, of "soul" (*psyche*) and "flesh" (*sarx*). This bears a close resemblance to the Buddhist analysis of man in terms of *nāma* (name) and *rūpa* (form). *Psyche*, like *nāma*, corresponds to the psychical aspect of man, which represents more or less those processes that come within the field of psychology, and *sarx*, like *rūpa*, corresponds to the physical processes with which the biologist is concerned. Both the Buddhist and the biblical view of man agree that there is no distinguishable, immortal soul within this psycho-physical *(nāma-rūpa)* aggregation which constitutes a person.

Creature and the Creator

Buddhism and Christianity come to a realization of non-egoity in two different ways. Christianity begins by stressing the greatness and majesty of God the Creator in relation to whom human beings are insignificant, fragile, and weak, and apart from whom they are nothing. Buddhism begins by looking inwards and seeing our nothingness and then something beyond is sought for. Perhaps the Buddha declined to say anything about God, for to assume that there is such a reality which gives a sense of security could be an obstacle for one to realize and understand the fact of non-egoity or self-emptiness. The Christian view, however, is that we understand our creatureliness—nothingness—in relation to the Creator. We are nothing-at-all in relation to the Creator, who is all-in-all.

The biblical doctrine of creation is a doctrine concerning the relationship between God the Creator and the creature. It is not a phenomenological account of how all things were brought into being. Its primary interest is in the Creator-creature relationship and not in an empirical description of the tangible world of sense experience. The interest in the empirical world is that it is the environment in which the creature is placed, and the nature of which the creature shares. It is pre-eminently a religious affirmation about the sovereignty of God and the absolute dependence of the creature. The intention of the creation story in Genesis 1 is not to analyze the essence of human beings or to define God's nature, but rather to indicate our task and our relationship as creature to the Creator.

The Creator-creature relationship is best expressed in the doctrine of *creatio ex nihilo*. This doctrine has a twofold significance in the context of Buddhism. It implies the absolute impermanence *(anicca)* of all things apart from the Creator, who maintains them in existence by the power of his Word. As they were created out of nothing at his Word, so they vanish into nothingness at his Word. As all things, including human beings, have been created out of nothing, so all things including them stand vis-à-vis the threat of nonbeing *(anatta* and *anicca)*. On the other hand it implies the absolute Lordship of God over existence. In other words God is the Uncreated, human beings are the created; God is the *Asaṃkhata* (Unconditioned), human beings are the *saṃkhata* (conditioned).

It is significant to note that the first meditation in *Introduction to the Devout Life,* by Francis de Sales, is on creation, in which our "nothingness" before the

Creator is stressed.[12] It could very well be called a meditation on *anatta* or *anatta-bhavana*. Thus we see the existential and spiritual significance of the doctrine of creation.

The Human Need for God

I believe that the biblical understanding of the Three Signata, especially *anatta,* can enable us to understand why we need God. It is my contention that, if *anatta* is real, God is necessary; it is in relation to the Reality of God that the reality of *anatta* can be meaningful. Because human beings are *anatta,* God is indispensable; because they are absolutely *anatta,* God is absolutely necessary. The conditioned (*saṃkhata*) has nothing to hope for unless there is an unconditioned Reality (*asaṃkhata*). It is in relation to the Unconditioned (God) that the full depth and significance of *anatta* can be understood.

To assert that we have within ourselves the intrinsic self-derived power to transcend conditioned existence is to deny the full import of *anatta.* If we can save ourselves, *anatta* is not real. Christianity takes the meaning of *anatta* in all its seriousness and denies any form of intrinsic power in human beings— be it karmic force or the power of mind, *viññāna*—by which they can save themselves. For Christianity *anatta* means *anatta* in its fullest sense. As Karl Barth puts it, "Man without God is not; he is neither being nor existence."[13]

To explain what this means we could employ the famous Udāna passage in the Pataligama Vagga of the *Khuddaka Nikaya*:

Monks, there is (*atthi*) a not-born (*ajatam*), a not-become (*abhuam*), a not-made (*akatam*), a not-compounded (*asaṃkhatam*). If that unborn, not-become, not-made, not-compounded were not, there would be apparent no escape from this here that is born, become, made, compounded. But since, monks, there is an unborn, unbecome, unmade, uncompounded, therefore is apparent the escape from this here that is born, become, made, compounded.[14]

The implication underlying this passage is that the unconditioned Reality is indispensable if human beings are to escape the conditioned; apart from the unconditioned there can be no escape for that which is conditioned. To put it in another way; if human beings are absolutely *anatta,* the hypothesis of the Unconditioned or some such other hypothesis becomes absolutely necessary if the error of nihilism (*uccedaditthi*) is to be avoided. Apart from the unconditioned Reality there can be no emancipation for that which is conditioned; all that can be expected is total annihilation.

The Meaning of the Term Christ

For the Christian the eternally existent unborn, unbecome, not-made and unconditioned—the Logos, the Word, the Dharma—was fully manifest in

Jesus Christ. He is pre-existent and eternally present reality—"Before Abraham was I am" (John 8:58). In him, in his Incarnation, there was a unique relation between the conditioned and the Unconditioned. This truth can be best understood in the light of the well-known passage, Philippians 2:7–11, in which St. Paul speaks of the *kenosis* of our Lord. The deep significance of Kenotic Christology can be understood in terms of the *Tilakkhana* when it is seen not as the emptying of the divinity of our Lord, but as the negation of the self in which the divinity of love is disclosed. In his self-emptying there is nothing of self to be seen— no notion of I, me, mine — but only the ultimate, unconditional love of God.

The essential principal of the divine *kenosis,* based on the conception of self-emptying, is that Christ negated himself without losing himself. By his identity with conditioned existence he negated himself; but because of his identity with the Unconditioned (God), he did not lose himself. This identity was a relationship between the conditioned and the Unconditioned. But it was unique in that it was a relationship concerning the unconditioned identity of the conditioned and the Unconditioned. This is the principle of *kenosis,* which has deep affinities with the Buddhist doctrine of *śūnyatā* (the doctrine of the void).[15]

To be in Christ means to experience *śūnyatā*—the simultaneous experience of emptiness and fullness (*śūnyatā-punnata*). In this experience the *saṃkhata* and the *asaṃkhata* become united. Jesus Christ is the critical point in history at which the conditioned and the Unconditioned meet in a unique way. But one comes to this experience through a process of sanctification which begins here and now and continues after death.

Progressive Sanctification

Modern theologians have found the notion that at death a person either passes into everlasting happiness in heaven or everlasting damnation in hell as literalistic distortions of biblical symbols. Today theologians speak of progressive sanctification which begins here and now and continues after death.

Heaven is a symbol for the fruition of life towards which people advance till they reach the goal which is identified with the "beatific vision"—that direct and indubitable awareness of God. We advance towards this goal by overcoming self-centeredness—the egocentric notion of "I," "me," "mine." We must realize that we are *anatta.* In the words of Romano Guardini, "Death upon death has to be endured so the new life may arise." It is by transcending the self that one grows into the likeness of Christ and so becomes "perfect as our heavenly Father is perfect."

Rightly interpreted then, heaven is neither mythological nor egocentric but the progressive fruition of life, the upper limit of which is fullness of being or perfect communion with God.

Some, mainly Protestants, prefer to call "progressive sanctification after death," the "intermediate state," and some, mainly Roman Catholics, "purgatory." In spite of the aversion Protestants have to the idea of purgatory, mistakenly thought of as a state of *mere* suffering, it is being increasingly recognized that this notion, when rightly understood, is entirely appropriate, for it points to the process by which one is purged of all egocentric elements, purified, and fitted for one's ultimate destiny. Hell, heaven, and purgatory are not sharply separated states, but form a kind of continuum through which one passes from even the "utter state" of near-annihilation which is called hell, to the closest union with God. Thus hell is also a phenomenon within this continuum and can be experienced here and now, or even after death, in varying degrees.[16]

Progressive sancification is, for the Christian, an alternative to the theory of rebirth. If *anatta* is real there cannot be natural survival. To affirm the continuity of one's own *karmic* force or memory contradicts the truth of *anatta*. If *anicca* and *anatta* are real, there can be nothing in us that can survive death. Survival is possible only if God creates a new being. This is what resurrection means. Resurrection is most meaningful in the context of *Tilakkhana*.

The doctrine of resurrection contradicts the notion of an immortal soul within us which survives death. It emphasizes the fact of our mortality, that we come to a total end at death. Therefore, we have to be recalled to life by a new act of creation. As Oscar Cullman puts it: "Resurrection is a positive assertion; the whole man who has really died is recalled to life by a new act of creation by God. Something has happened — a miracle of creation! For something has also happened previously, something fearful: life formed by God has been destroyed."[17]

Thus we see that the Christian hope of survival rests solely on the doctrine of God and not on any theory of a person's intrinsic capacity to survive. There is nothing in one, however noble, which does not bear the marks of *anicca, dukkha,* and *anatta* in the strictest sense of the words. Thus the doctrine of resurrection is wholly in keeping with the doctrine of *anatta*.

Eternal Life

The Bible teaches that human beings were created for communion with God but have fallen short of the ideal. The goal of life is to enter into perfect communion with God. This can be done through progressive sanctification, in which the egocentric life of craving and self-interest comes to an end with the realization that separate individuality bound up with the notions of I, me, and mine is a false notion. This realization in one sense could be called *nirvāna*. Therefore, progressive sanctification is a process of nirvanizing oneself: continually realizing one's non-egoity and the consequent sense of bliss.

In the Christian tradition there is something strikingly analogous to the Buddhist view of the need to strip oneself of the notion of I, me, and mine. Summarizing this central feature of Christian mysticism, Evelyn Underhill says:

All the mystics agree that the stripping off the I, the Me, the Mine, utter renouncement, or "self-naughting"—self-abandonment to the direction of a larger Will—is an imperative condition of the attainment of the unitive life. The temporary denudation of the mind, whereby the contemplative made space for the vision of God, must now be applied to the whole life. Here, they say, there is a final swallowing up of the wilful I-hood, that surface individuality we ordinarily recognize as ourselves. It goes forever, and something new is established in its room. The self is made part of the mystical Body of God; and humbly, taking its place in the corporate life of Reality, would "fain be to the Eternal Goodness what his own hand is to a man."[18]

The "unitive life" in which I-hood is swallowed up does not mean absorption but communion or participation. Communion is not absorption into distinctionless union, but is participation in which the person retains his differentiation as a person without the mark of exclusive individuality being expressed in it. The person loses his exclusiveness completely through participation but discovers authentic self-hood through communion. The I-Thou relationship in which alone a person exists on earth will be perfected and fulfilled in the end when the I and the Thou meet inherently in union and distinction. In communion, individual identity is preserved within a harmony without the implications of exclusiveness that the notions of I, me, and mine entail. In the end we shall be fully persons and cease completely to be individuals in the exclusive sense. We shall retain our differentiation as persons without that differentiation being expressed in exclusiveness of individuality. We shall retain identity within a complete harmony. The relationship in which we live on earth will be progressively sanctified until we reach perfect communion with God. This relationship is like the relationship of the center to the circle in which it is. The center is identifiable only within the circle. There is no question of dualism here. The I and the Thou meet inherently in union and distinction.

A Socially Relevant Ethic

What bearing has the theology we have outlined for a socially relevant ethic in the context of Asia's search for full humanity? To answer this question we have to ask the prior question: what do we mean by humanity? What is human nature? From our earlier discussion three points emerge—three aspects or dimensions of human nature. Christianity emphasizes *mutuality*, the I-Thou relationship; Buddhism emphasizes *non-egoity* or *anatta*-ness; and both emphasize *transcendence*, an ultimate reality towards which one inclines.

By mutuality we mean right-relatedness. That means to be rightly related to one another, overcoming alienation of one from another. It means to be other-oriented. Secular ideologies have stressed this aspect of human mutuality. Karl Marx said, "The human essence is no abstraction inherent in each single individual. In reality it is the ensemble of social relations."[19] Marx's social philosophy was based on an anthropology. He, being a Jew, owed much to the biblical view of human beings. Martin Buber refers to his view of humankind as a species of being existing in relationships as a Copernican revolution of modern thought. The person who is rightly related is one who has a deep concern for social justice and the removal of those things that create divisiveness between people. Thus, we could say that the concern of a Marxist for the abolition of class distinctions is a spiritual concern. Anything that is done compassionately to remove alienation of one person from another, whether by the so-called religious people or by the so-called secular people, is spiritual.

This understanding enables us to see morality in its right perspective, not as the observance of rigid absolute laws but as responsible living for the good of one another. Morality is not the adherence to inflexible absolute laws. Moral principles are situationally adaptable for responsible living for the common good of humanity. This is what it means to be a socialist. In Christian terms this is what "Love thy neighbor" means.

By non-egoity we mean the realization that one is nothing in himself or herself. It means that one is *anatta*. It means overcoming the notion of I, me, mine that stands in the way of right relationships.

To be rightly related to others one must be rightly related within, because the causes that separate people are within them. "What causes war, and what causes fighting among you?" asks St. James; "Is it not your passions that are at war in your members? You desire and do not have; so you kill. And you covet and cannot obtain; so you fight and wage war."[20] In one word it is selfishness or *taṇhā* and everything that promotes selfishness that must be removed.

Right relatedness often means a fundamental change in attitude, a basic change in mind, a prerequisite for change in society. Revolutionaries and peacemakers have recognized this principle. The well-known Cuban revolutionary, Che Guevara, recognized this truth. It is said that his whole outlook was governed by one fundamental principle "that no matter how much you change society, no matter how much you restructure it, unless you create a new man, unless you change his attitudes, it all ends up in greed, lust, and ambition."[21] And a statement of the purpose of UNESCO reads, "Since wars begin in the minds of men, it is in the minds of men that the defence of peace must be constructed."

To this end it is necessary that the egocentric life of craving and self-interest be conquered by the deliberate denying of the self. Jesus put it very strongly when he said,

If any man would come after me, let him deny himself and take up his cross and follow me. For whoever would save his life will lose it, and whoever loses his life for my sake will find it.[22]

The third dimension is transcendence. It is in the very nature of persons to transcend themselves, to incline towards an ultimate reality—Nibbana, God. Karl Jung pointed out that in us there is a psychic aptitude for the beyond, the transcendent. The love shining from the eyes of a bride, a scientist's devotion to his research, a mother's concern for her son or daughter, the haunting sweetness of music, the sense of wonder at the radiance of the sunset, the sense of immensity at the sight of the starry skies, the compulsions to reason and to question, the never ceasing creative urge to create something new and higher and not remain satisfied with what is, the experience of nullity or "*anatta*-ness" which makes one realize that there is something beyond the born, the made, the created, and the quest for meaning are all experiences that bring us to the threshold of something more.

Even in atheism there is a dimension of transcendence, for atheism is a protest in the name of hope for the not yet comprehended. We incline towards this something more in veneration, aspiration, hope, and worship. In Marxism and other social ideologies, transcendence finds expression in faith-decisions made in hope oriented towards a glorious future; it creates a sense of glory. In religions this hope is oriented to a glorious future even beyond the grave. This also creates a sense of glory which finds expression in worship. In theistic religions transcendence is based on a personal God. Transcendence is a summons from the Beyond that enables people to go beyond themselves, by which alone they can discover authentic selfhood.

The quality of transcendence is in everyone whether he or she is a materialist, a Marxist, a Hindu, a Buddhist, a Muslim, or a Christian. There is a beyond in science; the wonder and mystery of the immense range of depths in physical matter. There is a beyond in reason; an ever-receding something beyond the grasp of the mind—the inexplicable—what Buddhists have called *avyākata*. This points to an ultimate Beyond which gives meaning to the proximate beyonds—the experiences of transcendence in everyday life. Even after a hearty meal in a classless society there will still be a hunger for something *more*—for the *Beyond*.

Religions have generally tended to emphasize inwardness (a characteristic particularly of renascent religion) to the neglect of social action, and social ideologies have tended to emphasize social action to the neglect of inwardness. The understanding of human nature consisting of the three dimensions of mutuality, non-egoity, and transcendence will perhaps lead us to participation in a common spirituality linking inwardness with motion, solitary contemplation with mutuality, and transcendence with social involvement. A living theology should help link those two aspects which are essential for the realization of full humanity.

NOTES

1. Friedrich Nietzsche, *Thus Spake Zarathustra*, Pt. I, Ch. 9.
2. Paul Tillich, *Courage To Be* (New Haven, Conn.: Yale University Press, 1952), p. 27.
3. Ibid., p. 36, for a summary.
4. John McQuarrie, *Studies in Christian Existentialism* (London: SCM Press, 1966), pp. 115–116.
5. Edward Conze describes *dukkha* as existential anxiety, accepting that "the existentialist diagnosis of the plight of human existence agrees with that of the Buddhists." See *Thirty Years of Buddhist Studies: Selected Essays* (Oxford: Cassirer, 1969), pp. 210, 238. A. D. P. Kalansuriya draws parallels between Buddhist existentialism and modern existentialism. See *Buddhist Annual* (Colombo: M. D. Gunasona & Co., Ltd., 1967), pp. 75, 77.
6. Ps. 144:3–4; Ecclus. 10:8–11; Ps. 32:6; 2 Cor. 4:18.
7. See Lynn A. de Silva, *Problem of the Self in Buddhism and Christianity* (Colombo: The Study Centre for Religion and Society, 1975), Ch. 8.
8. Karl Barth, *Church Dogmatics* (Edinburgh: T. and T. Clark, 1956, 1963; Naperville, Ill., Allenson, 1969), Vol. III, Part 2, p. 382.
9. For a detailed exposition see Lynn de Silva, "An Existential Understanding of the Doctrine of Creation in the Context of Buddhism," in *A Vision for Man: Essays on Faith, Theology and Society,* ed. Samuel Amirtham (Madras: Christian Literature Society, 1978), pp. 89–90.
10. See an exposition of this passage in Lynn A. de Silva, "Theological Construction in a Buddhist Context," in *Asian Voices in Christian Theology,* ed. Gerald H. Anderson (Maryknoll, N.Y.: Orbis Books, 1976), p. 44.
11. St. Francis de Sales, *Introduction to the Devout Life,* ed. and trans. Allan Ross (Westminster, Md.: Newman Press, 1948), p. 50.
12. Ibid. There is a meditation on death too, p. 56.
13. Barth, *Church Dogmatics,* III, p. 345.
14. Lynn de Silva, "An Existential Understanding," p. 88.
15. See de Silva, "Theological Construction in a Buddhist Context," pp. 37–51.
16. James Alberione, *The Last Things* (Boston: Daughters of St. Paul, 1965), p. 46.
17. Oscar Cullman, *Immortalité de l'ame ou résurrection des morts?* (Neuchatel, 1956), p. 27.
18. Evelyn Underhill, *Mysticism: A Study in the Nature and Development of Man's Spiritual Consciousness* (New York: Noonday Press, 1955), p. 425.
19. Karl Marx, *Selections in Feuerbach,* p. 244.
20. James 4:1–2.
21. John Gerassi, ed., *Venceremos: The Speeches and Writings of Che Guevara* (New York: Simon and Schuster, 1969), p. 48. Note the similarity of the words "greed," "lust," and "ambition" to the Buddhist words *lobha, dosa,* and *moha.*
22. Matt. 16:24–25; Luke 9:23–24.

Editor's note: The founder of Buddhism was Siddhartha Gautama (563–463 B.C.). He was born the son of a king in the Himalayan foothills in what is now South Nepal. The word *Buddha* means enlightened. That is why in writings he is mentioned as the Buddha.

10

Orientations for an Asian Theology

Sebastian Kappen (India)

The aim of this paper is neither to summarize nor evaluate Asian Christian theology, past or present, but to suggest, tentatively, the direction theologizing should take in the future. Any such venture already presupposes a conception of theology. In the present case, the conception presupposed is itself the result of a protracted process of grappling with the problem of God and human beings in the Asian context, especially in the context of religious pluralism, Marxism, and the prevailing socio-political situation. Therefore, an elucidation of what I mean by theology will itself provide the framework for deriving guidelines for the future. It will also provide the frame of reference for a critique of past and present theologies. Admittedly, my views are largely shaped by the Indian experience. Whether and how far they apply to other Asian countries, it is up to the delegates from these countries to decide.

The fundamental notion that constitutes both the point of departure and the point of arrival of this paper is that theology is a critical reflection on our primordial encounter with God. Let me explain what this means.

God-Encounter: The Matrix of Theology

It is on purpose that I have used the word *encounter* in preference to *experience*. Experience is liable to be understood in a purely subjective sense,

Sebastian Kappen, S.J., is director of the Centre for Social Reconstruction in Madras.

as though God were a mere projection of the human mind. Encounter, on the other hand, involves a coming face to face with an "other," in this case, with the ultimate "Other," with the ground and goal of human beings and history. This "Other" is neither personal nor impersonal but transpersonal. In any genuine God-encounter, the absolute Other is experienced as the inmost *within* of the subject who encounters, be it individual or community. Encounter in this sense is not a function of any of the human faculties such as sensation, intelligence, or will. It takes place at the inmost being of the person, where feeling, knowing, willing, and loving have their common root. It is there that we are invaded and inhabited by the Absolute, where the transcendent becomes the immanent, where the in-breaking of the divine becomes an in-dwelling and an in-spiriting. To meet God in this manner is to be taken hold of by him, to be uprooted and swept off one's feet in such a manner that one is no more one's own master; it is, at the same time, to experience the relativization of everything else, whether it be job, security, fame, wealth, or even life itself. Such relativization is, in fact, the only guarantee that one has encountered the Absolute.

But where does our primordial encounter with God take place? It cannot be on the level of religious symbols—whether word-symbols (myths, legends, creeds, scriptures), act-symbols (cult, prayer, religious dance, ceremonies), thing-symbols (temples, altar, consecrated food, sacred utensils, sacred places), or person-symbols (priests, religious teachers, consecrated virgins). These are, at best, forms in which an original God-encounter expressed itself and, as such, are derivative in character. No form is adequate to the content; no symbol is capable of expressing the richness of the original experience, which is ineffable and unfathomable. Furthermore, forms and symbols which emerge subsequently can even distort what they are meant to convey and thus become alienated and alienating, especially when they become institutionalized. Finally, even the original God-encounter, which these symbols are meant to represent and to communicate, is itself historically conditioned and need not necessarily be relevant to the contemporary person.

It follows, then, that the primary locus of God-encounter is to be sought not within but outside and beyond religion in its institutionalized forms. This does not mean that symbols traditionally handed down are necessarily incapable of mediating religious experience. Whether they effect such mediation or not will have to be judged in each case on its merits. What I want to stress in this paper is that the primary focus of theological reflection should be our meeting with God in the contemporary historical situation; i.e., in the realities of practical life, individual and social, whose texture is made up of all that we do and of all that happens to us—dating and mating, sowing and reaping, producing and consuming, buying and selling, planning and organizing. This is the world of praxis, meaning the historical process whereby we transform ourselves in transforming our environment of things, persons, and structures (economic, social, political, and cultural). Praxis comprises not merely action but also passion: *passion-from* as openness to the mystery of life, and *passion-for* as striving for values, ideals, and goals. It is the world of praxis that mediates the presence and the in-breaking of the divine. For us, Asian theologians, this means that it is in the action and passion of our people, in their condition of bondage to systems of exploitation and domination, in their struggles to fashion a more just and humane society that we have to meet the living God.

How does this God confront us today? He comes to us, to everyone of good will, in the form of an *unconditional challenge* to shake off our shackles and to fashion a new home for the human family, a new society in which the free development of each and every one will be assured. In truth, there is no other way the divine can appear to human beings. For what is God but the absolute negation of all evil and the absolute affirmation of all that is good, true, and beautiful? Not in the sense that we form a *notion* of God by negating all limitations and imperfections, but in the sense that God is himself the act of negating, just as light is the act of dispelling darkness. To encounter God, therefore, is to become both a wielder of the sword and a herald of peace. Through the one who has encountered God, the divine No to misery, injustice, and exploitation and the divine Yes to whatever furthers the fullness of human beings reverberate in history and radiate to the ends of the earth. In other words, that person's response itself mediates the presence of God in the world. To have encountered and responded to God in this manner is the essential pre-condition for any valid theological reflection. But theologians should by no means confine themselves to their own personal God-encounter. They should bring within their purview also the God-encounter of others around them, to whichever caste, religion, or community they may belong. If God is the Absolute No to evil, it is obvious that theologians will find God not so much in the establishment—religious or secular—as in those social forces and trends which strive to break the fetters which the establishment imposes on people. For the establishment generally tends to imprison the human spirit in predetermined molds and prevents people from responding to the ever new invitations of God.

Theological reflection is genuine only when it forms a moment in the total human response to the challenge of God embedded in history. It is but one phase of a movement which originates from, and returns to, the world of praxis. But in any living process any one moment includes all the others. So, too, theologizing should encompass not only the God encountered but also the one who encounters God and the encounter itself; it should direct itself both to the divine challenge and the human response. Keeping this in mind, let us elucidate further the concrete task of theological reflection.

Let me state first what theology is not. It is not an attempt to flee from the concrete world of praxis to the world of sterile abstractions. It is rather a process of greater and greater immersion in reality, in the reality of God's challenge enfleshed in history. An analogy might prove useful here. Looking down from a plane as it flies at a high altitude one sees the landscape below but without being able to discern the various objects. But as the plane glides to a landing, objects begin to appear more and more distinctly, revealing their proper contours and colors. So it is with the course of theological reflection. Reflection leads one to perceive clearly what was already perceived, though confusedly, in the primordial God-encounter. Hence it is more like contemplation than like discursive reasoning. And yet, it is not mere contemplation; it is also a process of *becoming* what one contemplates and thereby attaining to a richer and fuller mode of *being*. For the same reason it can in no way be termed an "inscape" into the inwardness of one's self where one is alone with oneself. Such a self in isolation is but a fiction of the mind. For our deepest being is a being-with: with things, with other people, and with the Absolute Other. Centered upon ourselves, we are also centered upon our kind and upon God. In our inmost being we are openness to the mystery of existence, a hearer of words, a hearer of the Word. Theological reflection must, therefore, take place in a spirit of communion with all that is and of compassion for all who belong to the human family.

The Structure of Theological Reflection

The main thrust of reflection must be directed to rendering explicit (=thematizing) the dimensions of meaning implicitly contained in the original God-encounter. The dimensions of meaning to be thematized are many. Here I can do no more than indicate a few important ones. To begin with, there is the *existential* dimension. The experience of being taken hold of by the Absolute is what throws light on the deeper problems of existence such as our being-unto-death, the ambivalence of our freedom, our bondage to sin and guilt, and, finally, the ultimate object of our hope. For the divine that invades us is also power—power that enables us to conquer the forces of death and decay, to cast off all that smothers freedom, and to overcome the inner breach between what we are and what we *ought* to be. However, since the texture of personal existence is conditioned by the objective structures of society, the manner in which the existential meaning of one's God-encounter is perceived and responded to will show many variations depending on whether precapitalist or capitalist social relations prevail in any given place. That is why the answers which traditional religions like Buddhism and Hinduism give to existential human problems, however profound and valid they may be in themselves, cannot be taken as the last word on the matter. They need to be radically rethought and reformulated in the context of the contemporary social situation. This applies equally to the other dimensions of meaning to be discussed below.

A second dimension that needs to be thematized is the *social*. The divine challenge, the human response, and the something new which that response always creates, all these have a social significance. The divine challenge is mediated through a social situation, say, of exploitation or domination. Take, for instance, the oppression of landless laborers in a particular place. All who are sensitive to human values will see in it an unconditional, divine challenge to organize the affected laborers against the forces of oppression. The collective resistence that results is equally revelative of God, insofar as it makes the divine No to evil operative in the here and now of history. Finally, if as a result of organized struggle there is greater equality and justice in that area, that too has a theological meaning. For the splendor of God is then reflected on human faces, the divine reveals itself as the depth-dimension of the love that binds the many into one.

Our encounter with God has also a *cosmic* dimension. For our being-with-others is always mediated by things, whether given or produced by labor. Conversely, our relation to things is mediated by our fellow human beings. Hence the material world is something like the extension in time and space of our social existence. But in all societies dominated by the institution of private property—and Asian societies are no exception to this—nature and the products of labor act as principles of division and instruments of exploitation and domination. From being expressions of creativity, products tend to smother every authentic manifestation of the human. If so, for Asians the divine challenge assumes the form of a call to socialize property so that both nature and the products of labor become vehicles of human togetherness. Furthermore, in order that the world may radiate and manifest the glory of human beings and God it is equally necessary that the production of the useful is at the same time the creation of the beautiful. For the beautiful is that point of convergence where human transcendence unto (reaching out to) the divine and God's immanence (indwelling) in the world meet and fuse into one single incandescence. That is why the theology of the future will have also to be an aesthetics. Only then shall we recapture something of that reverence which the ancient seers of Asia felt for the earth and its fruits, for labor and its products. Only then shall nature cease to be something to be violated and ravished by lust for profit and power. This means that the goal of Asian development will have to be qualitatively different from the Western brand of gadget civilization.

Finally, the theologian must also focus on the *historical dimension* of God-encounter. History is not merely the stage on which the drama of our meeting with our Maker is enacted. It is essentially constituted by divine challenge and human response. What is history but the transcendence of God become the self-transcendence of human beings through project and praxis? It is the unconditional call of the divine which enables us to break loose from the ever-rotating wheel of cyclic time and march forward to the horizon of human-divine fullness, despite reverses and regressions. The goal of history, the realization of theandric fullness, too, transcends all concrete historical achievements. That is why it can be expressed more adequately through myth than through concepts. As examples one may cite the myth of the kingdom of

God in Christianity and that of the classless society in Marxism. The divine reveals itself not only in the challenge to create history and in the goal of historical development but also in the unto-deathness of praxis that aims at translating the ultimate project into reality. History is made only by those who are prepared to risk death so that others may have life, life in full measure and overflowing.

The dimensions of meaning inherent in our primordial God-encounter are essentially intertwined, one implying and flowing into the other. This underlying unity is only implicit in the original experience and must in its turn be thematized. It is the failure to do so that explains the fragmentation of Western theology into the dogmatic, the mystical, the spiritual, and so on. The Asian mind with its native genius for the unity of all is better equipped to avoid this pitfall.

The structured unity of meanings we arrive at should not be set up as an eternal and immutable dogma valid for all times. All dogmas point to the pathetic human attempt to reify the living God by housing God in fixed conceptual molds. Their emergence is understandable in the ages gone by, when people lived in a relatively stable universe in which the consciousness of historical time was all but rudimentary because of the low development of productive forces. But today God is encountered not so much as one *who is* but as one who *comes*. And his coming coincides with human *becoming,* which is history. That is why every knowledge of God must be subjected to critical revision in the light of subsequent historical experience.

Theologizing as Prophesy

If theological reflection is but a moment in the total human response to the divine challenge as revealed in history, it is obvious that it cannot stop at the stage of thematization. Theologians cannot remain neutral before the call of God as though they were mere onlookers. They are personally involved in what they are contemplating; they stand challenged by the same call from the Beyond which they are trying to fathom. To refuse to respond to it is to deny the living God. One cannot deny God and at the same time claim to theologize. On the other hand, to respond to God is to proclaim the challenge one has accepted of working for total human freedom. And what is this but to prophesy? Hence every theologian is also a prophet, one who challenges others to march forward to their ultimate destiny.

But the prophet is impelled not only to proclaim the new age of freedom but also to make it present in the world, here and now. Thus, through prophecy, theology becomes world-transforming praxis; knowledge becomes a power that renews the face of the earth. But theology can become power only if it is appropriated by the oppressed masses in whose interest it is to change the world. The Asian theology of the future—or any genuine theology for that matter—will, therefore, have to be one that expresses the mute longings of the downtrodden and the unwanted of the earth. So, too, the theologians of tomorrow will have to be people who have made an historic option in favor of the disprivileged and the disinherited. Only then will theology slough off its esoteric character, its elitist jargon, and its exclusivist, sectarian features. Herein is to be sought also the criterion for the validity of theology. Only that theological reflection is true which grips the masses and thereby becomes a power that changes the world. All theologies of impotence, therefore, stand self-condemned and must be discarded once and for all. Under this category fall all traditional theologies, whether Christian, Hindu, or Muslim. Where, on the contrary, theology becomes power, the resulting praxis will prepare the ground for ever more profound encounters with God. For, to eradicate injustice and oppression is to clear an open space where the divine can appear before human beings; it is to prepare the way of the Lord.

The Critical Function of Theology

We encounter God not in a vacuum but as men and women inserted in specific social relations and structures of power, and as bearers of a particular culture. We go to meet the living God with minds and hearts shaped by ideas, values, beliefs, attitudes, assumptions, myths, and symbols handed down to us from past generations. All these factors determine the way we are attuned to the total mystery of human existence and, therefore, also to God. The specific attuning we have received, the conditioning we have inherited, may be for good or for bad. For good, if it renders us perceptive to the various dimensions of meaning in our God-encounter; for bad, if it obscures or falsifies them. The aim of criticism is to identify the latter so that by eliminating them we may dispose ourselves the better for an adequate grasp of what the living God demands of us today. In this sense criticism is a preparation for theological reflection. Seen from another angle, it is also a constituent element of theological reflection. For we seldom, if ever, meet the naked God. God appears before us clad in the garb we ourselves have put on him. It is the role of criticism to remove the veils hiding his face, just as it should help remove the blinkers from our own eyes.

Here I shall dwell on three important biases which may blur, distort, or frustrate our encounter with God and our attempts at theologizing. They have to do, respectively, with money, power, and what I would call the *anti-God*.

The Renunciation of Money

Money is more than a mere means of hoarding. As the universal equivalent of all commodities, it confers control over production, circulation, and consumption. In the money form are expressed all the evils of an economy based on private property, competition, and exploitation. Money presupposes as well as creates the division of society into the propertied and the propertyless, into employers and workers, into consumers and producers. As the reification of all social relations, it expresses, as well, the alienation of people from other people. More than anything else it distorts our perception of reality, not excluding the reality of our primordial experience of God.

Where theologians—or any believer for that matter—either belong or owe allegiance to the moneyed classes, they are likely to use God as a means to legitimize their own class interests and as an accomplice in exploiting the poor. In the process, theology is degraded to the level of an ideology, and the divine to the level of a commodity. Money, the universal equivalent, can from now on be exchanged also for things divine. The rich can buy the favor of God by making donations to religious institutions or by having religious services held for their spiritual benefit. They can even buy theological expertise and use it to serve their economic interests. Thus we see the amusing phenomenon of the glitter of gold passing for the brilliance of theological reflection, and of theologians parading as ideologues of Mammon. If money can be exchanged for divine favors, no less can the latter be exchanged for the former. Those who claim the right to mediate the favor (grace) of God can convert it into money. In consequence, the higher the position one occupies in the religious hierarchy, the greater is that person's command over money—over production, circulation, and consumption. Similarly, those who have "accumulated" the knowledge of God can now indulge in the accumulation of capital or at least in hoarding. As a result, money is divinized and the divine monetized. The believer develops a religious attitude to money and a monetary attitude to God. But all exchange is on the basis of equivalence. If so, God and money must have a common essence which is nothing but abstract human labor. It follows then that the God who is exchanged for money is not the living God but a product of the human brain.

This is not just a possible but a real danger to Asian theology, if the situation of the Indian churches can be taken as typical of the whole of Asia. The individual theologian may not be a moneyed person or indulge in conspicuous consumption, but the theologian theologizes within the framework of churches which own immense property and whose economic interests coincide with those of the privileged classes. Besides, the system of values operative in church institutions and organizations is, more often than not, that of capitalism consisting of private interest, competition, individualism, and consumerism. No wonder that the theologies currently taught in seminaries largely tend to legitimate the status quo. They legitimate not only exploitation within the country but also economic imperialism, for the obvious reason that the financial nerve center of the Asian churches lies in the capitalist countries of the West.

In order to develop a theology that is faithful to the living God Asian theologians have, therefore, no other alternative themselves but to opt out of the institutional church or at any rate dissociate themselves from its practice, if not also from its theory. They have to make an historic option in favor of the poor and the oppressed; in other words, they have to declass themselves. Like the rich young man of the Gospel they, too, are called upon to sell what they have and give it to the poor.

Renunciation of Power

Power is understood here as the possibility some have to impose their options—ends and means—on others. As such, it is in principle opposed to God. For God is encountered as an unconditional demand to break all fetters and march forward to the reign of total freedom. Those, therefore, who exercise power or are in league with the wielders of power will either fail to encounter the living God or use God to sanction the existing structures of domination. This need not necessarily be a conscious process involving bad faith. It can coexist with good intentions. A classic instance of this may be found in Paul's advice to Christians: "Let every person be subject to the governing authorities. For there is no authority except from God, and those that exist have been instituted by God" (Roman 13:1). This God, too, is of human making and, therefore, can be exchanged for power, which is no less a human product. In consequence, religious authority is vested with secular power, and secular power with religious authority. God thus becomes kingified, and kings deified. In either case human beings are reduced to slaves.

Here, too, we are not describing a possible deviation that may affect religious practice and thinking. It describes more or less the actual course taken by religions, especially by Christianity. It is well-known that in medieval times there were magistrates who enjoyed episcopal powers, and bishops vested with magistrate's powers. Coming to our own times, the Indian churches have been using God to legitimize whatever regime happens to be in power. Very much to the point is the support given by the official churches to the dictatorial rule of Indira Gandhi. True, bishops are no longer in a position to exercise direct political power, except in the case of the bishop of Rome. This, however, is more than compensated for by the possibilities of exercising power within the Christian establishment itself. The structure of power embodied in church institutions is largely feudal, characterized by personal dependence and patronage. In the case of the Catholic Church it is also centralized and monarchical. The possibilities of domination are further enhanced by the inflow of foreign money. Such being the case, it is understandable that God is pressed into service to reinforce and consecrate ecclesial power structures. That is why the emergence of a theology of the living God will be possible in Asia only when theologians have the courage to renounce all power and, like Jesus, identify themselves with the powerless and the downtrodden of today.

Renouncing the Anti-God

The process we have described whereby people use God to legitimize their own interests of exploitation and domination already explains the birth of the Anti-God. But there are other factors too, which more directly contribute to his emergence, of which the chief are cult, dogma, and law.

Cult may be authentic or inauthentic. Cult is authentic when it is part of a person's response to the demand of God as revealed in history. It will then inevitably lead to creative, liberating praxis. Cult in this sense belongs essentially to the domain of prophetic-symbolic action, and never leaves the terrain of human self-transcendence in history. It becomes inauthentic, alienated and alienating, when it is detached from the dialectic of divine challenge and human response, and is set up as something autonomous. Where this happens cult is transposed from historical time to cyclic time in which nothing new ever happens. False cult is the result of our attempt to have a God whom we can manipulate and dispose of as we please. The God of such cult is a silent, passive God who is bound to make himself available where and when people choose. In this sense cult may be seen as a way of reifying the divine, which has for its counterpart the divinization of things (of the altar, the consecrated bread, etc.). Made in the image of alienated human beings, this God is neutral to the rich and the poor, and dispenses favors to the exploiter and the exploited. He is very much alive in Asian churches and his rule is reinforced by ever new and spurious cults imported from the West. He has his array of theologians, too, vowed to defend and extend his kingdom.

The Anti-God also breeds and is bred by dogma. Dogma, too, dehistoricizes and fixes God into eternal and immutable concepts. The reification that cult accomplishes at the level of symbolic action, dogma accomplishes through conceptualization. It, too, is the result of our striving to be the measure of our own Maker. The same tendency is noticeable in the development of religious laws. If dogma is the law of human thinking about God, law is the dogma concerning human action in response to God. Through law what human beings perceived as the will of God in earlier ages is absolutized as valid for all ages. Thus it, too, dehistoricizes the demands of God. Both deflect our attention from the challenge of the living God in the here and now of history. Both curtail human freedom: the first, freedom of thought; the second, freedom of action. Of the two, law is the greater source of unfreedom, because what passes for the law of God is often the sum of norms formulated by the privileged classes for the furtherance of their own interests. Besides, the religious laws operative in most Asian churches smack of ecclesiastical imperialism, imported as they have been from the West and imposed on us as normative for our thinking and acting. Fortunately, both dogma and the law are on the way out and the voice of the living God is beginning to be heard at least in certain Christian circles.

As far as Asian Christianity is concerned, the Anti-God is a domiciled foreigner. However, it should not be forgotten that he has his counterpart in indigenous religious traditions, with whom he stands in a certain relationship of cultural symbiosis. Though there is much that is beautiful and profound in the Hindu Scriptures, what these on the whole project is a class-God. For the Vedas, the Upanishads, the Epics, and the Puranas were either written or rewritten by the dominant caste of the Brahmins with a view to maintaining their supremacy and promoting the interests of the ruling classes. No wonder that they contain innumerable myths, legends, and discourses which provide ideological legitimation for the exploitation of the lower castes and the untouchables. A case in point is the famous Purusha-sukta (Creation Hymn) of the Rigveda, which describes the divine origin of caste. Furthermore, one can find in the religious lore texts sanctioning every conceivable form of inhumanity including rape, violence, war, and treachery. Such being the case, no theologians, whether Christian or Hindu, who are responsive to human values, can unreservedly identify themselves with the religious traditions of the past. They are likely to feel more at home with the socio-religious protest movements against Brahminism which have arisen time and again at critical periods in the history of India, such as Buddhism, Jainism, the medieval Bhakti movement, and more recently, the Dalit Panther movement, though all of them, excepting the last, became in course of time integrated into the caste system. This is not to say that we have nothing to learn from the past. We should by all means try to discover and assimilate whatever is authentic and humanizing in our religious traditions. But it is essential to keep in mind that the task is not a purely academic but an eminently practical one. For it is only in the process of collective subversive praxis aimed at the creation of a new society and a new culture that the masses will rid themselves of all forms of false consciousness instilled in them by the privileged castes and classes, and learn to discern what is of perennial value in their own cultural traditions.

Jesus and Asian Theology

The Christian theologizes between memory and hope—between the memory of Jesus and hope in the kingdom to come. If in our reflections we have focussed on the God of hope, we did so out of reverence for the memory of Jesus. In fact, his entire life and teaching goes to prove the validity of the approach of theology we have been advocating so far. To substantiate this, nothing less than a critical survey of the Synoptic Gospels is needed. Since that is not possible here, I shall confine myself to making a few general observations.

Jesus lived from one unique experience: his own primordial encounter with God. To judge by the Gospel narratives, that encounter took place on the banks of Jordan when, significantly, he identified himself with the common run of humankind by choosing to be baptized for the remission of sins. From then on he was a man possessed, taken hold of by the Spirit (power) of God, by that Spirit which was to lead him to the desert, to the villages and towns of Palestine, to confrontation with the powers that were, and finally to death on the cross. Every word he uttered, every deed of his, was in response to the challenge of the living God he encountered.

The God of Jesus is to be encountered in the domain not of cult but of history. God is *one who comes* to usher in a new age, in which there will not be any division of society into the rich and the poor (Matthew 5:3), in which the dispossessed will regain possession of the earth (ibid. 5:5), in which human hunger for justice will be satisfied (ibid. 5:6), in which class conflict will be replaced by brotherhood and the sword by peace (ibid. 5:9). Equally, it is in history that human beings *go* to meet God. The good Samaritan met him in responding to a human need (Luke 10:29–37); Zacchaeus in redressing the injustice he had done to others (ibid. 19:1–10); the rich young man was told that he should sell what he had and give it to the poor if he wished to have a share in the life of the new age to come (Mark 10:17–22). Jesus' teaching on this point reflects his own experience of God. It was in the heart of the world that he met his God—at weddings, at festal meals, by the lakeside where fisherfolk cast and hauled their nets, by wayside wells where townsfolk came to fetch water, at gatherings of people, in the company of outcasts, in the fellowship of his disciples, in the togetherness of friendship, and in the innocence of children, and, above all, in contesting the forces of oppression.

Jesus was no theologian in the sense of writing treatises on God. But there is no doubt that he did reflect on his own encounter with God and sought to grasp its implications for himself and for all people. His parables, discourses, and sayings gave expression to the various layers of meaning—existential, cosmic, social, economic, and political—embedded in his own God-encounter. I have elsewhere tried to bring out some of these dimensions of meaning (*Jesus and Freedom* [Maryknoll, N.Y.: Orbis Books, 1977]). Here I shall only comment on his language. He did not speak in abstract, desiccated concepts. Neither did he employ an esoteric language as do most theologians today. Instead he spoke in images, symbols, pictures, and parables. This is not to be attributed solely to the historical conditioning of a more primitive age. It shows rather that his thinking vibrated in unison with the life of his people. Besides, he was too involved in the unspeakable mystery of the God he encountered to be able to speak of God in the manner in which a scientist would speak of test-tube babies. He would not dissect God with the surgical knife of cold reason. For him knowing was also loving, speaking was also prophesying. It is in similar fashion that the Buddha spoke, that the ancient seers of India spoke of Brahman and the Atman. Asian theology will come into its own only when it will have made a complete break with the rationalism of Western theology and evolve a new manner of discourse about

God drawn from the life of God and God's people. We have to develop a new theological language which would express the fusion of thinking and loving, seeing and prophesying, vision and commitment.

For Jesus, reflecting and speaking were but aspects of his total response to the Father. And that response he himself summed up as one of preaching the good news to the poor, proclaiming release for prisoners, giving sight to the blind, setting free the oppressed, and restoring land to the landless (Luke 4:18–19). With him word became power, reflection became *prophecy* resonant with the divine force that re-creates the world. No wonder that, at his words, the blind saw, the deaf heard, the dead rose, and the paralytic took up his bed and walked away. The same force was at work in his fierce denunciation of the scribes and the Pharisees, whom he called a brood of vipers and whited sepulchers, (Matthew 23:33) and in his defiant appellation of Herod as a fox (Luke 13:32). If such words of force have long since been muted in the churches it is because theologizing has been divorced from encounter with God, and faith from practice. Where reflection starts not from one's own meeting with God but from the interpretations raised to the nth degree of the God-encounter which other people are supposed to have had, it will naturally end up in sterile speculation which changes neither the world nor the thinker. The springtime of Asian Christian theology will burst forth only when we refuse to theologize by proxy, i.e., when we refuse to be mere relaying stations for ideas fabricated elsewhere and muster enough courage to face the naked God and respond to his challenge to create a social order of justice and freedom.

Like the prophets of old, Jesus, too, instituted a severe criticism of wealth, power, and the Anti-God, a criticism which was a consequence of his own encounter with God. He rejected the service of Mammon as incompatible with faith in God and required of his followers that they sell what they have and give it to the poor (Mark 40:21; Matthew 6:24). Thereby he also repudiated the prevalent notion that wealth was a sign of divine favor, a notion manifestly born of an attempt to use God to legitimate the exploitation of the poor. No less severe was his criticism of power and of those who "made their subjects feel the weight of their authority" (Mark 10:42). He envisaged a society in which power will give way to service. For him the spirit of God was a subverter of all power, one who pulled down the mighty from their thrones, overthrew oppressors, and demolished prisons (Luke 4:18). True to this conviction he identified himself with the powerless: the simple, the uneducated, the little ones, and the socially despised.

An equally fundamental concern of his was the liquidation of the Anti-God. He would have nothing to do with a cult that does not change the world. For him worship that co-existed with unlove was an empty gesture (Matthew 5:23–24; Mark 12:32–33). Furthermore, he repudiated the distinction between the pure and the impure, between the sacred and the profane, which is the very basis of all religions (Mark 7:15). Of course he prayed; but his prayer was directly geared to meeting the immediate challenges that faced him in the critical phases of his life. It was rooted in history, not transposed to the realm of cyclic time. Nor was what came to be called the Eucharist originally a cultic act. It had its basis in the meals he had with the outcasts of society, with the publicans and the sinners, meals which anticipated the new humanity of the future, the festal gathering of the end-time, when "many will come from the east and west and sit at table with Abraham, Isaac, and Jacob in the kingdom of heaven" (Matthew 8:11). It may, therefore, more appropriately be called a prophetic action. Only subsequently was it interpreted in cultic terms. Similarly, even a cursory reading of the Gospels will show that Jesus was opposed to reifying God into dogmas and laws. He had no hesitation in radically reinterpreting the Law and the prophets. He even went to the extent of abrogating parts of the written law (Matthew 5:25–48). More significantly, he subordinated the law to the well-being of human beings and thereby rendered it relative and provisional (Mark 2:27). In short, his teaching is an emphatic repudiation of every manner of reifying God.

With no official cult, no set creed, and no legal code, what Jesus initiated could in no sense be called a religion among other religions. If anything, it was a prophetic movement reaching out to the ultimate horizon of the fullness of the age to come. Unfortunately, this movement, in passing through the mold of Greco-Roman thinking and culture and under the impact of pagan religions, was transformed into a dogmatic, cultic, law-ridden religion. Hope in the God *who is to come* was replaced by the cult of Jesus, the *already-come;* the kingdom of God was replaced by the churches. Disciples became Christians; pilgrims became settlers. What is worse, Christianity came to terms with money and power, and assumed the role of being a provider of legitimation to exploiters and oppressors. Though in recent years the churches have shown welcome signs of a return to the radical message of Jesus, it is not matched by any corresponding change in practice.

It follows that we have to return to the Jesus of the Gospels and make our own his vision of God and humankind. However, Jesus is more than a mere example to be followed in our quest after God. He is also one in whom we encounter God. And this is just what marks us out from other believers. These, too, meet God in the realities of life, just as we do. But, unlike them, we have met God *also* in the words and deeds of Jesus. However, these two modes of encountering the divine—in Jesus and in the world of today—do not run on parallel lines. They condition and illumine each other, forming unity in tension. Therefore, for us, disciples of Jesus, to theologize is to try to understand the Gospel in the light of our encounter with God today and, conversely to understand our encounter with God in contemporary history in the light of the Gospel.

A prophetic theology that does justice to God's self-revelation both in Jesus and in the world of today is more likely to emerge in Asia than in the West. In countries where Christians are the majority it is easy for them to nurse the illusion that the church is the center of the universe. And where the church is made the center, hope in the kingdom of God is rendered peripheral. In Asia, on the contrary, any exclusive claim Christians may entertain will fall to the ground when they see that they are no better in respect of concern for human values than the followers of other faiths. This makes it easier for them to recapture Jesus' vision of the kingdom of God which includes all—irrespective of caste or creed—who seek the well-being of their neighbors. However, even in Asia it is vain to hope that the Christian establishment will give the lead in fashioning a theology centered upon the kingdom, since it is still very much under the sway of the Anti-God. A relevant theology is more likely to emerge from those groups of dissenting Christians who in loyalty to Jesus have inserted themselves in the life of the people and are partners in their struggle for justice. It is heartening to note that more and more of such groups are being formed, at least in India. They are able to forget all denominational differences and meet on the common basis of discipleship under Jesus and of commitment to the new humanity he envisioned. They, in truth, anticipate the Jesus-community of the future which will transcend all human barriers. Understandably, such groups have no difficulty in joining hands with people of other religions or even with Marxists. The Christ of dogma divides; Jesus of the Gospel unites.

11

Faith and Life Reflections from the Grassroots in the Philippines

Carlos H. Abesamis (Philippines)

Psychological Prerequisite: Theology is the Respondent

In the moment preliminary to the doing of theology in Asia today, the question is not posed by theology. Rather the question is posed to theology. We sometimes meet the question: "What questions does theology pose nowadays?" In Asia and the Third World today, it is the history of our Asian and Third World peoples that propounds the question to theology rather than the other way around. "What does your religion and your theology say to our history of struggle and our history of hope? Are you with us or against us?" We fail to recognize the shifting roles of the interpellator and authority. Many theologians still look upon theology as the supreme teacher, in serene and unchallenged possession of the sources of revelation, giving a priori and

Carlos H. Abesamis, S.J., is coordinator of the Justice and Peace Department of the National Secretariat of Social Action in Manila. This article is based on notes for the talk given at the conference, the subtitle of which was "Towards a Theology from the Grassroots." Also, some of the ATC dynamics subsequent to the talk have been incorporated in this paper, particularly the reflection of the Philippine delegation, insofar as these shed light on the points discussed by the talk.

eternally valid formulations which people, the world, and history must know in order to be saved. In this outlook, theology is the teacher; the world and history, the passive recipient of its teaching. Though there are indeed periods in the life of the Church in which theology must teach, there are other moments (and I think we are living in one) in which a qualitatively new history exacts a new obedience from theology. Today, as has happened in decisive moments in the life of our religion (e.g., time of Moses, time of Jesus, Vatican II), history is the interpellator, theology the respondent.

For one who begins to do theological work in Asia today, the realization of the radically threatened position of theology is an indispensable psychological prerequisite. Moreover, at the very outset, the theologian will have to realize (1) that theology is response rather than dogma; (2) that what theology can eventually say is an inadequate second word in response to the question first spoken by the history of Third World peoples in our lands; (3) that one must go beyond Vatican II and even the recent theological developments elsewhere and proceed to make our peoples' contemporary history and God within that history the main preceptors of faith; and (4) that commitment to this Asian history and struggle is a prerequisite for one who engages in Asian theology today.

Such a realization is reflected in the theme chosen by our conference. We are first made aware of Asia's struggle for full humanity and then invited to work towards a relevant theology.

Sharing the Philippine Experience

What the Philippine delegates and I wish to share with you are our initial attempts in the Philippines towards such a theology. Our experience at doing theology is but one of several in Asia. Also, our experience is situated in a country where the population is predominantly Christian by religious affiliation—a situation which is not typical in Asia. It is with the consciousness of these limitations that we offer our experience as one model to be critically assessed and to be compared with your own way of doing theology. What we will share with you is not so much the content, for we believe that such a content does not and cannot yet exist. What we will share is rather what we see to be the way towards it.

Philippine Church Setting

We come from a country of which 90 percent of the population are baptized Christians, 85 percent being Catholic. Christianity was brought to us by our Spanish colonizers in the sixteenth century. The Philippine church today is, by and large, what it was thirty or forty years ago: the life of practicing Christians revolving around the Mass, baptism, and the other sacraments, prayers, good works, organizations promoting personal piety or charitable works. Within this faith-framework much deep piety goes on among our people, especially the older generation. This more or less traditional Christianity has undergone some face-lifting since Vatican II, such as a more personalist spirit in the living out of religion; the liberty and primacy of conscience; the indigenization of prayers, liturgy, and church architecture. By living within this faith context too, many, particularly those in the religious life, have overcome much of what was impersonal legalism of a former age.

But there has also emerged among us a new enfleshment of Christianity which goes beyond the concern for the salvation of souls or for the integral human development of the individual person. It is a form of Christianity that is concerned with the history of our people. It looks into the concrete historical forces working in the lives of men and women. It is committed to total life and total salvation for people and society. In its concern for the life hereafter, it does not forget the here-and-now; in fact, it sees the challenge to passionate commitment to the here-and-now as one of the principal challenges to religion(s) of our time. It is confronted by the glaring needs of people, hence it is committed to the struggle of the poor, deprived, and oppressed for full humanity. Its pastoral ministry includes as essential components the consciousness raising of the Christian community and the organization of the grassroots poor. Its apostolates of lay leadership, family life, health, media, prayer sessions, and Bible reflections have a thrust towards total human development, salvation, and liberation; and it concretizes this thrust by undertaking a conscientizing education and by catalyzing the organization of the oppressed for self-affirmation, self-determination, and self-reliance.

Accordingly, there has sprung up among us a movement, growing stronger every day, of building communities of peasants, workers, fisherfolk, poor urban dwellers, cultural minorities, with the integral component of conscientization and community organization for people's self-determination. In such communities, reflection and reflection sessions are an integral part of life. The people come together to reflect on their problems and experiences, do social analysis together, relate the meaning of their lives to the biblical message, pray, and celebrate the liturgy of the world and Eucharist, and plan their community action together.

Cebu-Malaybalay Consultation

It is people who belong to this stream of Philippine Christianity that we convoked to make the preparations for the Asian Theological Conference (ATC) and to put together the Philippine contribution to ATC. It was stipulated that the participants to this preparatory consulation should be people (1) who were either from the grassroots poor themselves or at least in direct contact with the grassroots, through conscientizing and organizing work; (2) who are familiar with and who have used social analysis in their reflection sessions; (3) for whom the Christian faith is biblical and history oriented, i.e., people whose main focus of faith is events in history and God's concern for total life and salvation; and (4) who are engaged in reflection sessions among the grassroots poor.

In all, we were able to gather about forty people, who met in two different places, Cebu City and Malaybalay. Of these forty there were about ten peasants and one worker; the rest were religious and laity who work among the grassroots as community organizers or reflection facilitators. We would have invited more people from the grassroots were it not for the problem of language and communication for the grassroots poor who might eventually have been chosen to be delegates to our ATC at Wennappuwa. Most of us Filipino delegates to the Conference were participants of the Cebu-Malaybalay preparatory consultation.

Initial Question

Curiously enough, the first significant question we had to tackle was: Who is the theologian? Who is the bearer, the doer, the producer of theology? Who is the subject-doer in a situation of doing theological reflection? This question was occasioned by the following observation: the preparatory circular sent by the ATC organizing committee was proposing, it would appear, that an interdisciplinary group composed of community developers, union organizers, sociologists, economists, pastors, professional theologians, artists, communications-media people, peasants, fisherfolk, minorities, youth, and women should reflect together on the situation of workers. It would appear from this that the subject-doers of theological reflection would be this interdisciplinary group. We asked ourselves: Do we agree with this? Based on our concrete experience and involvement, who did we think is or should be the theologian? Our collective answer was: assuming that it is worthwhile developing a theology, the theologians should be the grassroots poor themselves. They should be the subjects of theological reflection, not just the theological concerns to be reflected upon. I will develop this point more at length later, for it is, in any case, a cardinal point in our position as the Philippines group.

Search for the Meaning of "Theology" and "Theological Reflection"

Having resolved the initial question, it became clear that our task at the Cebu-Malaybalay consultation was to discover a way of facilitating or catalyzing theological reflection among the grassroots themselves. Especially those of us who belonged to the middle class asked ourselves: How do we perform our role as catalyzers and facilitators so that the grassroots themselves will do theological reflection and produce our Filipino theology? This question can be broken down as follows: (1) What do we ourselves mean by "doing theological reflection," the activity of doing theological reflection? (2) What do we mean by "theology," the theological product, the product of doing theological reflection? (3) What pedagogical methods or techniques do we use to assist the grassroots poor to bring to birth a relevant theology through their own activity? We tackled the first and second questions; the third, indirectly only.

What is "theology" and what is "doing theological reflection?" We started with no a priori prefabricated definitions. We agreed rather that we should consult our various experiences in doing theological reflection among the grassroots poor and work out our collective understanding from that perspective. It is important to underline the fact that what we offered at the Asian Theological Conference was taken from our actual and concrete experience and not from theoretical speculation. Our separate experiences, mutually and dialectically shared, became our collective experience, which remains a limited one, in the sense that the length of time during which we have engaged in this project of letting a theology evolve is, so far, short and limited. At any rate, most of us were involved in reflection sessions among the grassroots and we suspected that in such sessions was imbedded some kind of theological reflection in some form or other. We used a good part of the day to describe and to listen to each other's experiences in grassroots reflection in order to discover what "theology" and "doing theological reflection" meant to us.

Components of Theological Reflection

We eventually had before us a rich collection of experiences of how reflection among the grassroots is carried out, some experiences being quite common to many, other experiences, rare or unique. We proceeded to put some system into our collection of descriptive experiences by ferreting out what we would consider as "elements" or "components" of theological reflection. We made a list of such components and we put down everything that might remotely be connected with theological reflection. The resulting list of thirty elements ranged from traditional/indigenous culture to scientific tools of analysis; from prayer to mobilization for action; from biblical exegesis to the need for concrete experience.

Our next step at our Cebu-Malaybalay preparatory consultation was to identify which of these thirty components we considered to be the essential elements of theological reflection. In making this selection of essential elements, the large group of forty people was divided into four smaller independent groups, and the remarkable thing was that the four small separate groups, working independently, chose the very same five elements, with one group adding a sixth element. There was then practical unanimity in the components we chose:

1. contemporary life-situation and history
2. serious analysis of human life and society
3. faith-dimension: biblico-historical
4. leading to transforming action
5. authors: grassroots poor

One of the four small groups inserted still another component between the third and the fourth: native wisdom and native religion.

In a nutshell, what we are saying is this: theological reflection is an activity of interpreting contemporary life-situation in the light of the Faith, and that, accordingly, theological reflection is (1) based on contemporary life-situation and history (2) which is seriously and scientifically analyzed (3) and seen in the light of a faith which is biblico-historical (3a) and with the help of native wisdom or native religion; (4) such a theological reflection must lead to transforming action; (5) and the doers of theological reflection and the creators of a real Filipino theology are the grassroots poor themselves.

I shall now make an effort to explain what we mean by each of these five or six components, basing myself largely on what our Cebu-Malaybalay consultation group itself said.[1]

Contemporary Concrete Life-Situation and History

The principal focus and, one might say, the "raw material" of theology and theological reflection—far from being doctrinal truths which one seeks to organize into a system, and far from being biblical texts or truths which one seeks to apply to a given human situation—is contemporary Philippine, Third-World history, and life itself.

Underlying this way of looking at theology is the conviction that concrete reality and history is the principal fountainhead of all reflection and knowledge, even theological knowledge; and that our consciousness, even religious consciousness, is conditioned by the same concrete reality and history. The philosophy and theology we have inherited from our colonial past, whether it be neoscholastic or liberal-existentialist, being drawn and conditioned by the history and social systems of the West, can no longer be simply appropriated by us and applied to our Asian human situation; rather we must take a long meditative look at our own Asian life and history (in fact, be involved in its total life) and let this be the conditioning and source of our theological insight and formulations. From our experience, for example in seminary theology, when theology does not take the concrete Asian, Third-World experience as a serious point of departure, and one theologizes on the Asian scene by engaging in a-historical definitions of man and morality or in liberal-existentialist discussions on freedom and grace, and in the process generating artificial questions and even fears, there results a theology which is not life-giving to our people.

We feel the need to know Filipinos and Asians as they are—concrete, historical whole—not pre-packed for us by a metaphysical, dualistic, or existentialist philosophy or theology. Filipinos and Asians will be understood only in their concrete life-situations.

And the so-called indigenous theology, according to our Cebu-Malaybalay working group, will emerge only by humbly taking our point of departure from our reality and history, in fact by being immersed in it.

The primary focus of our theology, then, is the concrete human situation in the Third World, in Asia and in the Philippines today, especially with its main human realities of poverty and oppression, and the hope and struggle for justice and liberation.

The underlying theological persuasion for making history the source and material of our theological reflection is the conviction-in-faith that the God we believe in is a God who acts and speaks very especially in concrete events in history. God speaks the challenges of today through the sufferings and hopes of people today, and God acts out salvation in and through human efforts and movements towards a more human world. God's salvific acts are concretized in our time and in our Third-World Asia; the Asian theologians will accordingly search there for these raw materials of their theology.

We see, moreover, that in making history the focus and source of our theology, we are in good company in capturing something of the pristine spirit of our religion. The faith of the biblical people and the theology of the biblical authors were first and foremost about history. Their religious literature, the Bible, deals primarily with their social history, which they saw as the history of their God with their people and with the world. Today when theology fixes its gaze upon history to find its materials there, it is looking at the present stage of saving history which is being played out in our day.

Serious Analysis of Human Life and Society

As we do our pastoral work in the Philippines, and when we do theological reflection in the service of that pastoral work, we have experienced the need and importance of analyzing human life and society seriously. Having previously gone through a stage in which we understood human beings, human life, and ourselves in self-discovery seminars and T-group sessions with the help of the instruments designed by the science of psychology, we felt the need to go further and understand human life as it unfolds in its dialectic not merely with psychological forces but also with the social, economic, political, and cultural forces. As we went about our daily involvements, we saw that the poverty and subhuman life of our people were the most obvious and the most serious human problem we encountered, and that it was a problem for which the personalist psychology we had on hand had neither adequate analysis nor answers. For what we saw was a problem which was social in nature and for which we learned to tap also the resources of sociology, history, and political economy.

We thus began to uncover the hidden social forces at work in human life and society which, without analysis, remained hidden from our day-to-day consciousness. We began to understand the social order in which we live: the social structures, the social classes, the social relationships, the social contradictions. We discovered the oppressive dynamics that cause poverty and powerlessness, and the dynamics of liberating action for change. Thus, while not ignoring the personal and psycho-spiritual factors in our understanding and in our carrying on of life, we also saw the importance of identifying the societal and socio-political dynamics in the life of society and of our people.

It emerges from social analysis that the human problem today is structural oppression, and that participation in the transformation of the social order is an imperative. Serious analysis prevents the saving history of God, of which our Faith speaks, from being a safe and pious platitude; social analysis helps to give it a local habitation and a name within the struggle and history of the grassroots poor.

As a result of analysis, Christian discernment becomes authentic and complete. It ceases to be a merely solipsistic introspection into the inner spiritual and psychological forces in one's soul; it becomes a challenging confrontation also with the forces of social evil and social good and a questioning of one's role and responsibility in the bringing about of these social forces. Many of us, moreover, found out that analysis sharpened and strengthened our commitment to our people and our history as a nation.

We have made an attempt to impress upon people who use the tools of analysis that these tools are a hypothesis of work, not dogma; that these are a hypothesis to be tested by life and experience, just as they are born out of life and experience. We accept these tools of analysis which scientifically and truthfully clarify the life and struggle of the oppressed. The final test of these tools, or of any tool of analysis for that matter, is whether they help to bring about a more human life. Their validity will be proven or disproven not by the ambivalent middle class[2] but by the grassroots people themselves, who, in any case, must be allowed to appropriate and control these tools.

To recall the main point here: if the first component of theological reflection is human life and history as the raw materials upon which one does theology, we in the Philippines have discovered that that life and history must be seriously and scientifically understood in all its aspects: psycho-spiritual and socio-political — and thus the need for analysis of human life and society as an instrument for reading the signs of our times.

Faith-Dimension: Biblico-Historical

Theology has a faith-dimension. Here we are saying that reality and history, seriously understood and interpreted through analysis, are seen in the light of the faith, but we go on to say: in the light of a faith which is biblico-historical. Here the first question is: What does our Christian faith have to say to the portrait of contemporary reality which the analysis of human life and society reveals? What are the resources of the Christian faith which the theologian can tap to interpret this contemporary life in the light of the faith? The second question is: Which faith? Or, which formulation of the faith does one use in the light of which one sees contemporary reality: the biblico-historical? the Greco-Roman scholastic? the liberal-existentialist?

The biblical faith primarily confesses God's salvific involvement in historical events: in the exodus from the slavery of Egypt, in the possession of the land, and especially in the health-giving deeds of Jesus, in his life-giving death and resurrection, in his anticipated "second coming" which will usher in the "new heaven and the new earth" where people, nations, and the whole of creation will no longer know mourning nor tears nor suffering nor pain, because God will be all in all, and all things will be made new.

It is this biblical faith (and its spirit and presuppositions) which has struck a warm chord in our hearts. We have found it *historical* in outlook; i.e., a faith which has to do with history and events and *total* in concern; its concern is not just the salvation of the soul for heaven but of total persons, societies, nations, and the whole of creation for total life (grace, Spirit, health, peace, justice, human life, joy); and such concern for total salvation is not just for the life-after-death but also during the life-after-birth.

We are happy at the rediscovery of the ancient (Near) Eastern faith-outlook, particularly the biblical faith-outlook. We can with natural ease situate the struggle of our people and our own commitment to them within the history of God's total salvation. Those of us who have re-appropriated this biblico-historical framework feel that as our people create a counter-history of justice today, we are all part of a history which the biblical people experienced and which continues today. We are happy to go back to the root of our living faith, which is historical in spirit, and to remake the acquaintance of a living historical God interested in events, people, and total salvation.

The biblico-historical framework makes us feel the need of discerning the salvific moment of our day which belongs to a history which has a past, a present, and a promised future that sustains our hope. This realization in faith that a history of total salvation is being fashioned by God and our people today, and our self-questioning about what we are doing, become yet another motivation and goad to insert ourselves in today's liberating and salvific action, without thereby romantically playing down the several ambiguities which we must grapple with along the way.

Thus a new type of faith is born among us too, a faith — as some of us saw at the Cebu-Malaybalay consultation — born and nurtured by the experience of God and life in the history and struggle of our people, and not by abstract dogmas.

Thus as regards theology itself, this biblico-historical framework has helped us to make our passover from a domesticating theology to a liberated and liberating theology.

To conclude this section, one could briefly raise the question of another "faith-framework" for theology, or more precisely, of no preconceived framework at all. I know a group of people who have gone to join the workers in their life, work, struggle, and reflection, and who would like to see and to assist in the development of a new liberated culture—including religious culture and theology, whatever of it will emerge—born out of the history of the workers today. Into this involvement the group brings no pre-existent faith-framework. They want to allow either the natural or the existent religiosity (or the professed a-religiosity) of the workers to interact with the other elements in their struggle and in this way work out and arrive at a new religious culture and theology. I think that at a later stage, a possible linkage with the other forms of Christianity, especially the biblical one, is foreseen. This approach is attractive to me, but this is perhaps not the place to pursue this point further.

Native Wisdom and Native Religion

As different peoples and different social groups in Asia, we have specific ways of looking at life, world, God, society, and all of reality. These differing ways of looking at reality have been formed by the separate histories of our people. They have been shaped by the present and past forces that impinge upon our lives: geographical and ecological, genetic, biological and psychological, economic, political, social and religious. A certain ethos has been generated in our peoples and social groups. This becomes our particular ethnic or class outlook—our culture. We have certain values, symbols, customs, ways of acting and re-acting which are peculiarly ours. We have each our respective worldviews and meanings. This is our native wisdom: Indonesian wisdom, Japanese wisdom, Indian wisdom, or wisdom of peoples close to the sea or to the earth. And such a native wisdom would contain both liberating and nonliberating elements.

There is also among us in Asia a wisdom that is religious wisdom. This is especially true of those of us who are part of a people who belong to one of the great non-Christian oriental religions: Hinduism, Buddhism, Islam. Here we find a wisdom that is born out of centuries of religious philosophy and practice, asceticism, and piety. We are just beginning to awaken to the tremendous religious and moral riches which these other great religions possess. Like Christianity, they possess their own particular worldviews and explanations of humanity, the world, God, salvation, etc. This religious understanding and ethic is ingrained in the minds and hearts of the people among whom many of us live and work—certainly among those of other faiths, but even among our fellow Christians themselves; in fact, even among us in the degree to which we have not allowed a part of us to succumb to a Westernizing Christianity.

This native and/or religious wisdom must also play a part in doing theological reflection. It too must shed its own light on the meaning of life and history. Thus theology interprets concrete life with the help of (1) analysis, (2) Scripture, and (3) indigenous wisdom or religion.

These three are in dialectical relationship with one another. They complement as well as correct one another. For example, analysis, especially social analysis, can complement Scripture by giving a scientific understanding of contemporary human beings and society which Scripture cannot provide; Scripture can say that God and religion are concerned for justice, but it is social analysis that will uncover the structural injustices of our times. On the other hand, Scripture can complement social analysis by underlining the importance of the individual person, the reality of sin, the place of the psycho-spiritual aspects of life. Social analysis helps native wisdom and religion to understand the very real, though often nonconscious, economic and political forces that rule modern people and society, especially the forces that rule the lives of the unsuspecting poor. It can help to open one's eyes to the oppressive and domesticating role religion can and does play in society. It can also help to overcome the superstitious elements in religion, both Christianity and other faiths.

On the other hand, native religion can complement and even correct social analysis by recalling the values of inner liberation and personal conversion. Native wisdom can remind social analysis that any genuine reading of reality and any liberational action must take into account the culture of the people, the ethos and way of behaving and thinking of the masses. Scripture can complement the Eastern religions by its accent on history; the Eastern religions can remind Christianity of the place of silent interiority.

As one makes these three (analysis, Scripture, native wisdom/religion) in their dialectical complementarity bear upon concrete reality to interpret it, there would sometimes be the problem of which element corrects which. What is the criterion for judging? We in the Philippines still have to work this out in concrete practice, but I think we would ask, as we ask of anything related to our theory and action: Is it life-giving, liberating, humanizing, bringing about people's total salvation? And, very importantly: do the grassroots poor with liberated consciousness (and not professional people with middle-class values) judge it as life-giving and humanizing? We do not thus pretend to erase all ambiguities, but we have enough of a guide in the half-light in which we today must walk.

Liberation and/or Indigenization?

I have just described how we in the Philippines would see the place of indigenous culture and religion in the doing of theology. This might be the place to treat of a question that emerged in the course of our sharing and deliberations within the last few days of our conference. The experience and the social analysis that we, the Philippine group, brought with us from our country point to human liberation as the main stress of our indigenous theology. But in the concerns and interests voiced on the last day or so, the Philippine group was sensing that somehow this stress was getting lost in favor of considerations pertaining to Asian culture and Asian religions with their close relation to human liberation becoming looser and looser.

Here, then, I would like to paraphrase the thoughts which the Philippine group arrived at in our national group reflection: Asian theology, aiming to respond to the imperative put to it by Asian reality, has two basic characteristics: its "Third-Worldness" (with its thrust towards socio-political and total human liberation of the poor, the deprived, and the oppressed) and its "Asianness" (the peculiar Asian character, whatever that happens to be in our different situations respectively). Both of these characteristics are essential to today's theology and are inseparable, one from the other. However, the main and principal characteristic of a truly Asian theology is its "Third-Worldness." To highlight this primacy, we say: "Third-Worldness" is the substantive, while "Asian" is the adjective. The primary thrust and concern, therefore, of the Asian Third World theology is liberation, which, of course, to be authentic must be indigenous or inculturated. Inculturation, though an essential and unavoidable aspect, takes second place. Further, in our experience in the Philippines, we have found some inculturation approaches in theology which are totally devoid of a truly liberational thrust. These approaches either so exclusively focus on the religio-cultural aspects as to detach these from the other important aspects of Asian reality, especially the socio-political, or to treat human liberation as merely one of the themes which an indigenous theology must be concerned about. We think that such approaches neither reflect nor respond to the total human problem of our people nor do they focus on the most urgent human problem of Asia.

On the reverse side, if one is concerned with human liberation in action and in theology, and if one's action and theology are immersed in and emerge out of the history of the grassroots poor, such action and theology will most likely be indigenous. Commitment to and involvement in the concrete life and struggle of the concrete Asian is the guarantee that our theology will be both liberating and indigenous.

Leading to Transforming Action

We come now to what is for us in the Philippines the next component of doing theological reflection. We say that our theology today must lead to transforming action. Again, what underlies this persuasion is our belief in the imperative of human liberation. Our involvement in the struggle of the poor, our analysis, and our faith reveal all too clearly this imperative. At the same time, we see how the a-historical, individualistic, other-worldly kind of theology of the Christian churches has functioned as a nonliberating factor, giving legitimation to an unjust social order. Theology and religion can and should function as a liberating and transforming factor, because central to our faith is the belief in God's saving history of total salvation which, although it goes beyond history, already happens in history. Consequently, we Christians, seeing the imperatives of our day, should see to it that our theology not only can be but should be liberating.

It is in the praxis of involvement in the struggle of the poor and the realization of the need for a liberating theology that we also discover that theology cannot stop at reflection. It must lead to action. We always knew in some way that good theology must lead to good pastoral action, but somehow, our long association with Greek metaphysics has conditioned us to regard theology as abstruse speculation. Now, praxis, analysis, and the faith all conspire to make us see that for theology, too, the point is not to contemplate or explain the world but to change it. And so we speak of a theology that leads to transforming action. And whereas any good theology must lead at least to individual transformation, we see that today's theology must not only do this but go beyond this and contribute to total life through societal transformation.

Author: Grassroots Poor

We opened our Cebu-Malaybalay consultation by asking and answering the preliminary question: Who is the theologian? The grassroots poor, we said. We reaffirmed this in the course of identifying what for us constitutes the last component in doing theological reflection. If doing theological reflection is the activity of interpreting today's human situation in the light of the faith, we say that in such activity it is the grassroots poor who are the actors, the interpreters. They are the authors and the producers of the theological formulation we are in search of. They are the theologians.

Up to now, in the Christian tradition, beginning at least with the Constantinian era, the producers of meaning, even of religious meaning, have been the nobility, the aristocracy, the elite, the middle class. Today, as we live and strive in a Third World context, the producers of theological meaning must be the grassroots poor themselves. For too long has philosophical, cultural, and religious meaning been churned out by the upper portion of the social pyramid, within the ease and leisure upheld by a solid lower base of serfs and workers. The producers of society's victuals have not been the producers of its meanings. We feel that the peasants, workers, fisherfolk, and the poor must now come to the fore, and the voice from under, speak.

The view taken by us here is naturally premised on a great faith and trust in the grassroots poor. Most of the participants in our Cebu-Malaybalay consultation were either grassroots poor themselves or people from the middle class who were in direct contact with the grassroots. Our first-hand experience showed us that as the masses progressively raise their consciousness to a critical level they become more and more the trustworthy makers of their (and our) history. What we are now saying in reference to the making of religious meaning is that if the grassroots poor are the real makers of history in a Third World situation, they should be the makers of our Asian, Third World religious meanings and the reformulators of the faith. If without too much romanticism we can say that the conscientized grassroots poor are the trustworthy makers of history, they should also be the trusted makers of meanings.

We also felt that since theology is interpretation of life, the theologian should be one who actually experiences the typical life of the majority of Asians: the peasant, the worker, the fisherfolk, the youth. Along a similar vein, some of us felt that an indigenous theology, about which we speak so much nowadays, cannot come to be unless authored by the Asian who lives the typical life of the majority of Asians.

Crucial to this position that the grassroots themselves should be the subject-authors in the doing of theology is the following conviction: Every theology is conditioned by the class position and class consciousness of the theologian. Unconsciously we see and interpret reality according to our social class position and especially according to the class consciousness we carry with us.

People like those who participated in the Cebu-Malaybalay consultation are keenly aware that we and all Filipinos belong to a particular social class, depending on our access or non-access to the productive wealth of our society and depending on the place we occupy in its productive process: thus we have come to realize that we are bourgeois (elite), petty-bourgeois (middle class), or grassroots poor; and we see that our consciousness and way of looking at things, even theologically, is conditioned by class, i.e., by class origin, or by class position, or by the consciousness proper to one's origin or position, or, again, by a consciousness which by a deliberate choice has transcended one's origin or position. There is a theological consciousness of property according to which private property is an inviolable natural right. There is a petty-bourgeois theological consciousness which says that private property is indeed a natural right but profits should be shared more equitably with the workers. And there is still another theological consciousness according to which property, to be human and humanizing, must be collectively owned. We see all the more clearly, especially after having experienced the ambivalences and artificial fears of a theology that arises out of a middle-class consciousness among us in the Philippines, that the bearers of a truly liberating theology is the consciousness of the conscientized and liberated grassroots poor.

These experiences and convictions are what lie behind the reflections and questions raised by our Philippine group at the ATC during our national group reflection and from which I now again excerpt and paraphrase some of our considerations: Were we aware in this ATC of the petty-bourgeois character of our theologizing? Why was it that the only representatives of the working class among us at the ATC felt that our discussions were abstract and irrelevant? With the absence of an adequate representation from the basic masses in this ATC, it is relevant to ask whether our theologizing can ever be of use to the oppressed in their struggle for full humanity or whether the poor are rather not being used for the concerns and interests of the established churches, the ecumenical organizations, the theological schools, etc.

The basic question is: Who is theologizing, and for whom? We of the middle class must take infinite reserve in making claims of being the "voice of the voiceless." In our discussions in favor of the poor and the oppressed, we must take care that we present the concerns of these grassroots people, not as we (the middle class) perceive them, but as seen and formulated by the grassroots themselves, especially as they, through action and reflection, reach higher levels of critical consciousness. We need to affirm strongly that the formulation of the Asian theology which is really liberating to the masses of the poor and oppressed of Asia is the work of the Asian poor with a liberated consciousness. It is they who must reflect on and say what their faith-life experience is in the struggle for liberation. This trust in the people and belief that they can theologize and are the real theologians is central to our positon.

The grassroots poor, deprived and oppressed, as they break out more and more from their culture of submission and silence, are the real theologians. The act of doing theology must be theirs. The act of interpreting reality towards action must be theirs. What about those of us who belong to the middle class and who at present have control of theological production? What is our role in this scheme of things? As we see it in the Philippines, our main role is that of "technician," i.e., someone who is at present in possession of certain technical competences in exegesis, social sciences, languages, archaeology, or history, and who offers these findings in these different fields to the real theologians as materials to help them in the act of interpreting reality today from the perspective of the poor. Of course, such a person is one who makes real efforts both to transcend his or her middle-class consciousness and class habits and to possess a critical consciousness.

The real theologians are the grassroots poor; we of the middle class offer some necessary information about the Bible and its message, we catalyze their understanding of political economy and history, etc. But even here, we must create an atmosphere in which the grassroots feel very free to be critical about any piece of information, question, or instrument of enquiry we bring to them. Further, we must be careful not to overstay and prolong our role; the grassroots themselves must begin to acquire the technical skills of exegesis and themselves be the adept equals of professionals in what are now called the social and human sciences. We must hand over more and more these "means of production" to them.

Is the role of the middle class confined to offering information and sundry help garnered from one's field of technical specialization? Here again I recall the reflection of the Philippine national group during our national group reflection at the ATC: The middle class can engage in actual theologizing, provided that (1) they are rooted in the history and struggle of the poor and the oppressed; (2) they are attuned to the people's aspirations and faith-experiences in the struggle; and (3) they are remolded or converted from the petty-bourgeois to a truly liberated grassroots consciousness and lifestyle. For this it is necessary that they share in some form of collective life with the people.

Finally, to underscore how important for us is the role of class and consciousness, we point to a problem we experience of a progressive Asian theology which is not reflectively conscious of its elitist nature: Much is being made (and rightly so) about the need to liberate ourselves from European and American theological domination. But here is also a need to be liberated from any bourgeois, elitist, liberal theology, however indigenous and progressive it might be.

Theology, then, must be the production of the grassroots themselves, not in the sense that we of the Cebu-Malaybalay group, most of whom were from the petty bourgeois class, are programing a task for our grassroots people, but in the sense that, if theology is to be done at all, the authors of such a theology would have to be the grassroots people themselves, or at least, people who by origin or social position may not be grassroots but who are making efforts to remold their minds and hearts to see reality from the standpoint of the liberated grassroots poor.

In all this, what if the grassroots poor may not be interested or refuse? In this case, I think it would be better to have a respectful and fruitful silence rather than fill the vacuum with alienating theologies proceeding from alienated consciousnesses. The fact, however, is that there already exist grassroots communities of farmers, fisherfolk, workers, poor urban dwellers where one finds the ingredients for the making of a relevant theology. I think that after some significant length of time we will see the gradual emergence of such a theology. But even now, there already exist nuggets of a new theology embedded, certainly not in the learned periodicals of the contemporary ruling theology, but in the prayers shared by the grassroots poor among themselves at their prayer sessions, in their creative liturgy, drama, and songs, in their story-telling and attempts at poem-writing: all indicators to us of a new religious culture in the living journal of our people's lives.

Conclusion

At the Cebu-Malaybalay consultation, we arrived at a collective understanding of what is involved in theological reflection and theology from the grassroots. From our actual experiences, we culled thirty or so elements that somehow go into theological reflection. Out of these thirty we chose five or six essential elements: contemporary historical reality; analysis; biblico-historical faith; indigenous wisdom and religion; transforming action; grassroots theologians. We did not have time systematically and critically to share with each other the pedagogical methods we might use to bring these five or six components into play; i.e., how we go about helping the grassroots to grapple with their life situation, analyze, get introduced to a biblico-historical understanding of the faith, engage in various forms of transforming action. Meanwhile, realizing more clearly our respective roles, we went back to our separate areas of involvement to continue our work of helping in the coming into being of a theology from the grassroots. We hope that, as our grassroots people use, and eventually go as far as to appropriate to themselves the means of theological production, they will bring into existence fresh theological formulations, i.e., relevant life-themes, meaningful faith-formulations, a new culture springing out of the life and struggle of the oppressed, a meaningful ethic, a nondomesticating worldview, a liberated and liberating set of meanings, values, and symbols, a new book that thematizes the saving history of God and our people in our day.

NOTES

1. The views and convictions of the Cebu-Malaybalay group are, of course, held by many others who belong to the same stream of Philippine Christianity, sharing the same concerns and commitment.
2. See p. 136 for the use of this term.

12

Asian Theology: An Asian Woman's Perspective

Henriette Katoppo (Indonesia)

Introduction

For a long time, Asians were denied the right to theologize. Asian experience was denied validity. Asian expression was denounced as pagan.

We can relate this to the fact that Christianity had been the "white man's burden" for so long that European and American theologians did not accept independent Asian thinking. At the moment (January 1979), numerically the majority of Christians is still found in the so-called First World. However, the balance is shifting so rapidly that by May 1979, the majority of Christians will be in the Third World. Having grown so "strong in number" in relation to our First World Christian brothers and sisters, perhaps we can assert our right to be different, our right to be the Other.

In Asia's struggle for full humanity, woman are especially concerned in moving towards a relevant theology. A relevant theology for Asian women considers the Asian women's perspective about God, for theology, whether it is seen as a discipline or a critical reflection, is primarily about God. Done

Henriette Marianne Katoppo is a prize-winning novelist, journalist, and theologian who has served with a commission of the World Council of Churches in Geneva.

from a woman's perspective, this reflective process might be termed women's theology. I do not use the term feminist theology because the word "feminist" has become so loaded that it will take a long time before people will say "feminist is beautiful." Those who are eager to put everything in categories might say of women's theology that it is process theology (or more accurately, *theologia viatorum*) and that its methodology is inductive. In doing theology, however, an Asian woman has additional odds to overcome in order to assert her right to be different, her right to be the Other.

Being the Other

In order to clarify my position and to provide the context from which I speak, I should like to begin with my personal experience of being the Other and the problem of alienation that it entails.

Personal Experience

First of all, I am Asian. More specifically, I am Indonesian, from the Minahassa (Northern Sulawesi), which is about 2,000 kilometers from Jakarta, Java. Ethnically, linguistically, and culturally, there are very great differences between the Minahassans and the Javanese. Furthermore, the Minahassans are 99 percent Christian, while the Javanese are predominantly Muslim (90 percent).

Historically, the Minahassa has had its own peculiarities. Four hundred years ago, the Minahassa was under the Bishop of Manila, as Spain was in control of that entire region at the time. Two hundred years later, the Minahassa chieftains concluded a treaty with the Dutch against the Spaniards.[1] Around the turn of the nineteenth century, the Dutch seriously considered making the Minahassa "the twelfth province" of the Netherlands, the kingdom having eleven provinces at the time. Though this plan was never realized, it gave the Minahassa an image of being different, of being Westernized, an image that prevails until now.

After independence from the Dutch in 1945, the Minahassa first became part of the state of East Indonesia (Timor); then in 1950, when the United States of Indonesia was dissolved, Minahassa formally joined the present Republic (Republic Indonesia Serikat).

Secondly, I am a Protestant of the Evangelical (i.e., Presbyterian) Church of Minahassa. Together with six other churches of Eastern Indonesia, our church is a member of the Federation of the Protestant Churches of Indonesia (GPI).[2] One should bear in mind, however, that in Indonesia the Protestant churches are not so much determined by denominational as by ethnic factors. Hence we have the Minahassa Church, the Molucca Church, the Timor Church, rather than the Presbyterian Church, the Methodist, etc. Protestant Christianity is one of the six accepted religions in Indonesia, the others being Islam, Roman Catholicism, Hindusim, Buddhism, and Confucianism. Protestants and Catholics together constitute about 10 percent of the population,[3] the ratio being seven to three.

In the third place, I am a woman. Numerically, women are not a minority. Almost anywhere in the world, "women hold up half the sky." In Sri Lanka, for instance, women are 52 percent of the population; in Indonesia, 51 percent. However, in decision making, and the like, women are definitely treated as a minority in most areas in Indonesia. Minahassa, however, is the exception; women are raised in a more egalitarian atmosphere, *egalitarian* meaning less traditionally feudal and less sexist. However, since I moved to Jakarta as a child, I have continuously experienced being the Other: a Christian among Muslims, a "Westernized" Minahassa who was unfamiliar with the proper speech and behavior in a Javanese society, a girl raised to look upon boys as equals and not superior, a girl taught to think and not to cook.

To be the Other is an alienating experience in a society which is subconsciously still strongly influenced by concepts of cosmic balance, by the importance of ties of kinship and soil, etc. In such a society, the Other is the discordant note, the threat to harmony. Fortunately, Indonesia is now moving towards the Great Society, where national consciousness is supreme as opposed to the divisive regional chauvinist consciousness. In such a context, to be the Other can also be a liberating experience. One's "Other-ness" might be used positively to enrich national culture, as has been evident in the revival of many traditional tribal elements.

Philosophy and Theology of the Other

There is both a philosophy and a theology of the Other, the finer points of which I will not go into here. A few remarks are necessary, and at the same time sufficient.

God is the absolute Other. Since God is eschatological, the divine Self is not given entirely to us in history, but only at the end of history.[4]

People tend to worship idols of their own making, not only from nature, such as stones, trees, animals, or even human beings, but also systems and structures, capital, products, power. The prophets, in order to affirm God the Creator, had first to lash out against idols or gods that people had created for themselves.

Sin, all sin, is by nature an all-encompassing absolute. When we sin, we think we are all there is and are therefore divine. We deny the Other and believe that our own totalized order is the Kingdom of Heaven. We become, as the old Malays put it, "like the frog under the coconut shell, which cannot conceive of a world of light and vast open space beyond its world of darkness and limitations."

I must state that I find the theology and philosophy of the Other useful and relevant only inasmuch as they reinforce or help or develop my own.

Woman's Image of Herself

It has been established that, on the whole, the Asian woman's self-image is unsatisfactory. This can be attributed to culture and education. From an early age woman is conditioned to a subservient, submissive role. Her status is "derived"; instead of being a person in her own right, she is "daughter of," "wife of," or "mother of" a man.

In the case of Christian women, their poor self-image is the result of the church's tendency "to give male chauvinism . . . a theological and quasi-divine legitimation."[5] There are Christian churches where women have no awareness of having been created in God's image (*imago Dei*) because they are taught that woman was created to be a "helper" unto man. These churches have conveniently overlooked the implications of the Hebrew *eser* (which is translated as "helper"). In the Old Testament, *eser* is otherwise used only in reference to God, the Help of the helpless (cf. Psalm 107).[6]

Many Christian women are likewise unaware of the feminine aspects of divinity, which I will discuss in more detail later. There is need to emphasize these feminine qualities as well as the need to raise our awareness about them, if women are to improve their self-image.

The Liberation of Woman Is Also the Liberation of Man

From my personal experience as the Other, I came to realize that not only in society but in the church in general, woman is the Other.

If women are at all admitted to male-dominated institutions of higher theological education and to patriarchal church structures, they are expected to theologize by proxy: faithfully to relay the ideas fabricated in male chauvinist, white supremacist contexts. A woman's own experiences are denied validity, and her personal encounter with God is denounced as heretical or hysterical. In the first case one is figuratively burnt at the stake; in the second, people hasten to find her a husband.

To get ahead in patriarchal society, woman is expected to become a man and hence to cease being the threatening Other. In politics, whether of church or state, we often find that the few women who "reach the top" have often become so "man-ly" that they do the woman's cause far more harm than good. Some have become such dictators that some men self-righteously claim that this only goes to prove that women should never be given the chance to wield power, failing to recognize the underlying psychological process.

Many men are antagonistic to women's liberation, since they fail to perceive that it is also human liberation. Actually, this indicates how deeply engrained is their belief that woman is the Other. Man, being the norm, is human. Woman being the "deviation," is therefore not human.

There is the saying: "Men of quality are not threatened by women's call for equality." They realize that their worth as human beings is in no way threatened by women asking to be recognized also as human beings.

Men who feel threatened are those who fail to realize that women's liberation is concerned with the liberation of all people to become full participants in human society. They are not aware that their reaction is not rational, but emotional. It is caused by fear—fear of loss of status, fear of what will happen when patriarchal structures mutate, but, basically, fear of the Other.

And this fear will prevail as long as the church gives male chauvinism not only a practical expression but a theological legitimation. I am claiming the right for a woman to be the Other, to be a human being in her own right, not as an afterthought, a derivation, a deviation, a subordinate in reference to man.

Only recently have Asians been "granted" the right to their own perspective of history. We may hope that Asians will formulate their own theology (with the caveat that there will never be a pure Asian theology). Why is it so difficult, then, to accept the fact that Asian women may have their own insights to contribute to the richness of Asian theology?

When will Asian churches learn that, unless they admit the right of their women to be the Other and use this Other-ness positively, they will alienate them totally?

The Other: I am—You are.

I am free—You are free.

But where I am, what I am, you cannot be.

Where you are, what you are, I cannot be.

Am I encroaching on your freedom?

Are you intruding on mine?

Have I the right to be what I am?

Can we be fully human, you and I, each in our own way?

Can we enrich another, by being the Other?

Socio-Political Realities

The Exploitation of "Non-Persons"

Women are members of the same sexual caste, whether they live in Sweden or Saudi Arabia.[7] Women are used as objects in many different ways. A look at almost any advertisement confirms this fact. Whether it is to sell cars or cameras or bathroom tiles or inexpensive tours abroad, women are prominently displayed. When one is conditioned to think of categories or groups of people as "non-persons" then one subconsciously sees them as objects to be used or disposed of as one pleases. Sexism, racism, imperialism, exploitation, are all expressions of the same attitude, which denies the Other (non-persons, objects, etc.) the right to exist. The rape of women, of races, of any human or natural resource therefore become justified for the mode of existence of a few. Conquest is the watchword when it is far better to strive for conviviality!

Women in the Rural Areas

The nutritional situation in the underdeveloped countries has generally not improved since before World War II; in many countries, it may even have deteriorated. In Southeast Asia, people spend two-thirds or more of their income on foodstuffs, yet the FAO has pointed out that the majority of people in those countries suffer from undernutrition or malnutrition. I shall not discuss here the roots of this situation. It is well known throughout Asia that power and especially economic power is ordinarily held by a very small section of the population, and the rest of the population is simply the "non-persons" who serve the interests of this upper class.

In Indonesia, women as "non-persons" are doubly exploited from the very start of their lives. Statistics show that 85 percent of all female children under five in Indonesia are undernourished. In the rural areas, people often live at subsistence levels. Seen in the overall context of poverty, the undernourishment of female children may not be surprising. There are in fact entire villages where children are cretins because of the malnutrition. However, the undernourishment of female children can also be attributed to the fact that they are often the ones who get the least food, fathers and brothers getting first priority.

Women in the Urban Areas

If the female child survives her early struggles, her plight is unlikely to be brighter as a young woman. Many young women of the rural areas are lured to the big cities with promises of work in the factories or as domestic servants. Once in the urban centers, their dignity is continuously insulted and these women, having come from conditions of the most abject poverty, are easily driven to prostitution. Once forced into this way of life, they are ashamed to return to their homes. It becomes almost impossible to get away.

It has been estimated that 60 percent of the women in certain areas are prostitutes. Where prostitution is not legalized, it is localized.

At Kramat Tunggak, Jakarta, there is a localized prostitution complex surrounded by a high fence. There are about 100 houses, with at least eight women in each. The total number of prostitutes in Jakarta has been estimated at 3,000, including 500 Christians. Some Ursuline nuns started a program for Bible study and general knowledge lessons for the prostitutes, held at an office across the road. Before the Department of Social Service intervened, the madame used to charge the women who attended the nuns' program for "being away from work."

The hotel industry is also involved in the prostitution racket. Tourism and prostitution almost always go together. I find it interesting that in the tribal societies of old, prostitution was not known. It came with increased mobility and commercialization. Does this not indicate the degree of alienation a person has to experience to start treating sex as a commodity?

Prostitution has not only been commercialized or legalized; it has even received ideological support through the Indonesian language itself.

In Bahasa Indonesia, the national language which evolved from the commercial Malay (the *lingua franca* of the archieplago), the word for prostitute was *pelaour*, which means "a person who sells him/herself." A few years ago, the trend was to use complicated Sanskrit words, even when there were perfectly good words in Malay. Hence "prostitute" became *wanita tuna susila*, "woman without morals." Interestingly enough, there is no corresponding *pria tuna susila*, "man without morals."

Is there any significance in the fact that the Risen Christ first appeared to Mary Magdalen who, according to tradition, was a prostitute?

The Dowry

A further exploitation of women is the dowry system still practiced in some areas in Indonesia. In these areas, dowry means "brideprice," that is, the amount the man's family has to pay for the bride. It is in this very sense that in the U.N. Declaration against the Discrimination of Women "dowry" is especially mentioned as "one of the forms of slavery" still to be combatted.

Some Indonesian churches, e.g., the Nias Church, have condemned the practice of giving dowry or accepting it. Those members who still do it are refused Holy Communion.

In my opinion, however, the abolition of dowry should not be imposed "from above," but should come from the grassroots level through a proper understanding of "personhood." Admittedly this will be difficult in a tribal society which attaches great importance to cosmic balance. Here it is the tribe, not the person, which is important. The *adat* or customary law which was originally intended to preserve the tribe from all evil, often has become itself an evil, insofar as it oppresses the people instead of protecting them. The church does not always take a clear stance here, failing to realize that the *adat* has become a manifestation of the Anti-God.

The Political Participation of Women

There is a growing awareness of women's exploitation and status in Indonesian society and it began prior to the country's independence. Women's movements and organizations began to be formed. In their early days, the burning issues for women were co-education and marriage, the latter covering polygamy or polygyny, child marriage, and a woman's lack of voice in her own marriage. However, women's concerns and activities went beyond mere social protest. They were as active as the men in Indonesia's struggle for independence. Political parties and youth organizations began to have women's units and, in some cases, to accept women as full members. In fact, one of Indonesia's great statesmen said in 1939: "The women's movement was born in the twentieth century as a full sibling (*adik kandung*) of the Indonesian nationalist movement."[8]

In these different organizations, men began to realize that women were good comrades-in-arms, possessing equal capabilities as well as rights and responsibilities. Another positive effect of the inclusion of women in the organization was the overcoming of regional chauvinism as well as the breaking down of male chauvinism. Members began to consider themselves as Indonesians rather than Javanese or Sumatrans or Amboinese, reflecting the words of the *Sumpah Pemuda* (Oath of the Youth) of 1928, which said: "We, the sons and daughters of Indonesia, vow to have one motherland, bne nation, one language—Indonesia."[9]

Partnership of Men and Women in Society

What is actually emerging is the growing consciousness of the indispensability of a partnership between women and men in the process of liberation and change. This partnership is an important point in Asian culture which we need to rediscover and to recover. In the agricultural societies of the past, great value was attached to this partnership, but as societies moved towards industrialization, the partnership tended to become obscured. We must seriously ask ourselves whether development takes place only at the expense of others, or the Other? Are both consumerism and the commercialization of women the inevitable product of development? Should not our struggle for full humanity be motivated by love for life, for the Other? It is in this challenge that we shall encounter the absolute Other—God.

Theological Motifs

The Concept of God from the Feminist Perspective

If our theology is to be relevant, then our concept of God has to be relevant. For this we must learn to read the Bible again. For so long, masculine imagery has dominated the text; the feminine images have been conveniently overlooked. The text which has come to us has indeed been the product "of a society driven to choose male metaphors by virtue of partriarchal structures predicated upon sexual inequality."[10] We have further flattered ourselves into thinking that while patriarchal structures have remained, we no longer have sexual inequality.

If that were really true, then why is the name of God, Yahweh, which is a verb, not a noun, still consistently translated as Lord? To quote Hanson again, "This masculinization does seem to be a conspiracy spanning three millennia."[11] It is a fact that where the original texts make no indication of gender it has been supplied gratuitously by the translators, who were usually male. The Dutch theologian Maria de Groot, also a linguist, draws our attention to the way in which the domination of the male hyperboles and male symbols has gravely impaired our understanding of revelation. Most of us do not really take Genesis 1:27 seriously. It is not really accepted that woman is created in God's image, nor is it accepted that it is just as valid to ascribe feminine qualities to God as it is to ascribe masculine qualities.

In the Old Testament, the word *rahamin* is used for God's mercy, compassion (cf. Exodus 3:6). Literally it means "movements of the womb." Yet some male theologians will perform the most extraordinary contortions exegetically, in order to avoid relating this to the motherliness of God. Isaiah 49:15 is another example of the motherliness of God. So is Hosea 11:1–4.[12]

When we call God "Father" this does not necessarily limit God to being male. *Father* is intended to express the loving concern of God. Clement of Alexandria sings:

> God is Love
> God can only be perceived in love
> Father is his inexpressible being
> Mother is his compassionate pity for us
> In his love for us
> The Father became woman
> The great sign for us is this:
> He who was born.

Clement has the deep insight of the ecstatic love for Christ in the early church, when (as Karl Rahner remarked somewhat wistfully) theologians were still poets, and able to see the greater context. We must point out, however, that it is not quite right to say that only "in his love for us, God became woman"; God is Father and Mother in all eternity.[13]

Anselm of Canterbury sings of Mother Jesus: "And Thou, Sweet Lord, art Thou not a mother, who tasted death in order to give life to us?" Even Pope John Paul I referred to God as our Father-Mother. There is nothing new or strange in acknowledging the feminine aspects of divinity. Yet why do so many still recoil from the thought?

In the tradition of the ecclesiastical West, the Holy Spirit is conceived of as he. This is due to the fact that the feminine *ruach* of the Hebrew was first effectively neutered in Greek, then made masculine in Latin. Is it coincidence that the symbol for the Holy Spirit is the dove (*peristera* in Greek: "Bird of Istar")? The battle between Yahweh and Istar, "the Great Mother," seems to be going on still.[14]

In view of the quality and the function of the Spirit as God who creates, who comforts, it is not surprising that in the Gnostic writings (such as the Gospel of the Hebrews) the Holy Spirit was explicitly called "Mother of Jesus" or (in the Acts of Thomas) "Mother of all creatures."

Some people do not feel that it is oppression to force people to relate to an all-male Trinity. Yet they would laugh at those who are still firmly convinced that "God is an Englishman."

For a more relevant theology, perhaps we could do some more reflection on the significance of other feminine aspects of the divine besides *ruach*, such as *hokmah* (wisdom) and *shekinah* (presence). We will confine ourselves to *hokmah*, which had the good fortune to remain feminine in the "sacred" languages (Greek: *sophia;* Latin: *sapientia*). Since "wisdom" is feminine in most languages, it is interesting to note that women are often accused of lacking wisdom.

Post-exilic literature shows how *hokmah* (as eventually *shekinah*) was almost personified: "A female form of great refinement and beauty, whose utterances were most profound and radiant."

She inspired love. She was love. In Proverbs, the Book of Wisdom, and Ecclesiasticus (Ben Sira), whenever Hokmah was the subject, even the most desiccated hagiographer would wax lyrical in praise of her.

In the light of the New Covenant, rather than personifying wisdom, should we not see Hokmah as God's personal inclination to the world? As a form in which God is with us, and wants to be sought by us?

And it is interesting that in the early Church there seems to have been an identification of Hokmah with Jesus.

Mary: the Fully Liberated Human Being

I would like to devote this last portion of the theological section to Mary, the Mother of Jesus. To me, Mary was the fully liberated human being. It might be startling that I, a Protestant, should make this claim. Protestantism, especially the Calvinist variety, has not displayed any great interest in Mary. Except for children's pageants at Christmas and Easter, Mary is invisible in the Protestant Church.

Many feminists, including feminist theologians, have rejected the model of Mary. One can readily agree if one looks at the standard portrayal of Mary: sugar sweet, fragile, with eyes downcast or turned up to heaven, not quite here-and-now. This is in line with her supposed submissiveness. After all, did she not say: "I am the Lord's servant; may it happen to me as you have said"?

We fail to realize that Mary's submission to the will of God is in no way the abject submission of the slave who has no choice. Rather, it is the receptive submission of the truly liberated human being, who put the will of God first. It is the creative submission of the fully liberated human being who, not being subjected to any other human being, is free to serve.

This, too, is the deepest meaning of virginity. It is a positive stance, rather than a negative substance.[15] The image seeks to convey that God takes the initiative and the human being should be responsive.

In women's theology, "virgin" can be the symbol for the autonomy of woman. Virgin then would not primarily mean a woman who abstains from sexual intercourse, but a woman who does not lead a "derived" life (as "mother of," "wife of," "daughter of"), a woman who matures to wholeness within herself as complete person, who is subject of herself, and who is open for others, for God. Through this maturing process, she is fertile, she gives life. Not only "Virgin," but also "Mother," attains a new power of imagery, and this may liberate women from the previous concept of Virgin-Mother, a biological impossibility which was held up to them as model. It is no coincidence that lately more importance is being given to Mary, both in Catholic dogma and in Protestant thinking.

Asian Catholics, for example, are beginning to see Mary no longer as "the fairy queen oozing out sweet piety," to quote Aloysius Pieris, S. J., "but as the peasant mother who cheerfully wore herself out to feed and clothe her carpenter son; the worker's wife wearing holy furrows on her face, an image reflected in millions of Asian village mothers today."

Protestants, who have learned to overcome their initial fear of "Mariolatry," might find their sign of hope in her as the first fully liberated human being, whose Magnificat is central in the theology of liberation.[16]

In my opinion, it speaks for itself that Gutiérrez, the famous liberation theologian, for example, makes little mention of Mary, although the Magnificat is generally attributed to her. Is this perhaps an example of the way women are constantly eclipsed in history—this occurring so often and so naturally that we simply forget that things should be different?

The thanksgiving and the joy in the Magnificat are addressed to God, but "true liberation will be the work of the oppressed themselves; in them God saves history."[17] Human liberation often seems a grim and joyless struggle. The Magnificat shows otherwise. And I exult in the fact that this Asian woman, this Mary, upon her encounter with God bursts out in this great song of thanksgiving and joy. Mary is the truly liberated, fully liberated human being, subject to no other human being, submitting only to God. Receptive to God's action, and creative in as much as she shares in bringing the good news of salvation to the world, she is the model not only for woman, but also for man. She is the new human being (man-woman), receptive before God, who calls him/her to be *imago Dei*: compassionate and free.

NOTES

1. One of the most interesting clauses of the treaty is the solemn undertaking of the chieftains "to abolish the abominable practice of headhunting."

2. The Federation of the Protestant Churches of Indonesia (GPI), together with 42 other churches, forms the Indonesian National Council of Churches.

3. The present population of Indonesia is 144 million, making it the fifth largest country in the world.

4. Enrique Dussel, *Ethics and the Theology of Liberation* (Maryknoll; N.Y.: Orbis Books, 1978), p. 13.

5. Tissa Balasuriya, *The Eucharist and Human Liberation* (Maryknoll, N.Y.: Orbis Books, 1979), p. 52.

6. See also Ps. 10:14; 30:10; 54:4; 71:12; 94:17.

7. Mary Daly, *Beyond God the Father: Toward a Philosophy of Women* (Boston: Beacon Press, 1973, 1974), p. 2.

8. Adinegoro, "Soal Ibu," *Keutamaan Istri*, April 21, 1939.

9. The Indonesian *tumpah darad*, which I have translated as "motherland," literally means "bloodshed," obviously in its context referring to the process of childbirth.

10. Paul Hanson, "Masculine Metaphors for God and Sex Discrimination in the Old Testament," *The Ecumenical Review* 27 (October 1975).

11. Ibid.

12. Cf. D. Preman Niles, "Old Testament: Man and the Holy," in *The Human and the Holy*, ed. Emerito P. Nacpil and Douglas J. Elwood (Quezon City, Philippines: New Day Publishers, 1978; Maryknoll: Orbis Books, 1980), p. 18.

13. Eulogia Würz, "Das Mutterliche in Gott," *Una Sancta* 32 (1977), pp. 268–269.

14. Gerhard Voss, "Maria in der Feier des Kirchenjahres," ibid., pp. 308–309.

15. Catharina Halkes, "Eine, andere-Maria," *Una Sancta,* ibid., pp. 323–337.

16. Cf. Gustavo Gutiérrez, *A Theology of Liberation* (Maryknoll, N.Y.: Orbis Books, 1973), pp. 207–208.

17. Ibid., p. 208.

13

The Final Statement

Preamble

We, Christians from Asia, along with fraternal delegates from other continents, gathered in Wennappuwa, Sri Lanka, from January 7 to 20, 1979, motivated by our solidarity with our people in the struggle for full humanity and by our common faith in Jesus Christ. Bringing with us the experience of the struggle in our own countries, we came to share in the life and situations of the masses striving for justice in Sri Lanka, through our four-day "live-ins."

During the days that followed, we became more aware of the commonalities and divergences in our backgrounds, which sharpened our understanding both of the richness and the anguish of our people in Asia.

As Asians, we recognize the important task before us. Our reflections, already begun in our local realities, helped us to enrich the process of interaction and sharing among us who have committed ourselves to the struggle of the poor in Asia. At the same time, we realize that these reflections are only part of the beginning of a collective and continuous search for a relevant theology in Asia.

The Asian Context

Asia suffers under the heels of a forced poverty. Its life has been truncated by centuries of colonialism and a more recent neocolonialism. Its cultures are marginalized, its social relations distorted. The cities, with their miserable slums, swollen with the poor peasants driven off the land, constitute a picture of wanton affluence side by side with abject poverty that is common to the majority of Asia's countries. This extreme disparity is the result of a class contradiction, a continuous domination of Asia by internal and external forces. The consequence of this type of capitalist domination is that all things,

152

time, and life itself, have become marketable commodities. A small minority of owners dictates the quality of life for the producers (workers, peasants, and others) in determining the price of their energy, skills, intelligence, as well as the material benefits needed to sustain these. What is produced, how and where it is produced, for whom it is produced, are the decisions of transnational corporations in collusion with the national elites and with the overt or covert support of political and military forces.

The struggle against these forces has been courageously taken up by the advocates of socialism. This socio-political order corresponds to the aspirations of the Asian masses both in the rural and urban areas since it promises to them the right to take their lives into their own hands, to determine both the social and economic conditions that govern their well-being. A very large part of Asia has succeeded, after long struggles, in establishing this socialist order. However, it must be added that the socialist transformation in these countries is not yet complete and that these countries must continue to liberate themselves from all distortions in an on-going self-criticism.

Neither will socialist movements in Asia be thorough in their struggle for full humanity without an inner liberation from self-seeking and exploitative instincts. The rich traditions of the major religions of Asia (Hinduism, Buddhism, Islam, and Christianity) offer many inspirations. The richness is expressed not only in philosophical formulations but also in various art forms such as dance and drama, poems and songs, as well as in myths and rites, parables and legends. It is only when we immerse ourselves in the "peoples' cultures" that our struggle acquires an indigenous dimension.

However it is equally true that the social function of religions or cultural systems is ambiguous. In the past, religions and cultural systems have played the role of legitimizing feudal relationships, yet the self-critical principle inherent in them can be a source of liberation today from the domination of capitalist values and ideologies.

Hence we feel that the Asian context which dictates the terms of an Asian theology consists of a struggle for fuller humanity in socio-political as well as psycho-spiritual aspects. The liberation of all human beings is both societal and personal.

The Issues

We realize that if large numbers of men and women find themselves socially deprived and progressively thrown further and further away from the center of life and meaning, it is not a mere accident or the effect of a national catastrophe. In fact, from Pakistan to Korea, passing through the southeast subcontinent and Southeast Asia, practically all parliamentary governments, with the exception of Japan, have at some time given way to military governments or authoritarian regimes of one form or the other. In these countries not only political rights are suppressed, but also the rights of workers to strike in the cities and the rights of peasants to organize themselves in the countryside. Many leaders and people holding political views contrary to the ruling group are condemned to spend several years in prison, often without due process of trial.

Behind the facade of "law and order" are Asia's cheap and docile labor and laws that leave the country open to unrestricted exploitation by foreign capital with the profit going to a small elite. A deeper logic is to be found in the dual economies of these countries. The industrial sector, monopolized by the national elite, has developed along the lines of an export economy that does not correspond to the needs of the local population. It also depends heavily on foreign capital and technology. And as a result of unequal trade relations and the weakness of these countries, their indebtedness and dependence grew to an extent beyond their control. International banks and transnational corporations have become the new masters of Asia's politics and economics.

At the same time the rural sector in these countries has remained stagnant. The so-called agrarian reforms did not change the unequal social relations of production in the rural areas. The benefit of the "Green Revolution" went only to the middle and big landowners who could afford its technology. A great number of peasants were driven off the land in the process and ended in the slums of the swollen cities of Asia. On the other hand, the rural surplus thus accumulated is often re-invested in crops for export or channeled into urban industries, preventing the growth of production of food. As a result, Asia, which is potentially rich in agriculture, is importing food and the amount is increasing continually at an alarming rate. Hunger and poverty will be the fate of the Asian masses for many years to come.

A hopeful sign is the growing awareness among the oppressed peoples that leads to the growth and increase of peoples' organizations in both the cities and the rural areas. The majority of Asian countries have witnessed peasant uprisings and urban disturbances. Put down by bloody oppression and intimidated by imprisonment and torture, many of these movements have gone underground and turned to a protracted struggle as the only means of changing their societies. While not necessarily condoning the use of violence, which is most often unavoidable, we question and object to the enforcement of "law and order," which consolidates the control of the power elites while thwarting the organized conscientious objections of the deprived majorities. When legalized violence leaves no room for peoples to free themselves from their misery, are we surprised that they are so compelled to resort to violence? Have the Christian churches sufficiently understood the message of revolutionary violence in the Asian struggles for political independence, social emancipation, and liberation from the built-in violence of the present economic and political structures?

The youth in Asia, who form a large segment of the Asian population, are continuously victimized. They constitute the growing number of unemployed and underemployed labor forces. A lack of proper educational facilities and decreasing employment opportunities in the rural areas where the majority of youth come from lead to the irreversible process of migration to urban centers; in the urban areas, the youth are the targets of consumer culture and in turn become vehicles of deculturation. We emphasize also that some students, youth, and workers have been playing the important role of a critical and committed force in the struggle for the basic rights of the oppressed people. At the same time, they are also made pawns in the power politics of politicians and other interest groups, thus losing their genuine relevance, and are even sacrificed in abrupt physical violence.

The educational system, linked to the established centers of power, is geared to perpetuate the domination of youth. It serves as a mere channel for the transfer of technical skills and alienated knowledge without reference to humanistic values. The pyramidal elitist structure of education is used to fabricate losers, who are continuously exploited.

We recognized deeply that women are also victims of the same structures of domination and exploitation. In the context of the Asiatic religions and cultures, the relationship between men and women is still one of domination. This situation is worse in the poorer classes of society. Thus women face an unforgiveable double oppression.

In the economic sphere, a male-dominated society reduces the "price" of woman-labor and limits the scope of women's participation in the process of production at all levels—the local, national, regional, and consequently the international levels. In the political sphere, women are aware of the political situation in their countries, but here too their competence and activity are greatly stifled.

Women are sexually and intellectually vulnerable in a society where an interaction of traditional and modern forces (especially tourism) compels them to compromise with consumeristic values of capitalist society. It also compels them to prostitution. Instead of condemning the system that forces women into prostitution, the men who exploit the women also condemn them.

We recognize the existence of ethnic minorities in every Asian country. They are among the most deprived sectors at all levels, including the economic, political, and cultural. They are struggling for self-determination against heavy odds, yet their authentic struggle is often utilized by the centers of power in playing up racial antagonism to camouflage themselves and disrupt the unity among the marginalized.

Mass media, including the printed word, films, and television, are controlled by the ruling elite to propagate their dominant value systems and myths, providing a dehumanizing, individualistic, consumerist culture. Despite this domination, we also witness the emergence of a more creative micro-media that portrays realistically the struggle of the dominated people.

We need to mention also the increasing impact of urbanization and irrational industrialization. Women, children, and men together face narrowing opportunities for education, housing, and health services as these social needs are determined by market forces. With the transfer of the platforms of production and mechanization from industrialized countries, environmental pollution surfaces in most of the Asian countries, causing ecological imbalances. Here we join with our fisherfolk in their struggle against the unscrupulous practices in certain countries like Japan, Taiwan, and South Korea.

We realize also the legitimizing role of religion in the course of history within the Asian context. Religions form an integral part of the total social reality, inseparable from all spheres of action. Much interaction has taken place between religion and politics in Asia down through the ages, and today there are significant movements of social renewal inspired by religion outside the traditional institutions. We need to stress the critical and transforming element in religion and culture. A serious socio-political analysis of realities and involvement in political and ideological struggles should be seen as vital elements of religion in its role as a critic. Here we realize the creative force of culture in bringing people together and giving them an identity within their struggles. Critical cultural action would destroy old myths and create new symbols in continuity with the cultural treasures of the past.

Towards a Relevant Theology

We are conscious of the fact that the vital issues of the realities of Asia indicate the ambivalent role of the major religions in Asia and pose serious questions to us, hence challenging the dehumanizing status quo of theology. To be relevant, theology must undergo a radical transformation.

Liberation: Area of Concern

In the context of the poverty of the teeming millions of Asia and their situation of domination and exploitation, our theology must have a very definite liberational thrust.

The first act of theology, its very heart, is commitment. This commitment is a response to the challenge of the poor in their struggle for full humanity. We affirm that the poor and the oppressed of Asia are called by God to be the architects and builders of their own destiny. Thus theology starts with the aspirations of the oppressed towards full humanity and counts on their growing consciousness of, and their ever-expanding efforts to overcome, all obstacles to the truth of their history.

Subject of Theology

To be truly liberating, this theology must arise from the Asian poor with a liberated consciousness. It is articulated and expressed by the oppressed community using the technical skills of biblical scholars, social scientists, psychologists, anthropologists, and others. It can be expressed in many ways, in art forms, drama, literature, folk stories, and native wisdom, as well as in doctrinal-pastoral statements.

Most participants asserted that every theology is conditioned by the class position and class consciousness of the theologian. Hence a truly liberating theology must ultimately be the work of the Asian poor, who are struggling for full humanity. It is they who must reflect on and say what their faith-life experience in the struggle for liberation is. This does not exclude the so-called specialists in theology. With their knowledge they can complement the theologizing of the grassroots people. But their theologizing becomes authentic only when rooted in the history and struggle of the poor and the oppressed.

Liberation, Culture, and Religion

To be authentically Asian, theology must be immersed in our historico-cultural situation and grow out of it. A theology that emerged from the people's struggle for liberation would spontaneously formulate itself in religio-cultural idioms of the people.

In many parts of Asia, we must integrate into our theology the insights and values of the major religions, but this integration must take place at the level of action and commitment to the people's struggle and not be merely intellectual or elitist. These traditions of Asia's great religions seem to understand liberation in two senses: liberation from selfishness both within each person and in society. These religious traditions also contain a strong motivation for personal conversion of life. These religions, together with our indigenous cultures, can provide the Asian sense in our task of generating the new person and the new community. We view them as a potential source of a permanent critique of any established order and a pointer towards the building of a truly human society. We are conscious, however, of the domesticating role religions have often played in the past, so we need to subject both our religion and our culture to sustained self-criticism. In this context, we question the academic preoccupation to work toward the so-called "indigenization" or "inculturation" of theology divorced from participation in the liberational struggle in history. In our countries today, there can be no truly indigenized theology that is not liberational. Involvement in the history and struggle of the oppressed is the guarantee that our theology is both liberating and indigenous.

Social Analysis

Theology working for the liberation of the poor must approach its task with the tools of social analysis of the realities of Asia. How can it participate in the liberation of the poor if it does not understand the socio-political, economic, and cultural structures that enslave the poor? The vision of full humanity and the complexity of the struggle leading to its achievement are continually challenged and distorted by the meshing of mixed motives and interests and by the interweaving of the apparent and the real. This analysis must extend to the whole length and breadth, height, and depth of Asian reality, from the family to the village, the city, the nation, the continent, and the globe. Economic and socio-political interdependence has shrunk the earth to a global village. The analysis must keep pace with the ongoing historical process to ensure a continuing self-criticism and evaluation of religions, ideologies, institutions, groups, and classes of people that by their very nature run the hazard of a dehumanizing bureaucracy.

Biblical Perspective

Because theology takes the total human situation seriously, it can be regarded as the articulated reflection, in faith, on the encounter of God by people in their historical situations. For us, Christians, the Bible becomes an important source in the doing of theology. The God encountered in the history of the people is none other than the God who revealed himself in the events of Jesus' life, death, and resurrection. We believe that God and Christ continue to be present in the struggles of the people to achieve full humanity as we look forward in hope to the consummation of all things when God will be all in all.

When theology is liberated from its present race, class, and sex prejudices, it can place itself at the service of the people and become a powerful motivating force for the mobilization of believers in Jesus to participate in Asia's ongoing struggle for self-identity and human dignity. For this, we need to develop whole new areas of theology such as understanding the revolutionary challenge of the life of Jesus, seeing in Mary the truly liberated woman who participated in the struggle of Jesus and her people, bridging the gaps of our denominational separation, and rewriting the history of the Asian churches from the perspective of the Asian poor.

Spirituality and Formation

The formation for Christian living and ministry has to be in and through participation in the struggle of the masses of our people. This requires the development of a corresponding spirituality, of opting out of the exploitative system in some way, of being marginalized in the process, of persevering in our commitment, of risk bearing, of reaching deeper inner peace in the midst of active involvement with the struggling people (Shanti).

Our fellow Christians who have become regular inmates of the Asian prisons bring us new elements of fidelity to our people inspired by Jesus. To them we too send a message of humble solidarity and prayerful hope. May the suffering of today's prisoners in the Asian jails give birth to a genuine renewal of ourselves and our communities of believers.

Future Tasks

Coming to the end of this conference, we feel the need to continue the search we have initiated here. To keep alive our efforts towards a theology that speaks to our Asian peoples, we see the following tasks before us.

1. We need to continue deepening our understanding of the Asian reality through *active involvement* in our people's struggle for full humanity. This means struggling side by side with our peasants, fisherfolk, workers, slum-dwellers, marginalized and minority groups, oppressed youth, and women so that together we can discover the Asian face of Christ.

2. Our theology must lead us to transform the society in which we live so that it may increasingly allow the Asian person to experience what it means to be fully alive. This task includes the transformation of our church structures and institutions as well as ourselves.

3. We shall continue to assist in the development of a relevant theology for Asia through constant interaction and mutual respect for the different roles we have in the struggle, as professional theologians, grassroots workers, and church people.

4. We seek to build a strong network of alliances by linking groups who are struggling for full humanity nationally and internationally. The following concrete actions taken in the course of the conference show the beginnings of this network:

a. A letter of solidarity with seventy-six boat people in Hong Kong who were arrested on their way to petition for better housing.

b. A public statement by the Sri Lankan delegation pledging to support the Tamil-speaking people in their struggle for their just rights.

c. A message to Bishop Tji of Korea, supporting the Korean struggle and regretting the absence of the entire Korean delegation at the conference.

d. A letter to Kawasaki Steel Corporation, Japan, protesting the export of pollution to other Asian countries.

e. A telegram to the Latin American Bishops as well as to Pope John Paul II, expressing deep concern for the CELAM conference in Puebla, Mexico.

f. Solidarity with the Filipino participants in their protest against the pollution caused by the transfer of high pollutant industries and the erection of nuclear power plants.

5. We are concerned about formation programs in our training institutions and the lifestyle of our pastoral leaders. The experiences of the conference make it clear that there must be new emphases in our theological and pastoral policy. We need to evaluate our parish and diocesan structures to assess where they alienate us from the poor masses of Asia and give us the image of might and power. We urge that necessary adjustments be made so that our

religious personnel may be more deeply in touch with the problems of our people.

6. In order to facilitate the implementation of our tasks, we have formed the Ecumenical Theological Fellowship of Asia.

For two weeks eighty of us, participants at this Asian Theological Conference, have tried to grapple with the contemporary call of the Asian poor and oppressed.

The prayerful silence in worship and the unity in faith helped to keep our communion in dialectical and creative tension.

As Christians we see the urgent tasks of renewing ourselves and the churches in order to serve our people.

To this sacred and historic task we humbly commit ourselves and invite all Christians and people of good will everywhere to participate in this ongoing search.

Part Four

Assessments

14

Notes on the Asian
Theological Conference

Dalston Forbes (Sri Lanka)

Purpose

The Conference was prepared with a definite purpose in mind. It was not meant to produce a total systematic theology for Asia, but only to handle and tackle the question of the poverty and religiosity of Asia and what Christian theology has to say about this.

The aim was to do theological reflection. The theme made this clear: "Asia's Struggle for Full Humanity—Towards a Relevant Theology."

Form and Shape of the Conference: Methodology

1. The Conference was sponsored by the Ecumenical Association of Third World Theologians. It was supported by the Commission on Theological Concerns, Christian Conference of Asia (CCA), Singapore, and the Research Department of the Office of Human Development of the Federation of Asian Bishops' Conferences (FABC), Manila. Actual organization was in the

Dalston Forbes, O.M.I., represented the Catholic Bishops' Conference of Sri Lanka.

hands of the Centre for Society and Religion, Colombo. So there were various thrusts and influences in the organization.

2. Practical areas of concern were identified and studies had been made in preparation for the ATC. In Sri Lanka these were: peasantry in the villages; industrial workers; plantation workers; slums; youth; condition of women; national minorities, mainly the Sinhala-Tamil problem.

Each national delegation was supposed to do its own preparation, but the work was unequal. Good preparation was done mainly by the Philippines, India, and Sri Lanka.

3. Representation was of three categories—activists and social workers from the grassroots and the base, church officials like bishops and administrators, theologians and specialists. There were too many activists and too few theologians.

4. The actual conference began with a live-in of three days where delegates lived in the seven problem areas earmarked above with Sri Lankan companions. This was followed by the actual conference in Wennappuwa. The live-ins were too short and superficial. The reports made in the Assembly showed this deficiency.

There was also a real difficulty in theologizing about the issues that emerged. Issues were identified, but there was no time to connect them with biblical and theological reflection.

5. Many position papers and documents were presented, some in dossiers before the conference and others at the conference. They were of unequal importance and standards and there was no time to study the material. Though the documentation was good, it had no real impact on the Assembly.

6. The Final Statement was rushed. It appeared only on the last morning. There was no procedure to allow for amendments on the first draft in the Assembly. The Editorial Committee had to correct, amend, abridge, and write it up after the delegates had left.

Tensions

There were many tensions that the delegates faced which were not always solved.

1. What is theology? The Filipino view was that theology is the work of the Asian poor with liberated consciousness. It is they who must reflect on and say what their faith-life experience in the struggle for liberation is. Others, like the Indian and Sri Lankan groups, felt that theology is a process which should start from real-life situations in the matrix of history, but then includes biblical and theological specialists, social scientists, church officials, etc. There can be a level of systematic synthesis. The Final Statement is a compromise!

2. Who does theology? One view: The people at the grassroots. Another

view: The specialist, though he or she must be in organic contact with the life situations of the Christian and human community.

3. Social Action vs. Theological Reflection.

It was not clear whether the conference had as its objective social analysis and consequent action or theological reflection on Asian reality and society. The structural analysis, often Marxist inspired, was used to describe situations, but not consistently. There was thus this constant interference of the lines of reflection and action. The organizers and the delegates made no clear options.

4. Social Reality vs. the Religiosity of Asia.

Some delegates wished to stress the importance of a theology of Asian non-Christian religions. They felt Christians could not work alone and must find/need allies in the other living religions of the continent. Others saw Asian religions as dehumanizing and exploitative, and did not see the importance of the religious pole in the conference.

The Final Statement

The Final Statement gives only the formal conditions for a liberational theology of Asia. It does not get down to the material content of such a theology. It is clear that the Statement marks only the beginning of a long train of theological reflection.

I have summarized the theological section as follows:

The Statement accepts the dehumanizing role, often ambivalent, of religion and theology in Asia, Christian and others.

Our theology in the context of poverty must be liberational.

First act is commitment to the challenge of the poor and their cause.

The locus and matrix of theology is the struggle for liberation of the Asian poor. We must meet God in the experience of history.

Theology must ultimately be the work of the Asian poor. But specialists have their role to play as facilitators and catalysts.

Theological reflection must be faith-inspired and biblical.

Theology can be strongly motivational in the struggle for justice.

Other religions can help especially in the liberation of the person from selfishness.

Spirituality must be related to the struggle for justice. Formation of church personnel must be in the same sense.

Evaluation

The Statement does not bring out the riches of the Asian Theological Conference. The preparatory studies were quite good and much richer. The speeches and interventions on the floor of the Assembly and the dynamics of exchange were also helpful and formative. Their accents are not brought out in the Statement. The ATC must be seen as one moment or part of a process of theological reflection. The really positive contribution is the interest of socially active Christians in Asia for theology. This is a good thing and augurs well for the future.

15

Reflections by Korean Theologians on the Final Statement of the Asian Theological Conference

Certain Protestant theologians in Korea welcome the Asian Theological Conference's Final Statement in its basic theological direction and appreciate the good spirit and efforts of the ATC towards the Final Statement.

It is generally felt that the Statement is a thorough and comprehensive analysis of the socio-political and economic situation of the peoples in Asia. It carries and communicates the suffering and struggles as well as the dynamics of the people and those who take the liberating gospel seriously in the midst of their personal and social existence. It is an accomplishment of the theologians who for many years had spoken Western-style jargon and theological ghetto language.

Some theologians think that there should be some attempts to reconcile two trends in contemporary theologies, namely, liberation theology and the theology of indigenization. The former tends to put emphasis on contemporary issues while the latter on cultures and traditions. They must come together to form a theology which can liberate the total person and the total society in which contemporary issues are so closely interrelated to past history.

There are, however, some critical comments by the Korean theologians.

On "The Asian Context"

1. The paragraphs on socialism reduce too drastically the aspirations of the Asian peoples to the socialist ideology. There is also too blanket an endorse-

ment of the existing social orders of the socialist countries. There is need for more discussion of the socialist ideology and the socialist order: limitations as well as advantages, some of which are reflected in the paper.

2. The third paragraph is fine, but it seems to curiously contradict the second paragraph. Traditionally, Asian people's aspirations were expressed by and large through traditional great religions, although they are now shackles of bondage for the peoples in Asia in many cases.

The Statement legitimately presents "liberation" as the center of concern as it is the center of concern throughout the Bible. However, it does not carefully work out from what the oppressed are to be liberated and this is an important omission. At the outset the Statement enumerates the external obstacles which dehumanize the Asian people as it describes the Asian context and presents the issues to be tackled. It also urges all theologies to be liberated from race, class, and sex prejudices which one might call internal hindrances. It, however, fails to mention distorted faiths, ideologies, and varieties of prejudices which we inherit from our past culture and traditions as well as from any dominant contemporary culture.

Closer attention should have been given to the roles which traditional cultures and religions have played in domesticating or liberating the oppressed. It is not enough simply to say that "the rich traditions of the major religions of Asia (Hinduism, Buddhism, Islam, and Christianity [why omit Confucianism?] offer many inspirations" or "in the past, religions and cultural systems have played the role of legitimizing feudal relationships." A religion is born out of a set of views on life. The basic orientation of the view can contribute to the liberation of people, or domesticate them. And the orientation of the view is determined by the position which the founder or the founders of the religion take either on the side of the oppressed or of the oppressors. Confucianism, a religion looking at life from the point of view of rulers, therefore, is basically for the domination of the oppressed. Other religions must be examined in a similar way and their histories studied along the same line.

3. In paragraph 3 one reads, "Neither will socialist movements in Asia be thorough in their struggle for full humanity without an inner liberation from self-seeking and exploitative instincts." The term "instincts" is an unfortunate one and should be avoided. It is too Freudian and will bring about unhappy consequences. If self-seeking and exploitative tendencies are from instincts, one cannot eliminate them, but can only suppress them, which is harmful always in the long run. It is not the self-seeking tendency which is wrong, but the selfishness which comes from the wrong use of human freedom stemming from a mistaken view of life. Therefore, the self-seeking tendency should not be suppressed, but directed properly in the light of a healthier view of life.

On "Towards a Relevant Theology"

4. The paper should have taken seriously a theological critique of the Asian churches; merely ideological criticism is not enough and should recognize existing attempts that are emerging in the national situation, no matter how feeble they may be.

5. The Statement correctly insists that the oppressed people must be the subject of theologizing. While agreeing with this argument wholeheartedly, one of the Korean theologians feels that the real issue still remains—how can the oppressed people become the subject? It is easy to talk about this, but it is something else to bring it into reality. Very often we see the oppressed people roused up to claim their rights. However, we also see them manipulated by cleverly formed ideologies created by power-hungry elites. A person can be truly the subject only when there is freedom from external manipulation as well as internal prejudices. This freedom can be attained when a person has real sensitivity toward life and gives life the utmost value. Then a person can truly judge what is good for life and what is harmful.

Unfortunately, however, the views which the oppressed hold about themselves, about the oppressors, and about the world are so damaged that they are unable to become the subjects. Here is where the doctrine of incarnation must come in. Someone must come down to them with real respect and concern, sharing the life with them and learning of them in depth. Through such intercourse of life, the oppressed will gradually learn to respect themselves, to uphold the value of their own lives—and to judge what is good for their lives and what is not. It is only through such a loving incarnation that the oppressed people can become subject and do their own theologizing. Thus we see that the oppressed are not doing the theology alone, but with the incarnated people who share life with them in dialogue.

We are to do our theological reflections upon our experiences. When we say the oppressed are more qualified to do theology, it means that their experiences have a special meaning and significance. In general the inner experiences of the oppressed people as they struggle to be human beings in an inhuman world are not elaborated in the Statement. This may indicate the fact that really oppressed people were not represented in the deliberation or that their voices were not heard in the process of making the Statement. Therefore, there should be a more sincere attempt to penetrate the complexity of the inner experiences of the oppressed, or bring it to consciousness for our deeper understanding.

6. Concerning the phrase "new humanity," such a short theological statement cannot, of course, elaborate what the phrase really means. Nonetheless, it is hoped to see at least in which context this phrase is being used. Is it used in the context of Christology, or eschatology, or something

that is entirely different from the Western theological concept? If the latter, it has to be explained a bit more fully.

7. The final but small point is on Mary (see Biblical Perspective) as "the truly liberated woman, etc." We would like to question whether theology of liberation of women has concurred on this particular point. We are not questioning the traditional Catholic stance on Mariology, we are only questioning the Statement's consistency. The Statement is searching for the new image for a theology in Asia and of the Asian people. Then why is it that the Statement could not look for an Asian image for the liberated woman in the Asian context. Another problem is that on the one hand it is a good thing for the Protestants to look into the status of Mary in the light of liberation, but on the other hand this statement might exclude some of the Protestant feminists from the struggle.

16

From Accra to Wennappuwa: What Is New? What More?

Rose Zoé-Obianga (Cameroun)

The Conference on Asian theology was held from January 4 to 20, 1979, at Wennappuwa in Sri Lanka (formerly Ceylon).

One year earlier, in December 1977, the Pan-African Conference of Theologians of the Third World took place in Accra (Ghana).[1] Both of these conferences were the result of decisions taken during the first meeting at Dar es Salaam from August 5 to 12, 1976.[2]

Being the only African woman who participated in both the Pan-African Conference of Accra and in the Conference of Asian Theologians, I was asked, not only to share my impressions of the Wennappuwa Conference to which I was privileged to have an invitation, but also, and this was even more important, to compare the two conferences and to describe relationships between the two theologies, or more exactly, to compare the main characteristics which are present in these two theological options.

But before introducing the subject of this article, I just want to state that my participation is, in no way, an exhaustive analysis of African and Asiatic theologies. The point of this article is much more modest.

Rose Zoé-Obianga is lecturer in arts and sciences at the University of Yaounde and is doing postgraduate studies in Europe and the U.S.A.

The first point of comparison to speak about is the methodology followed at the two conferences. In fact, there is a vast difference between the way in which Accra and Wennappuwa evolved.

The inductive method, used at Wennappuwa, allowed both groups, grassroots people and academicians, to experience an original type of conference. There was no question, as at Accra, of sitting at the feet of different orators (of whom I was one) to listen and absorb their laboriously prepared lectures.

On the contrary, from the outset, we were divided into groups according to our interests (villages, factory workers, tea plantation workers, coconut plantation workers, fisherfolk, women, youth) and were sent to specific places chosen in accord with the different aspects of the theme of the Wennappuwa Conference.

Thus from January 7 to 11, 1979, the women's group, of which I was a member, went to southern Sri Lanka, to the village of Baddegama. The main purpose of these "live-in" experiences, which made up the first part of the conference, was to allow us to share the rude and difficult life of the poorest of the working class in a Third World country (in this case, Sri Lanka).

The basic purpose of this methodology consisted in this: to make a theology for Third World people coming uniquely, from now on, from the deepest perception of the reality of our people and our country—that is, the experience of exploitation, misery, and hunger.

The meeting between man or woman with God does not and will not henceforth take place in an ethereal world, but rather in the midst of Third World humanity (John 17:1–19). It is now seen as inadequate, even useless, to attempt to theologize in Africa, Asia, Latin America, in the Caribbean, in the Pacific, or among North American minorities without an examination and a detailed analysis of the poverty and exploitation which are the lot of men and women of the Third World.

It is true that for all of us the experience of exploitation, misery, and hunger is not so extraordinary (some will smile with contempt or indulgence), recognizing that we in Africa share with Asia the same daily reality of a permanent struggle to survive and for recognition of the dignity of the human person; of exploitation at every level of the peasant and the worker; of "law and order" oppression in our different systems; of domination of women by societies fashioned, above all, for the benefit of the male; of the menace (one cannot explain why) of youth; of racial, sexual, and religious discrimination; of the humiliating indignity of minorities in our different countries; of the (oppressed) masses of refugees caused by fratricidal wars which are destroying our young states.

We found all this, not only in different "live-in" situations spent with the most disenfranchised in our host country, but also through the diverse documents from different countries represented at the conference in Wennappuwa.

From the outset then, it went well and we congratulate the local organizers of this conference and also the government of Sri Lanka for its courageous support. It is not always easy to uncover for foreigners what is not immediately evident in one or about oneself.

The second element which provides a good comparison between the two conferences is the composition of the delegations sent to Accra and at Wennappuwa.

1. At the conference at Wennappuwa the percentage of women was larger than at Accra. I cannot say the same about young people.

2. The presence of grassroots representatives was also an extremely important factor at Wennappuwa.

3. The fraternal participation of representatives of other great religions in Asia (Buddhism, Hinduism, Islam) reveals the reality of the search and the achievement of a more sincere dialogue between the different world religions. It would have been better at the Accra conference had the Independent Churches, the traditional African religion, and black Islam been able to share this extraordinary experience with us.

There were certain theological differences between Accra and Wennappuwa, but there were similarities as well.

It is always easier to discover differences in making a comparison. I will speak only of one significant difference—the percentage of Christians on the two continents. In Asia, the Christian population is estimated at 2 percent. In Africa, it has been estimated (by Barret and Neill) that Christians will represent more than 50 percent of the population by the year 2000.

On the other hand, the presence of other great religions (Hinduism, Islam, Buddhism) gives a remarkably different coloration to Asian society.

I am not going to spend time listing differences, for I am in agreement on this point with James Cone's claims about African theology and black theology:

My contention is that black and African theologies are not as different as has been suggested and that their common concerns require a dialogue that is important to both.[3]

Turning now, to what African and Asian theologies have in common:

There was a considerable measure of agreement in the area of the need to do theology in context as described above; furthermore, we recognize that our countries have common problems. The analysis of the social, economic, political, cultural, racial, and psychological situations showed clearly that the countries of the Third World have had similar experiences of which account should be taken in the task of theologizing.[4]

In this context, Accra and Wennappuwa affirm the need of a thorough analysis of Asian and African reality.

The Living Word of the Lord has led us to consider the realities of Africa today.[5]

Our reflections, already begun in our local realities, helped us to enrich the process of interaction and sharing among us who have committed ourselves to the struggle of the poor in Asia.[6]

Also the primary source of theology in Asia and in Africa is the Bible.

The Bible is the basic source of African theology, because it is the primary witness of God's revelation in Jesus Christ.[7]

For us, Christians, the Bible becomes an important source in the doing of theology.[8]

Theology in Asia and Africa is liberational, a struggle to transform the living conditions of men and women.

Because oppression is found not only in culture but also in political and economic structures and the dominant mass media, African theology must also be *liberation theology*.[9]

In the context of the poverty of the teeming millions of Asia and their situation of domination and exploitation, our theology must have a very definite liberational thrust.[10]

It seems that on the two continents, the situation of women has not yet been taken seriously. It was unanimously recognized that woman is above all a victim of the structures of domination and exploitation. Although she frequently constitutes the majority in congregations, her presence in decision making in the church, for example, is still minimal.

But, at the same time, a reorientation of mentality and of structures was decided at the two conferences. The Accra statement gives hope about the future participation of women. I quote it:

Throughout this document, we have referred to the need to struggle against *sexism*. If that struggle is to be taken seriously by the church, then our seriousness will be reflected in the way we do theology. We recognize that African women have taken an active role in the church and in the shaping of our history. They have shown themselves to be an integral part of the liberation struggle. But we cannot ignore their exclusion from our past theological endeavors. The future of African theology must take seriously the role of women in the church as equals in the doing of theology.[11]

Similar sentiments were expressed at the Conference in Wennappuwa. Finally, the future perspective, in general, is the same. It is necessary to understand our socio-economic, political, cultural, and religious realities and to transform them for the well-being of the Asian and African population. On the other hand, the need to teach African and Asian theology is all the greater.

Conclusion

In conclusion, there are two points to emphasize:

1. Among the objectives of the Dar es Salaam meeting was: "promoting the exchange of theological views through writings in the books and periodicals of Third World countries."[12]

However, we discovered at Wennappuwa that it was not so much a question of exchanging books and periodicals. The Third World is poor—they have neither the means nor the publishing houses to accept what they really want to publish. Our Third World theology must be first of all an existential theology.

2. I agree with James Cone when he talks about the future of African theology:

I contend therefore that indigenization and liberation belong together. The future of African theology, and all Third World theologies, is found in the attempt to interpret the Christian Gospel in the historical context of the people's struggle to liberate themselves from all forms of human oppression.[13]

Theology in the Third World cannot be anything other than a struggle, for Third World theology takes the totality of the human being seriously. It is a fight for the total development of the human person.

But then, one might ask, what is so new about Wennappuwa? Did they really say anything new there?

In my humble opinion: yes. Yes, because we ourselves have said it; it is we, ourselves, who will speak henceforth, in our own words. Eboussi says:

The Truth is his [the African and the Asian] to make, here and now; he cannot make it for any one else, and no one can take his place.[14]

Paulo Freire observes that oppressed peoples live *in silence*. They speak, yes, but they use the words of their oppressors. Liberation requires that the oppressed find their own words and name their own world.

The theology of Africa, and that of Asia, have something new and something more to say because they speak their own words.

Translated by Sister Joan Kirby, R.S.C.J.

NOTES

1. Pan-African Conference of Third World Theologians, December 17–23, 1977, Accra, Ghana; proceedings published as *African Theology en Route,* ed. Kofi Appiah-Kubi and Sergio Torres (Maryknoll, N.Y.: Orbis Books, 1979).

2. Ecumenical Dialogue of Third World Theologians, August 5–12, 1976, Dar es Salaam, Tanzania; proceedings published as *The Emergent Gospel: Theology from the Underside of History,* ed. Sergio Torres and Virginia Fabella, M.M. (Maryknoll, N.Y.: Orbis Books, 1978).

3. James H. Cone, "A Black American Perspective on the Future of African Theology," in *African Theology en Route,* p. 178.

4. Final Statement in *The Emergent Gospel,* pp. 270–271.

5. Final Communiqué in *African Theology en Route,* p. 190.

6. Final Statement of this Asian Theological Conference, Document 13, p. 152.

7. Final Communiqué in *African Theology en Route,* p. 192.

8. Final Statement of this Asian Theological Conference, Document 13, p. 158.

9. Final Communiqué in *African Theology en Route,* p. 194.

10. Final Statement of this Asian Theological Conference, Document 13, p. 156.

11. Final Communiqué in *African Theology en Route,* p. 194.

12. Communiqué in *The Emergent Gospel,* p 273.

13. Cone, "A Black American Perspective, op. cit., p. 184.

14. F. Eboussi Boulaga, "The African Christian in Search of Identity," in *The Churches of Africa: Future Prospects.*

17

A Black American Perspective on the Asian Search for a Full Humanity

James H. Cone (U.S.A.)

What has Asian theology to do with black theology? This is the question that defines the focus of this essay. To answer this question is not easy, because there has been a limited dialogue between Asian and black theologians. In contrast to many conferences and workshops dealing with the relationship of black theology to African, Latin, and Caribbean theologies, no such conferences or workshops have been organized for the purpose of examining the relations of black and Asian theologies. When black theologians and churchpeople have encountered persons born in Asia and who presently live and work on that continent, usually it has been in the context of the World Council of Churches with an ecumenical agenda not related to the unique concerns of Asians and black Americans. Because of our difference in cultural origin and the large geographical distance that separates us, the assumption has been that Asians and blacks do not have much in common with each other.

For comparison, it is important to note that a similar assumption has not been made in regard to black theology's relation to African, Caribbean, and Latin theologies. That black theologians have something to talk about with African theologians is obvious by our common racial origin. During the

James H. Cone is Charles A. Briggs Professor of Systematic Theology at Union Theological Seminary in New York City.

1960s, it was not unusual to hear black nationalists say that "we are an African people," and the publication and television production of Alex Haley's *Roots* reinforced the significance of Africa for the masses of black people. But even prior to the rise of popular black nationalist groups in the 1960s and before Alex Haley's *Roots*, the significance of Africa for the identity of black Americans had been emphasized in the religious and secular contexts of black life in the United States. Marcus Garvey's "black to Africa" movement and W. E. B. DuBois' pan-Africanism are prominent examples of the importance of Africa in the political and intellectual life of black people.[1] Because many blacks believe that who we are and what we shall become cannot be separated from our African heritage, it was only natural for black theologians to seek to deepen their theological vision by turning to Africans for mutual dialogue on the common faith and struggles of our peoples.[2]

As we pursued our historical roots in Africa and began to investigate the African slave trade, there was no way we could ignore the significance of Latin America and the Caribbean for the African world. There are more black people of African descent on the continent of South America than in North America. This fact alone suggests that black, Caribbean, and Latin theologians have something of mutual interest to talk about. When the theme of *liberation* and its relation to race and class is introduced into our discussions, the dialogue between black, Latin, and Caribbean theologians is deepened.[3]

Unfortunately when black theology is related to Asian theology, their common interest is not easily recognized. What has an essentially black, racial struggle for justice in North America to do with an Asian struggle for full humanity in the context of immense poverty and the perpetual dehumanizing effects of European colonialism? Because black and Asian peoples' knowledge of and personal contact with each other is limited, their respective cultures and life-experiences seem vastly different and far removed from each other. But is that assumption correct? I do not think so. In fact, I contend that Asians and black Americans have far more in common that what is immediately obvious, and that this commonality arises from a similar experience of ultimate reality in the historical context of our struggle against slavery and oppression. In this essay, I want to explicate my assumption about the common interests of Asian and black theologies by examining three experiences I have had on the continent of Asia.[4]

Japan and Korea: May 1975

The first occasion in which I had to deal with the relation of black and Asian theologies occurred in May 1975 when I was invited by the Korean Christian Church in Japan to lead workshops for church leaders on the theme: "The Church Struggling for the Liberation of the People." After my nearly three-week stay in Japan, I also visited South Korea at the invitation of struggling Christians in that country. Before these experiences in Japan and Korea, my knowledge of and personal contact with

Asian people had been limited to the contexts of the World Council of Churches, the diaspora Asian communities in the United States, and the speeches and writings of white scholars and missionaries. None of these contexts adequately prepared me for the creative challenge that Asia would provide for the theological perspective through the Korean Christian Community in Japan and the Korean struggle for democracy and justice in South Korea.

In Japan, it was not difficult to perceive the similarities between the Korean experience in that country and the black experience in the United States. As blacks were stolen from Africa by Europeans and enslaved in the Americas, Koreans were taken against their will from their homeland and brought to Japan in order to serve Japanese people. Like blacks who expressed their struggle for justice by creating songs of liberation derived from the biblical account of the Exodus, Korean Christians in Japan expressed their determination to be free in a similar fashion. As blacks experience discrimination in employment and in every other aspect of American society, Koreans have an analogous experience in Japan.[5]

White racism against blacks and Japanese racism against Koreans are so similar that I was tempted to suggest that the latter was derived partly from the former. In fact, after only a short stay in Japan, I could easily determine the composition of my audience, even though there are no obvious physical differences between Korean and Japanese peoples. I could tell who was in my audience by the kinds of questions asked, the reactions to liberation struggles of poor people, and the respect for the openness to learn from another people's culture. Japanese people had an attitude of superiority and their questions about the attitude towards oppressed people were very similar to whites in the United States. Almost without exception, in churches as well as seminaries and universities, Japanese Christians were hostile towards the liberation-focus of the Christian faith and were more interested in analyzing the dominant theologies of Europe and North America. I found it very strange that the theological systems of Barth, Brunner, Tillich, and Niebuhr still occupied important places in Japanese theology with almost no reference to liberation theologies in Asia, Africa, and South and North America.

In contrast to Japanese people, Korean Christians reminded me of black people in their openness to the liberation theme in the gospel. The four workshops, several worship services, and many private conversations provided excellent occasions on which to talk about the black experience in North America as well as to hear about the Korean experience in Japan from the people who have lived it. Initially, however, some Koreans were suspicious of my emphasis on liberation in the gospel, because the translation of that term into their language had many negative implications for their situation. But when they realized that my interpretation of liberation was derived from my people's struggle against slavery and injustice, they immediately identified with black people's fight for justice in a white racist society and expressed that identification by readily accepting me as one of their own. To be at home in such a totally different culture from my own was a very strange but rewarding experience. The language and other cultural barriers were transcended through a mutual openness to each other's struggles, and through a common recognition that the universalism in the gospel is found in God's will to liberate all oppressed people from the shackles of human bondage.

I will never forget my experience with Korean people in the four workshops as we discussed the biblical meaning of salvation. Having such a "conservation" orientation towards the Bible (as is also true of blacks in the United States), Koreans first wanted to explore where I stood regarding the biblical view of salvation. I centered my interpretation of salvation in the Bible as it is defined by the Exodus, articulated by the prophets, and consummated in the life, death, and resurrection of Jesus. I contended that to be saved is to be liberated. And as evidence, I pointed to the liberation of Israelites from Egypt, the prophets' stand on justice, and Jesus' claim that he came "to preach good news to the poor," "to proclaim release to the captives" and "to set at liberty those who are oppressed" (Luke 4:18 RSV). I emphasized that my perspective on the scripture was not derived primarily from white scholars and missionaries, but rather from the history and culture of black people who have been struggling for justice and freedom for nearly four hundred years in North America. Black people in North America are an historical representation of the hermeneutical privilege that God gives to the poor in order that they may recognize that their struggle for freedom is also God's struggle.

In order for Koreans to hear the black folk expression of this view of salvation, I recited such spirituals as "Go Down Moses," "Oh, Freedom," and "Oh, Mary, Don't You Weep." When Koreans heard the lyrics of these songs, they realized that my view of salvation was not an abstract philosophical concept but rather a reality that has been derived from the lived-experiences of black people. We both also realized that the Korean experience in Japan is similar to the black experience in the United States, and we spent much time talking about our common interests. While we recognized our obvious differences, these did not separate us, but instead brought us closer together in our struggle against the racism of both Japanese and white peoples.[6]

When I left Japan for Seoul, Korea, I realized for the first time that blacks and Asians do have some things in common. But the Korean experience in Japan had not prepared me for my subsequent experience in Seoul. It is one thing to read and hear about a political dictatorship, but it is quite another thing to have a concrete, existential experience of one. When I arrived, the famous "Presidential Emergency Measure No. 9" had just been issued (May 13, 1975), which allowed the police to arrest and imprison any person who criticized the Park regime. The universities had been closed for several months but were allowed to re-open just before my arrival. It was thought best that the university context would not be the appropriate place for my lectures, since the government had threatened to close them again if I were allowed to speak. Many persons who had been associated with my visit had been arrested, and others anticipated arrest and imprisonment at any moment.

During the time between my arrival at the airport and my first lecture at the YMCA (about one hour), I was told about the political repression and the difficult struggle for democracy and justice now taking place in Korea. Because I did not understand clearly the complexities of the Korean political situation, I asked several persons about what should be the theme of my lecture, and what especially should I avoid. I did not want my particular perspective on the gospel to cause anyone any unnecessary pain and suffering. But their reply was: "Speak the truth of the gospel, and do not worry about us." But what is the truth of the gospel in this Asian situation of extreme political repression? How could I speak about the gospel's empowerment of people in the struggle for justice, and also remain sensitive to the immediate political dangers of my Korean friends? I agonized over these and related questions in the presence of nearly fifty Korean CIA agents and about three hundred people who had taken the political risk to hear my lecture.

I decided to lecture on the theme of "God the Liberator as Found in the Black Slave Songs in North America." This theme enabled me to express my solidarity with the Korean struggle for justice and democracy, and to partly camouflage my utter distaste for the current Park regime. The impact of my lecture on the Korean situation far exceeded my expectations. Because of the conspicuous presence of so many Korean CIA agents, it was thought best not to take any unnecessary political risks by entertaining questions. The audience simply joined hands and sang: "We Shall Overcome." That was indeed a very moving and spiritual experience. To know that the black struggle for justice in the United States was a source of empowerment for Korean Christians engaged in a similar struggle enhanced the possibility for a creative dialogue between Koreans and blacks.

I have traveled extensively in many parts of the world, but no experience anywhere is comparable to this frightening experience in South Korea. The only analogous experience was work in the southern parts of the United States during the Civil Rights Movement of the 1950s and '60s, and especially in Mississippi and Alabama. The conspicuous presence of Korean CIA agents reminded me of southern policemen and other white supporters of the "white way of life." In both contexts, to create the fear of arrest, torture, and death in those who would challenge the "law" defined the character of the government. I was afraid in both situations, but much more in Korea than in Alabama or Mississippi. The reason was obvious. In the South, the place of my birth and early training, I had had enough experience with white folks there to be able to predict fairly accurately what responses they would give to anything I said or did. But not so in Korea. All I knew was the volatile situation in which I found myself, and that perhaps the lives of my friends depended upon how well I could speak the truth of the gospel without being stupid politically.

Initially I thought about the safety of my life, but soon realized that the most that was likely to happen to me personally would be my deportation from the country. But Korean Christians engaged in the struggle for democracy did not have the luxury of deportation as an option. And that fact alone made a radical distinction between them and me. Their only option was passivity or struggle, and the latter could easily lead to arrest and imprisonment. In this Korean context, I realized once more how relative our verbal pronouncements about justice are. The radical nature of any political challenge to injustice, whether in words or deeds, is dependent on the situation in which it is made.

Something happened to my theological perspective in Korea that is difficult to explain. What I encountered in that country was not so much "new" theological concepts that could be added to the current theological discussion. Rather than ideas, I met people whose commitment to the gospel in their struggle for justice and democracy was so clear (despite the risks) that I was simply awed by the humility and lack of self-righteousness which characterized their presence and speech. When I compare the modest attitude of Korean university students and professors with the self-righteous attitude of their North American counterparts, I feel compelled to say that the latter is possible because of a sense of privilege that characterizes their class position in the United States.

In this small community of Korean Christians, I knew that I had much to learn which would confirm my theological conviction about liberation and also compel me to relate liberation to a larger cultural and political context than my present focus on black Americans. For the Koreans who were engaged in the struggle for justice and democracy reminded me of my own people who have made similar commitments in order to fight against white racism. It was not a matter of being absolutely right and the government being absolutely wrong. It was a simple matter of taking a stand for human rights and the dignity which governmental policies did not seem to take seriously. They knew that their stand meant that it would possibly cause their arrest, torture, and imprisonment. In the context of living, talking, and being with these Korean Christians, Gustavo Gutiérrez's reference to theology as the "second step"[7] was reinforced in my theological consciousness. The first step is the political commitment on behalf of the poor and weak in society. The Korean Christians I met in May 1975 had taken the first step, and they have paid a heavy price.

Sri Lanka: January 1979

The Korean experience (in both Japan and South Korea) did much to prepare me for the Asian Theological Conference held at Wennappuwa, Sri Lanka, January 7–20, 1979.[8] But there was much that I learned in that two-week conference that went beyond the Korean experience. For example, my experience among Koreans had been primarily limited to Christians, and thus the Christological center of my theology had not been seriously challenged. Such was not the case in Sri Lanka. In the three-day live-in experience, I stayed with a very poor Buddhist family in Ratmalana. During the day, I met many Buddhist labor leaders engaged in the struggle for justice on behalf of industrial workers. This three-day live-in encounter radically challenged the Christological perspective of my theological and political commitment. The challenge did not arise from the verbal questioning of Buddhists about the absoluteness of Jesus Christ. No Buddhist even indirectly questioned my commitment to Jesus, even though they knew that all of the members of our group were Christians. They simply wanted to know where we stood on justice and liberation in terms of the concreteness of our political commitments.

The raising of the Christological issue in my theological consciousness was forced upon me by the Asian religio-cultural and socio-political context. I simply said to myself that if I had to do theology in an Asian context, the political and the cultural situation would require a reinterpretation of Jesus Christ so as to be effective in communicating precisely what the biblical Jesus represents. When I came to that conclusion, my theological perspective was deepened by its new-found openness to experiencing the heart and soul of Asia as lived by the people and expressed in their culture.

In questioning the Western formulation of the Christological emphasis in theology, I had to ask, what is the source from which Christian theology arises? In classical Western theology, the Bible or revelation has often been given as the answer to that question. But my participation in a three-day live-in at Ratmalana and my subsequent involvement in the Conference itself at Wennappuwa prevented me from accepting a pre-fabricated Western answer to an Asian question. Therefore during my first days in the Conference, I did not say much, because I was trying hard to listen to Asians as they struggled to make sense out of the complexity of their situation.

By merely hearing Asians speak about and struggle with the plurality of issues in their various situations (they came from eleven countries), I realized once again that theology arises out of life and not from theological textbooks. Therefore, the critical question is: Whose life does your theology represent? Theology is not applied to the situation as if it exists apart from it. Rather theology arises out of concrete life-situations and derives its reasons for being from people who are seeking to make sense out of their lives. If Asian theology (or any theology for that matter), is to be accountable to poor people's struggle for justice, then it must arise from their situation of struggle, and not from some abstract European concept of revelation. Most persons participating in the Asian Theological Conference seemed to recognize this fact, even though they often disagreed on the practical theological consequences of this assumption.

Although Asian theologians and church officials criticized the Western church and its theology, some young workers felt that the Asian church establishment was too closely tied to the Western interpretation of Christianity. If the European missionaries who introduced Christianity to Asia also brought with them the culture of the West, and if Christianity was and still is in the hands of the Asian ruling classes, how is it possible to create an Asian theology that is accountable to the liberation of the poor? If the phrase "Asian theology" means more than "theology in Asia" and thus reflects an "Asian sense," how can this Asian sense be created in theology if theology in Asia is in the hands of rulers who are Western in sense? These are some of the questions that were hotly debated in small groups and plenary sessions.

At this point, it may be useful to point out one significant difference between black theology and Asian theology. The rise of black theology is inseparable from an independent black church movement that is nearly two hundred years old.[9] In fact, ninety percent of all black Christians belong to independent black churches. Even most blacks in white denominations have an independent black consciousness which means that they are much closer to other blacks in independent churches than they are to whites in the same denominations. In this sense, black theology is not and has never been in the hands of the white church establishment. Rather it represents an independent black church constituency whose religious consciousness is defined by black people's struggle for freedom. That is why black theology could say that the white church and its theology represents the anti-Christ. We black theologians knew that our accountability was and is located in the oppressed black community, even though we have not always reflected that accountability as clearly as we should have.

When one turns to the church establishment in Asia, whether Catholic or Protestant, the radical independence found in black Christianity is absent. That was why so many young workers at the Conference questioned even the possibility of an Asian theology. How can there be a true Asian theology when the church structures are accountable to Western theology? As I listened to this discussion between church officials and young workers, I began to perceive the creative possibilities in the black church and its theology. But these possibilities have not been realized, and it does not appear that their realization is near at hand. Because the black church is independent, it is only natural that one would expect some radical expressions of this independence in action and words. During the eighteenth, nineteenth, and most of the twentieth centuries, it was not difficult to find creative expressions of the black church's commitment to the righteousness of God as revealed in the human struggle for justice. Martin Luther King, Jr., was an international symbol of that commitment.

But when I examine more critically contemporary black church denominations, I am very disappointed with their inordinate concern with themselves and their own institutional politics. With more resources at their disposal than ever, black denominations do less in creating justice and liberation for their people than they did in the nineteenth century. Why is it that no black church denomination has created a distinct confession of faith, defined by the liberation struggle of its people? Why is it that there is no ecumenical structure that unites black denominations so that they can be more effective as creative agents of liberation?[10]

While Asian churches are not independent, there are ecumenical structures that transcend the Western identity of their ecclesiastical institutions. An important example is the Christian Conference of Asia (CCA). This ecumenical body has resisted the importation of European theologies and church structures into Asia. It has convened conferences in order to examine the relation of the "Confessional Families and the Churches in Asia." The CCA has continued the discussion by asking what it means to confess the faith in Asia today?[11] Therefore, whatever may be said about the dependence of Asian theology and church structure on their European counterparts, the CCA consultations and the Asian Theological Conference clearly reveal an ecumenicity that is genuinely creative and could serve as a useful example for black Christians.

The Asian Conference delegates' stress on the particularity of their theological enterprise raised for me the question of the universality of the Christian gospel, a point that is applicable to any theological expression. I found myself asking, in what way does the Asian struggle for a full humanity embrace other human strivings for liberation? I realized that there is a serious danger inherent in the question, for it may serve as a distraction from the urgency of the present situation as found in Asia. Dr. Preman Niles has expressed a strong warning against this danger:

Asian theology is suffering from a crisis of identity, for it is often dominated by theological thinking in the West and, more recently, by Latin American and Black American liberation theologies. Indeed it is difficult to perceive what is distinctive about Asian theology. If theology in Asia is to have its own identity, it must cease to be merely an extension of Western theologies, and instead speak meaningfully to and within the context of Asian suffering and hope. The true identity of Asian theology will emerge only when we begin to perceive and articulate the relevant word in our situation.[12]

It is within this context that we ought to understand the small number of non-Asians invited to the Sri Lanka Conference and their status as fraternal delegates.[13] Asians were rightly concerned about the distinctiveness of their theology. That is also why there is a sharp resistance among Asians to Latin American liberation theologians who are often perceived by them (and also by some Africans and black Americans) as being arrogant and dominant in their relations to other Third World peoples. While most participants were not resistant to Marxism and class analysis, they did resist what some perceived as the dogmatic approach of the Latin Americans. Unlike most Latin theologians, Asians could not avoid the religio-cultural situation of Asia as they spoke about socialism and class analysis. In fact one of the most heated debates was generated in the conference regarding the relation between the religio-cultural and the socio-political situations in Asia. This issue was sharply raised by Aloysius Pieris' paper, "Towards an Asian Theology of Liberation: Some Religio-Cultural Guidelines." He emphasized that, unlike Latin American liberation theology, an Asian theology of liberation cannot avoid the "multi-faceted religiosity" of the Asian context. But the delegates from the Philippines gave an equally sharp reply in their emphasis on "socio-political liberation of the poor, the deprived, and the oppressed." Neither Pieris nor the Filipinos denied each other's emphasis, but each was concerned that their own emphasis did not receive the proper recognition.

I was fascinated by this debate between culture and politics among Asians, a discussion that was especially useful to me in my struggle with a similar issue in the black North American context.[14] But while every theology must wrestle with the particularity of its cultural and political context, we must be careful not to become imprisoned in our starting point. We must be careful that we do not allow our own historical reality to blind us to the universal dimension of humanity that transcends our particular locality. This radical universality is not to be confused with European intellectual abstractions. I believe that it is a universalism that embraces and illuminates the struggles of the oppressed throughout the world. Therefore, black theologians must ask: What is it in our particular analysis of the Christian faith that embraces the Asian search for a full humanity? Asian theologians should ask: What is it in the Asian search for a full humanity that expresses solidarity with the black struggle for justice in the United States? And both theologies must extend this question to other oppressed peoples.

By the time we reached the point of writing the "Final Statement," no one questioned that liberation will occupy a central focus in Asian theology. But it would not be a mere repetition of its meaning as found in black theology or Latin American liberation theology. The Asian emphasis on liberation would affirm some continuity with other Third World theologies, but it would also express its own uniqueness. Thus the "Final Statement" begins its first major section with the "Asian Context" and then moves to the "Issues." Both the context and the issues set the stage for the distinctive approach to Asian theology in the next section under the heading of "Towards a Relevant Theology." Liberation is made the chief focus of Asian theology, because the poor, in the struggle for freedom, are its subject. It is within the context of struggle that poor people's culture is emphasized as a source of empowerment, and social analysis is introduced as indispensable for accomplishing the goals of freedom.

The biblical perspective was introduced in the Final Statement's section on Asian theology not as an afterthought nor as an absolute, objective authority. The delegates at this conference were at least partly aware of the Western influence in what is often called the "biblical perspective." Therefore while there was not much discussion about the relation of Asian and biblical histories, there was an underlying assumption that the latter could not exercise an absolute authority over the former. Many delegates seemed to be aware of earlier discussions of this matter in the writings of Choan-Seng Song and Dr. Preman Niles.[15] Therefore they affirmed the authority of the Bible in the context of Asia's struggle and not separate from it.

I left the Asian Theological Conference with the realization that Asian theology represents one of the most distinctive and creative theologies on the world scene.

Japan and Korea: May 1979

During my visit to Japan in May 1975, I also had the privilege of speaking at the organizing meeting of the Citizen's Movement in Ichinomiya. This was not a Christian movement, but rather a small group of Japanese citizens concerned about justice and liberation for all human persons. I remember clearly the public testimonies of children and adults, the physically handicapped, and Koreans—all of whom were united in the struggle for freedom. In that meeting, I experienced a unity among people that transcended physical, mental, racial, and cultural differences, thereby giving sociological concreteness to the oneness of humanity. That small community of people symbolized for me the universal humanity that philosophers and other intellectuals often talk about, but they seldom take the political action necessary for its realization in society.

In May 1979, four years later, I was invited to return to Japan by this same citizen's group, which is now known as the National Association for the Protection of Children's Rights. At their May 5 national meeting in Tokyo, their concern was limited to the "Re-evaluation of Children's Day in the International Year of the Child," and they chose as their central theme: "Children Cry." May 5 is "Children's Day" in Japan, a national holiday that has always emphasized the ritual and festival dimensions of this event, thereby completely ignoring the suffering of the children of the poor. In order to express another perspective, the National Association for the Protection of Children's Rights invited people from all over Japan so that they could collectively register their solidarity with the victims, that is, the children of people who are ignored by the governmental officials in Japanese society. I was invited to make a presentation on the suffering of black children in the United States so as to give an international focus to their concern.

I was impressed by this gathering of nearly four hundred people, whose main commonality was not a particular confession of faith but rather a socio-political concern for the right of children to survive in a world free of suffering and inhumanity arising from the insensitivity of adults. Because only two Christians were present, the limitation of a rigid Christological approach was clearly revealed. As to be expected, I also found out that not all Japanese people are insensitive to human suffering. The meeting lasted for nearly five hours, and I heard testimonies from the mothers and fathers of dead children, from parents whose children had been seriously injured, and from Japanese children themselves. I was struck by their mutual solidarity and determination to make structural changes that would recognize the right of children to survive with dignity.

In this meeting was disclosed a dimension of Japanese humanity that I hardly saw at all in 1975. Most of the Japanese people I met in 1975 were university and seminary students and faculty, church people, and their pastors, very few of whom seemed particularly concerned about poor people's struggle for justice. But in the 1979 visit, I saw a different side of Japanese society which represents an unusual concern for the liberation of oppressed people. This fact alone increased my openness to the Asian reality.

From Japan I went for the second time to South Korea, and I found very little change, except an increased determination by Korean Christians to resist the Park regime. In four years, almost all of my friends were either in prison or had served their time there, expecting to return at any moment. We had more time and an appropriate context to talk theology, because one of my books (Black Theology and Black Power) had already been published in Korean.[16] I was especially surprised and also pleased that Korean Christians struggling for justice have expressed so much interest in black theology.

Korean theologians spoke a great deal about the "theology of people" (minjung)[17] which they claim embraces both the socio-political struggles of Koreans and also the cultural foundation of that struggle. Black theology's emphasis on culture in the context of political struggle and our exploration of our culture through an examination of the songs, prayers, and sermons of our people appealed to many Korean theologians. I also found their analysis of a "theology of people" to be creative, even though there is much work still to be done. I was invited to return in order to share in their struggle to give some shape to their theological vision. I readily accepted this challenge, because I know that black theology has much to learn from Asians generally and Koreans in particular. I only hope that we blacks will have as much to give to them as they to us.

NOTES

1. For an excellent documentary history of the development of black nationalism, see Black Nationalism in America, ed. John H. Bracey, Jr., August Meier, and Elliott Rudwick (New York: Bobbs-Merrill, 1970). See also Gayraud S. Wilmore, Black Religion and Black Radicalism (New York: Doubleday, 1972).

2. For an account of the dialogue between African and black theologians, see my analysis of it in Gayraud S. Wilmore and James H. Cone, eds., Black Theology: A Documentary History, 1966–1979 (Maryknoll, N.Y.: Orbis Books, 1979), pp. 492-501.

3. For an account of the dialogue between Latin and black theologians, see ibid., pp. 510-530.

4. For my early reflections on the relation of Asian and black theologies, see my analysis of it in ibid., and my "Asian Theology Today: Searching for Definitions," *Christian Century*, May 23, 1979.

5. My invitation by the Korean Christian Church in Japan was partly determined by their perceptions that blacks and Koreans have a similar experience. See the report of the "Consultation on Minority Issues in Japan and Mission Strategy," May 6–10, 1974, Kyoto, Japan, *IDOC*, No. 65, September 1974. See also Ha Lee, "Race and Minority Issues in Theological Perspective" in *Towards a Theology of People: I*, published by the Urban Rural Mission and the Christian Conference of Asia, 1977.

6. The fact that two of my books had already been translated into Japanese greatly aided my dialogue with both Korean and Japanese peoples. *Black Theology and Black Power* (New York: Seabury, 1969) was published in Japanese in 1971 by Shinkyo Shuppansha Publishing Co., Tokyo, Japan. *A Black Theology of Liberation* (Philadelphia: Lippincott, 1970) was published in 1973 by the same company. My *God of the Oppressed* (New York: Seabury, 1975) was published in Japanese by the same company in 1976, and *The Spirituals and the Blues* (New York: Seabury, 1975) is presently being translated.

7. See his *A Theology of Liberation* (Maryknoll, N.Y.: Orbis Books, 1973), p. 11.

8. For an earlier account of this conference, see my essay "Asia's Struggle for a Full Humanity: Toward a Relevant Theology" in Gayraud S. Wilmore and James H. Cone, eds., *Black Theology: A Documentary History, 1966–1979;* also my "Asian Theology Today: Searching for Definitions," *Christian Century*, May 23, 1979.

9. The best historical account of the development of the black church is Gayraud S. Wilmore, *Black Religion and Black Radicalism* (Garden City, N.Y.: Anchor Press/Doubleday, 1973). More recently, even white historians have begun to give prominent recognition to involvement of the black church and its preachers in the abolition of slavery. For an account of black slave religion and its independence from white religion, see especially Albert Raboteau, *Slave Religion* (New York: Oxford University Press, 1979); Olli Alho, *The Religion of the Slaves* (Helsinki: Soumalanen Tiedeakatemia, 1976); and Eugene D. Genovese, *Roll, Jordan, Roll: The World the Slaves Made* (New York: Pantheon Books, 1972).

10. The National Conference of Black Churchmen represented such a structure during the 1960s and early seventies. However it is not nearly as effective as it once was. For an account of NCBC, see Wilmore and Cone, eds., *Black Theology: A Documentary History, 1966–1979*. See also Gayraud S. Wilmore, *Black Religion and Black Radicalism*, and Leon W. Watts, "The National Committee of Black Churchmen," *Christianity and Crisis* 30 (Nov. 2 and 16, 1970).

11. See especially *Confessional Families and the Churches in Asia*, a report from a consultation convened by the East Asia Christian Conference (now called the Christian Conference of Asia) and held at Kandy, Ceylon, Dec. 6–8, 1965; and *Confessing the Faith in Asia Today*, a statement issued by the consultation convened by the East Asia Christian Conference and held in Hong Kong, Oct. 26–Nov. 3, 1966. The role which CCA has played in uniting Protestant churches in Asia is enormous. And it has served as a context for the development of Asian theology. See especially *Christian Action in the Asian Struggle* (Singapore: CCA, 1973); Yap Kim Hao, ed., "Asian Theological Reflections on Suffering and Hope," *Asia Focus*, no. 661, 1977; and *Towards a Theology of People: I*.

12. See his "Towards a Framework of Doing Theology in Asia," in *Asia Focus*, no. 661, 1977.

13. There were only seven non-Asians invited to attend, two each from Africa, Latin America, and the United States and one from the Caribbean. There were some questions raised about both the number and the fraternal status of the non-Asian delegates, since this conference was being sponsored by the Ecumenical Association of Third World Theologians. When the fraternal delegates requested a meeting with the Organizing Committee, it was readily granted. And the members of this committee explained that their effort to make sure that the development of Asian theology would remain in the hands of Asians alone accounted for both the small number of non-Asian delegates and also their fraternal status. Our openness to respect their concern increased our participation in the Conference. To my surprise, I was even selected to serve on the writing committee for the "Final Statement."

14. For my discussion of the politics-culture debate among black theologians, see my essay, "An Interpretation of the Debate among Black Theologians" in Wilmore and Cone, eds., *Black Theology: A Documentary History, 1966–1979*.

15. See Choan-Seng Song, "From Israel to Asia: A Theological Leap" in Gerald H. Anderson and Thomas F. Stransky, eds., *Mission Trends No. 3: Third World Theologians* (New York: Paulist Press, 1976), pp. 211–222. An enlargement of this discussion is found in his *Christian Mission in Reconstruction: An Asian Attempt* (Maryknoll, N.Y.: Orbis Books, 1977). For Dr. Preman Niles' critique of Song and Song's reply, see "Reviewing and Responding to the Thought of Choan-Seng Song" in *Occasional Bulletin of Missionary Research,* vol. 1, no. 3 (July 1977).

16. It was published by Cheong-Sa Press in Seoul in 1979.

17. See the important essay by Y. Kim, "Christian Koinonia in the Struggle and Aspirations of the People of Korea" in *Asian Theological Reflections on Suffering and Hope,* ed. by Yap Kim Hao; and also *Towards a Theology of People: I.*

18

A Latin American View of the Asian
Theological Conference

Sergio Torres (Chile)

I

I was once of the few non-Asian participants in the Asian Theological Conference held in Sri Lanka. As a member of the Association of Third World Theologians I have been part of this process of the contextualization of theology in the different continents of the Third World and I looked very much forward to the Asian Conference.[1]

Since Dar es Salaam in 1976 I have been puzzled and intrigued by the dialogue with the Asian theologians. Because this was just the start of the dialogue, many questions remained unanswered.

I knew that Christianity was a minority group in Asia. But it was different to experience this reality in the Buddhist context of Sri Lanka.[2] In Latin America, more than 90 percent of the population belongs to either the Catholic or Protestant churches. In Asia, only about 2 percent are Christians. As Aloysius Pieris reminded the Assembly in his presentation, "with four centuries of missionary presence the Christians are numerically and qualita-

Sergio Torres is a Chilean priest working among Puerto Ricans in New York City. He is executive secretary of the Ecumenical Association of Third World Theologians.

tively an insignificant minority: a mere 2 percent of the Asian masses."[3] This overwhelming reality makes a difference in the existential approach of Asian Christians exploring the meaning of salvation in Asia and trying to formulate their theology. But I was more perplexed when Pieris added: "Asia, as circumstances clearly indicate, will remain always a non-Christian continent."[4]

This affirmation did not sound pessimistic in his presentation. In fact, it presented a challenge as he continued, saying that this situation offered "enormous opportunities for more creative modes of Christian presence in Asia" or it could simply "repeat past mistakes in . . . new ways."[5]

I was immediately caught by this challenge and was impressed by the group searching for these "creative modes" of presence in Asia.

II

The Asian Theological Conference reflected a healthy search for an Asian identity. This search came from two different sources. One was the need for unity and common understanding among the different countries with diverse traditions, religions, and cultures. The other came from the need for independence and self-affirmation in relation to the colonial heritage. On the theological level there was a rejection of the cultural and theological imperialism of the West. This rejection came at different times and in different ways in the process of the Conference.

Tissa Balasuriya, the organizing secretary, wrote in preparation for ATC: "If we do not accept the Euro-American worldview of history, geography, economics, technology, and culture, we find that many elements in the Christian teaching are not relevant to us."[6]

Carlos Abesamis from the Philippines was more explicit: "The philosophy and theology we have inherited from our colonial past, whether it be neo-scholastic or liberal-existentialist, being drawn and conditioned by the history and social systems of the West, can no longer be simply appropriated by us and applied to our Asian human situation."[7]

I was attracted by the actual experience of this movement towards theological affirmation by the Asians. It is interesting to note that all theological efforts of contextualization and affirmation have started with this first step of rejection. Black theology in the U.S.[8] and in South Africa[9] has rejected the dominant theology as irrelevant for black people. Feminist theology[10] has also challenged the male interpretation of Christian symbols by Western dominant theology.

We in Latin America also have made the attempt of looking for our own Christian and theological identity. It has been very difficult for us, because we are located geographically in the West. I was both surprised and disappointed when people in Asia identified me as "Western."

It is true that historically and culturally Latin Americans have been part of the European culture. We were colonized by European countries, Spain and Portugal, for 300 years and we speak their languages. However, there are other elements we need to consider. The cultural domination never reached the totality of the population. Today there are still about 30 million Indians who have not been assimilated by the dominant society. They still use their own languages and have kept their culture.[11]

There are other segments in Latin America that have disassociated themselves from the dominant way of life influenced by European values. They do not equate Christianity with Western civilization.

In this process of self-affirmation some Latin American social scientists have elaborated the "theory of dependency."[12] This theory offers a scientific interpretation of the relation between dominant countries and oppressed continents, between the "center" and the "periphery." On the theological level a number of Latin American theologians have attempted to express the identity of our theology, focusing on dependency and liberation.

We see a difference in the responses of European and Latin American theologies to the different challenges. Theology in Europe after the Enlightenment has been a response to the intellectual difficulties of the *nonbeliever*. In Latin America, the response is to the stark reality of the dialogue with the *nonperson*, the poor and oppressed. In Europe the question is how to believe in God in the world of modernization and science. In Latin America, the question is how to change the world so it will be possible to live as children of God.[13] This is what has been called an epistemological shift from an abstract to a praxis-oriented theology.[14]

Both Asians and Latin Americans are thus concerned with identity and self-affirmation on the theological level. We should continue the dialogue and help each other in the reconstitution of an independent and relevant theological thinking.

The rejection of the Western interpretation of revelation is, however, only the first step in the process for the search for an Asian theology. As was affirmed in the ATC, the next step is the formulation of the framework from which a relevant theology could spring. This is the part of the Conference I want to analyze now.

III

For me, the best contribution came from Aloysius Pieris. Talking about the starting point for Asian theology, he said that the theological axis of our deliberations should have as its two poles Asia's "overwhelming poverty" and "its multifaceted religiosity."[15]

The Filipino delegation agreed with the two poles. However, concerned with some alienating efforts of inculturation in their own country, they warned against the emphasis on the pole of "religiosity." In their national group position paper, which had lasting effect at the Conference, the

Filipinos stated that "the main and principal characteristic of a truly Asian theology is its Third-Worldness: [this is] the substantive, while 'Asian' is the adjective."[16]

There was consensus that the starting point of theology in Asia should be the discovery of the revelation of the living God in the masses of the poor struggling for full humanity. But God has already been at work in the traditional Asian soteriologies, especially in Buddhism, Hinduism, and Taoism.[17] Therefore, the framework of an Asian theology should be twofold: (a) the presence of God among the poor and (b) the traditional religions, which are the cultural environment of these poor.

It will be necessary to distinguish in the traditional religions the seeds of liberation as well as the alienating aspects. But there is no other choice. Asian theology has to be rooted in the traditional religions and cultures.[18]

Until recently this discussion about culture and religiosity seemed irrelevant in Latin America. Liberation theology was perceived as centered on the faith reflection that is conditioned by economic and political structures. This has been true. The emphasis has been on the level of structures although the discussion on culture has always been present but on a secondary level. Recently however, two issues have come to the surface in Latin America.

The first one is the reflection on Latin American culture. This theme entered the theological scene as one new and important element, completing the analysis of class in the study of Latin American reality.[19]

The second element is popular religiosity. Although religions like Buddhism and Hinduism do not exist in Latin America, there exist the beliefs and practices of the Indian cultures (Maya, Aztec, Inca, etc.), which have remained in the life of the people and have been incorporated into the Catholic rites.[20]

The key to understanding popular religiosity is the fact that the people are both believers and oppressed. The popular religious practices are manifestations of the religious and cultural identity of people resisting modernization and cultural domination.

These two examples show how the reflections of Asian theology on culture and religion are very important for Latin Americans.

IV

I also want to consider some aspects of the methodology of Asian theology as it was explained in the ATC.

There was a lively discussion about the subject of theology: the participants were divided on this issue. The academic theologians present at the Conference felt challenged by the grassroots persons, who clearly asked for a radical revision of the traditional approach.

The Filipino delegation asserted that "the formulation of an Asian theology which is really liberating to the masses of the poor and oppressed of Asia is the work of the Asian poor with a liberated consciousness." They said that the academic theologians still have a role to play "provided that they are rooted in the history and the struggle of the poor and the oppressed." Theologians could be considered as "technicians" and should assist grassroots people in their process of theologizing.[21]

Recently, Gustavo Gutiérrez, the leading liberation theologian in Latin America, expressed a similar idea when he wrote that what is needed is "the death of the professional theologian."[22] He explains that this paradoxical affirmation means two things. First, physical death. The prophets of the Old Testament, as well as John, Paul, and Luke, were theologians and several of them were killed for their expression of faith. To speak out in Latin America today about God and the poor is to take a real risk of being sent to prison or being killed.

Second: symbolic death. When Paul quotes the Scriptures in his letter to the Corinthians, "I will destroy the wisdom of the wise" (1 Cor. 1:19), he is talking about the abstract theological speculation which is not relevant and must die. When theologians lose their relevancy, they too must "die."

Another point of similarity is about the role of theology in the churches and in society. According to the Final Statement, "Every theology is conditioned by the class position and class consciousness of the theologians."[23]

In Latin America this point has been emphasized in different ways. We agree with Asian theologians when they say that "theology is never neutral." This is also a clear challenge to Western theology, which has not been aware of its European conditioning. We have been told that European theology was a universal theology. We do not find this to be true and we are in the painful process of finding a new relationship with that tradition.

V

There is a final question that I would like to raise. Is there a Third World theology? The ATC was convened by the Ecumenical Association of Third World Theologians. It seems important to see if ATC helped to answer this question.

The question was taken by two of the most influential theologians in the conference, Pieris[24] and Abesamis.[25] Both affirm that Asian theology must be part of a Third World theology.

On the other hand, there was much discussion about the "Asian sense," about the Asian style, about the Asian-ness of theology. Pieris said that the condition of being a minority in Asia will push the Asian Christians to create a "Third World theology that will radically differ from the South American and the African theologies."[26]

It seems that although we can distinguish some common elements of a theology in the poor countries of the so-called "Third World,"[27] we cannot talk at this moment of *one theology of the Third World*. It would be better to talk about the theologies in the Third World. The movement towards contextual and relevant theology is growing, but further study and research are necessary in each continent for defining Asian, African, Latin American, and black (U.S.) theologies.

I believe that the Spirit of God is at work in the churches of the Third World and that our theologies will enrich the traditional theology and contribute to the life of the universal church.

NOTES

1. See my opening address in Dar es Salaam, in Sergio Torres and Virginia Fabella, eds., *The Emergent Gospel: Theology from the Underside of History* (Maryknoll, N.Y.: Orbis Books, 1977), pp. 1–6.

2. Sri Lanka (the former Ceylon) has a combination of various ethnic and religious groups. Buddhists account for 67.3 percent of the population, the Hindus, 17.6 percent, and Muslims, 7.1 percent.

3. Aloysius Pieris, S.J., "Towards an Asian Theology of Liberation: Some Religio-Cultural Guidelines," Document 8, p. 80 above.

4. Ibid.

5. Ibid.

6. Tissa Balasuriya, *Towards the Liberation of Theology in Asia,* Dossier 39, July 1978 (Sri Lanka, Centre for Society and Religion, mimeo), p. 5; included here as Document 2.

7. Carlos H. Abesamis, "Faith and Life Reflections from the Grassroots in the Philippines," Document 11, p. 128 above.

8. See James Cone, *A Black Theology of Liberation* (Philadelphia: Lippincott, 1970), p. 25.

9. Allan Boesak, *Farewell to Innocence: A Social-Ethical Study on Black Theology and Black Power* (Maryknoll, N.Y.: Orbis Books, 1978).

10. Feminist theologians in the U.S.A. have written extensively on this issue and developed a new theological approach. See Rosemary R. Ruether, ed., *Religion and Sexism* (New York: Simon and Schuster, 1974); Letty M. Russel, *Human Liberation in a Feminist Perspective: A Theology* (Philadelphia: Westminster, 1974); Sheila Collins, *A Different Heaven and Earth* (Valley Forge, Pa.: Judson Press, 1974).

11. The Indians live especially in Mexico, Central America, Ecuador, Peru, and Bolivia.

12. Some of these social scientists are F. H. Cardoso, "Desarrollo y dependencia: perspectivas en el análisis sociológico" in the anthology *Sociología del desarrollo* (Buenos Aires, 1970); Celso Furtado, *Obstacles to Development in Latin America*, trans. Charles Ekker (Garden City, N.Y.: Anchor Books, 1970). A good synthesis in English is the book by James D. Cockcroft, Andrè Gunder Frank, and Dale L. Johnson, *Dependence and Underdevelopment: Latin America's Political Economy* (Garden City, N.Y.: Anchor Books, 1972).

13. Gustavo Gutiérrez, "Two Theological Perspectives: Liberation Theology and Progressivist Theology," in Sergio Torres and Virginia Fabella, eds., *The Emergent Gospel* (Maryknoll, N.Y.: Orbis Books, 1978), pp. 227–259. Jon Sobrino, *"El conocimiento teológico en la teología europea y latinoamericana,"* in *Liberación y cautiverio* (Mexico, D.F.: Imprenta Venecia, 1976), pp. 177–209. Hugo Assmann, *Theology for a Nomad Church* (Maryknoll, N.Y.: Orbis Books, 1976), pp. 111–129.

14. Alfred Hennelly, S.J., "Theological Method, the Southern Exposure," *Theological Studies* 38 (December 1977): 708–735.

15. Pieris, Document 8, p. 75 above.

16. Abesamis, Document 11, p. 134 above.

17. Pieris, Document 8, pp. 75–95 above.

18. Final Statement of this Asian Theological Conference, Document 13, p. 157 above.

19. See Proceedings of the Latin American Bishops' Conference (CELAM), Puebla, Mexico, January 27–February 13, 1979, nos. 385–443 in *Puebla and Beyond: Documentation and Commentary*, ed. John Eagleson and Philip Scharper (Maryknoll, N.Y.: Orbis Books, 1979).

20. Proceedings of the Latin American Bishops' Conference, nos. 444–469 in *Puebla and Beyond.*

21. Abesamis, Document 11, p. 137 above.

22. Gustavo Gutiérrez, "La fuerza histórica de los pobres," in *Signos de lucha y esperanza* (Lima: Centro de Estudios y Publicaciones, 1978), p. XXXVIII.

23. Final Statement of this Asian Theological Conference, Document 11, p. 157 above.

24. Pieris, Document 8, pp. 75–95 above.

25. Abesamis, Document 11, pp. 123–139 above.

26. Pieris, Document 8, p. 80 above.

27. Sergio Torres, Opening Address, in Kofi Appiah-Kubi and Sergio Torres, eds., *African Theology en Route* (New York: Orbis Books, 1979), pp. 5–7.

19

Hope for the Future

Justinus Cardinal Darmojuwono (Indonesia)

This conference is a probing search, on facing our Asian reality, towards a renewal of our attitude. Renewal presupposes adaptation to the reality. That means probing, searching, digging into the Asian soil, the Asian world. That implies also the feeling of being uncertain, mixed with a lively longing for the future that is already present—somehow.

A factor that should be taken into consideration is that we come from so many Asian countries, with so many backgrounds and situations, not forgetting the so-called modernization that is taking place in our countries. It makes our meeting the more difficult.

Another important factor to be considered is the fact that the participants are personally invited, that is, not as official representatives of certain churches. Hence we cannot consider their opinions as the official opinions of their churches.

This conference, however, could be seen as the expression of how our churches are trying to adjust themselves in this present Asian situation together. We learn from one another. We come to know what happens in the other countries. That can give a push to one another's effort in incarnating one's faith in Asia.

I have the impression that as a whole the preparation of the participants was unsatisfactory. I hope it will be better in future meetings. God has given us the strength to meet. He will also give us the courage to continue this effort, whatever difficulties there might be. We shall overcome!

Justinus Cardinal Darmojuwono is archbishop of Semarang (Java), Indonesia, and is president of the Indonesian Bishops' Conference (MAWI).

List of Participants

Bangladesh

Rt. Rev. Joachim Rozario, C.S.C., Bishop's House, P. O. Box, 152, Chittagong

Rt. Rev. Barnabas D. Mondal, Dacca Diocese, St Thomas' Church, 54, Johnson Road, Dacca - 1

Hong Kong

Mr. Cheng Ching Fat, c/o 57 Peking Road, 4/F, Tsim Sha Tsui, Kowloon

Mr. Hui Kwan Cheung, Christian Ind. Committee, 57 Peking Road, 4/F, Tsim Sha Tsui, Kowloon

Mr. Leung Kin Sang, Christian Ind. Committee, 57 Peking Road, 4/F, Tsim Sha Tsui, Kowloon

Rev. Stephen Tam Kwan, St. Theresa's Church, 258, Prince Edward Road, Kowloon

Sr. Christian Tse, Justice & Peace Commission, Catholic Diocese Centre, 16, Caine Road, 13/F, Hong Kong

Mr. Shau Shing Tang, 6 Rue de la Limite, 1030 Brussels, Belgium

India

Dr. J. Russell Chandran (Organizing Committee), United Theological College, 17, Miller's Road, Bangalore, 560046

Mrs. Christina Rajkumar, 580 Anna Salai, Madras, 600006

Sr. Gladys D'Souza, R.S.C.J., Sophia College, Gurukul, Cumballa Hill P.O., Bombay, 400026

Rev. Samuel Rayan, S.J., 23 Raj Niwac Marg, Delhi, 110054

Dr. Gnana Robinson, Principal, Tamilnadu Theological Seminary, Arasaradi, Madurai, 625010

Mrs. Florence Deenadayalan, St. Paul's Church, Robersonpet, Kolar Gold Fields, Karnataka

Rev. C. A. B. Tirkey, Gossner Theological College, Ranchi, 834001, Bihar

Bishop Poulouse (Mar Poulouse), Metropolitan's Palace, Trichur 680001, Kerala

Indonesia

Justinus Cardinal Darmojuwono (Organizing Committee), JLN Pandanaran 13, Semarang

Rev. Bernard S. Mardiatmadja, JLN Abubakar Ali No. 1, Yogyakarta

199

Dr. J. Riberu, Taman Cut Mutiah 10, Jakarta Pusat

Rev. Natan Setiabudi, JL Korawa 13, Bandung, West Java

Mr. Emmanuel Subangun, 66 Sekip Ujumg RTO 12/14, No. 12, Utan Kayu/ Atinegara, Jakarta Timur

Japan

Rev. Munetoshi Maejima, 2-14-58, Sukematsu-Cho, Izumiotsu-Shi, Osaka, 595

Sr. Mary Elizabeth Omizo, C.N.D. (Organizing Committee), 3-55, Shimoishihara, Chofu-Shi, Tokyo, 182

Rev. Noel Keizo Yamada, S.J., Sophia University, 7, Kioicho, Chiyodaku, Tokyo

Pakistan

Rev. J. Louis Mascarenhas, O.F.M., Darakhshan, 250, Catholic Colony 1, Karachi, 0502

Mr. Kenneth Louis Fernandes, St. Patrick's Tech. School, Ahmed Nuhir Road, Saddai, Karachi 3

Mr. Edward Parshad, Principal, St. Joseph's English Medium School, 3/G Shad Bagh, Lahore

Philippines

Rev. Toribio Cajiuat, Peace Formation Programme, 877, Edsa, Quezon City, Metro, Manila

Mr. Carlito Gaspar, Mindanao-Sulu Pastoral Conf. Secretariat (MSPCS), Rm. 203, Susana Building, J.P. Laurel Street, Davao City

Rev. Florencio Jacela, C.SS.R., Redemptorists Church, Tacloban City, Leyte

Bishop Julio X. Labayen (Organizing Committee), Bishop's Residence, Infanta, Quezon 3918

Sr. Angelita L. Navarro, I.C.M., I.C.M. District House, 61, Banawe Street, Quezon City

Rev. Rene C. Nachura, Bishop's House, Calbayog City

Sr. Virginia Fabella, M.M. (EATWOT Liaison), Maryknoll Sisters Center, P. O. Box 92, Maryknoll, New York 10545, U.S.A.

Mr. Gaudioso A. Sustento, Comm. Media Center, Malaybalay, Bukidnon

Mr. Oscar D. Francisco, National Secretariat of Social Action, 2655 F.B. Harrison, Pasau City

Thailand

Rev. Luan Nakpansa, Worasarn School, Thawee Watthana Lance, Chan Road, Bangkok 5

Miss Rakawin Phoomitrakul, c/o Fr. Miguel, Xavier Hall, 70/9 Victory Monument, Rajavithi Road, Bangkok 4

Mr. Sompot Somboon, Catholic Council of Thailand for Development (CCTD), 2, Soi Saensuk, Prachasongkroh Road, Huaÿkwane, Bangkok 10

Bishop Bunluen Mansap, P.O. Box 5, Ubon Ratchathani

Dr. Vithavas Khongkhakul, Faculty of Political Science, Chulalongkorn University, Bangkok

Taiwan

Rev. Aloisius Gutheinz, S.J., Fujen Catholic University, Faculty of Theology, 242, Taipei-hsien, Hsin-chuang

Pacific Islands

Rev. Galuefa Aseta, Pacific Conference of Churches, P. O. Box 208, Suva, Fiji Islands

Rev. Leone Vasole Raselala, Pacific Regional Seminary, P. O. Box 1200, Suva, Fiji Islands

Sri Lanka

Bishop Leo Nanayakkara (Co-Chairman), Bishop's House, Badulla

Bishop Lakeshman Wickremasinghe (Co-Chairman), Bishop's House, Kandy Road, Kurunegala

Rev. Tissa Balasuriya, O.M.I. (Organizing Secretary & Convenor), Centre for Society & Religion, 281 Dean's Road, Colombo 10

Mrs. Bernadeen Silva (Program Co-ordinator), Centre for Society & Religion, 281 Dean's Road, Colombo 10

Mr. Ainsley Samarajecva (Program Co-ordinator), 123A Galle Road, Dehiwela

Rev. Michael P. Rodrigo, Sevaka Sevana Ministries School, Bandarawela

Rev. Philip Setunga, Catechetical Centre, Chilaw

Mr. Jeffrey Abayasekera, 88/2 Danbar Road, Hatton

Miss Anita Fernando, 3/1 Talahena, Malabe

Miss Audrey Ribera, 33 Rupasinghe Avenue, Dehiwela

Rev. Dalston Forbes, O.M.I., Oblate College, National Seminary, Kandy

Mr. George Gnanamuttu, 4, Chelsea Gardens, Colombo 3

Rev. S. J. Emmanuel, National Seminary, Ampitiya, Kandy

Rev. Lynn de Silva, 490/5 Havelock Road, Colombo 6

Sr. Marlene Perera, F.M.M., Franciscan Convent, St. Joseph's Street, Tillanduwa, Negombo

Sr. Josephine Mendis, H.F.C., Holy Family Convent, Maradana, Colombo 10

Sr. Mary Maude, A.C., Carmel Convent, Colombo 10

Sr. Milburga Fernando, S.D.S., Provincial House, Malkaduwawa (N.174), Kurunegala

Dr. Preman Niles (CCA Liaison), CCA Office, 480 Lorong 2, Singapore, 12

Mr. A. Wimalathasan, P. O. Box 81, Jaffna

Resource Persons

Rev. Sebastian Kappen, S.J., H - 129/5, 34th Cress Street, Besang Nagar, Madras, 600090, India

Dr. K. Matthew Kurien, Indian Institute for Regional Development Studies, Kottayam 686002, Kerala, India

Dr. Feliciano Carino, Philippine Christian University, Cor Taft Avenue, P. O. Box 907, 8, Pedro Gil Malate, Manila, Philippines

Dr. Gahani Corea (Sri Lanka), UNCTAD, CH - 1211, Geneva 10, Switzerland

Miss Henriette Katappo (Indonesia), World Council of Churches, 150, Route de Ferney, Geneva 1211, Switzerland

Rev. Carlos H. Abesamis, S.J., Loyola House of Studies, P. O. Box 4082, Manila, Philippines

Prof. Fasal A. Shamsi, 55/26, G/4, Islamabad, Pakistan

Rev. Aloysius Pieris, S.J., "Tulana," Nungamugoda Road, Kelaniya, Sri Lanka

Dr. Piyasena Diesanayake, Director/Registrat, B.C.I.S., c/o B.M.I.C.H., Dauddhalaka Mawatha, Colombo 7, Sri Lanka

Fraternal Delegates

Mrs. Rose Zoé-Obianga (Cameroon), 527 Riverside Drive (Apt. 1A), New York, N.Y. 10027, U.S.A.

Mr. Kofi Appiah-Kubi, University of Science & Tech., Humasi-Ghana, West Africa

Rev. Sergio Torres (Chile), (Exec. Secretary, EATWOT), 1290 St. Nicholas Avenue, New York, N.Y. 10033, U.S.A.

Dr. James H. Cone, Union Theological Seminary, 3041 Broadway, New York, N.Y. 10027, U.S.A.

Dr. Cecil Corbett, Executive Director, Cook Christian Trg. School, 708, South Lindon Lane, Tempe, Arizona 85281, U.S.A.

Mrs. Eunice Santana de Velez (Caribbean), P. O. Box 6244, Arecibo, Puerto Rico 00612

Prof. Enrique Dussel, Dr. Balmis 199-202, Mexico 7, D.F., Mexico

Rev. Ngindu Mushete, B. P. 823, Kinshasa XI, Republic of Zaire

Special Staff

Mr. Victor J. Asumin, P.O. Box 909, Kumasi, Ghana

Sr. Terosa Dagdag, M.M., Young Workers Centre, 23 Block 28, Sau Mau Ping, Kowloon, Hong Kong

Mr. R. J. Rajkumar, 464 K. Blk. 179, Toa Payoh Central, Singapore 12

Rev. Gondulf Hoeberichts, O.F.M., 250 Sadhu Hiranand Road, Catholic Colony 1, Karachi, 0502, Pakistan